30th May 2001 -

For Tom Maplesden,

With all my grateful, and
most appreciative thanks, for
all your years of help and
care to so many people -
you will be much missed -
With very good wish, for
very many happy years
of retirement, and with love,
from Mary Shakemore

Reports of the Research Committee of the Society of Antiquaries of London, No. 63

GLAMIS CASTLE

Glamis Castle and the avenue

GLAMIS CASTLE

Harry Gordon Slade

The Society of Antiquaries of London

First published 2000
by
The Society of Antiquaries of London
Burlington House
Piccadilly
London W1V 0HS

ISBN 0 85431 277 3
ISSN 0953-7163

British Library Cataloguing in Publication Data
A CIP catalogue record for this book is available from the British
Library.

Original series design by Chuck Goodwin, London W2 5DA
This book typeset and laid out by Steve Moloney and
Caroline Spoors, SJM Design Consultancy
Printed and bound in Great Britain by BAS Printers Ltd,
Over Wallop, Hampshire

Contents

ILLUSTRATIONS

FOREWORDS

Glamis Castle first came into my life in 1955 when I became engaged to Fergus Bowes Lyon. I admit to finding it at that time rather gloomy and sad, and I was thankful that my home was to be an army quarter in Germany! When, unexpectedly, it became our responsibility in 1972 I was filled with foreboding and sadness as I knew it meant leaving our own house in East Lothian where we had been so happy for ten years. But Glamis soon worked its magic on me, as it does on so many people.

It was a mammoth task to turn the public side into a successful business operation for corporate entertaining and the ever-increasing number of daily visitors, but most of all it was a great challenge to make a cheerful self-contained home for ourselves and our three children. Our architect James Dunbar-Nasmith's inspired idea to turn the back courtyard into our private entrance and make a new front door and *porte-cochère* made it possible to live a relatively normal life and is an oasis of calm at the back of the Castle even in the midst of the busiest of days in the public side. So Glamis evolved yet again as it has done so often over the centuries.

My late husband's family has lived at Glamis since 1372 and the task that Harry Gordon Slade took on when he decided to write the architectural history of the Castle was a Herculean one and is the first major study ever done of the building. I am sure no one could have done it better. His interest and knowledge know no bounds. His visits over the years have always been an enormous pleasure and my family owes him a great debt of gratitude for writing this book. My only bone of contention has been that almost all of the stories I and many other people used to tell visitors have been proved false. Anyone who saw that brilliant play *Lettuce and Lovage* will know what I mean! That, however, is a small price to pay for such a brilliantly researched and architecturally correct history of Glamis Castle.

The Castle that filled me with such foreboding in 1972 has become so very much loved. It is one of my greatest pleasures to know how many thousands of visitors are as entranced by its magic and history as I am, and also that it is still a much-loved home for my family after so many centuries.

MARY, COUNTESS OF STRATHMORE
JUNE 2000

This book happily brings together the special interests of two Fellows of the Society of Antiquaries of London. The first is Her Most Gracious Majesty Queen Elizabeth, The Queen Mother, a Royal Fellow since 9 January 1958. Her Majesty has always shown herself interested in the history of Glamis Castle, her ancestral home. Indeed, when in 1983 Her Majesty was unable to attend the Society's lecture on the works of her direct ancestor, Patrick, the 3rd Earl of Kinghorne and Strathmore, at Glamis Castle, given at Burlington House by Dr Michael Apted FSA, her regret was such that a special session was arranged at Clarence House. And when, on 1 November 1990, Harry Gordon Slade lectured on Glamis Castle the occasion was rendered unforgettable by the presence of Her Majesty and that of the Earl and Countess of Strathmore.

The second Fellow is the afore-named author of this book, Harry Gordon Slade. As befits a true antiquary, Harry's enthusiasm and knowledge range wide and deep. His style is idiosyncratic, his approach eclectic. In editing his book the Society has attempted to preserve that personal favour, while trying to introduce consistency where it was felt needed, adding translations of the Scots and Latin, and seeking to identify some of the more obscure literary allusions for a lay audience. Problems with Harry's health and eyesight have led to the Society playing a larger role than it usually hopes to in the production of the final text. We are particularly indebted to our Fellow Geoffrey Stell, as academic reader, to the Royal Commission on the Ancient and Historical Monuments of Scotland (RCAHMS) for its extensive assistance, and to the Society's Library staff, especially Adrian James, to our Publications Manager, Kate Owen, and to the copy editor, Ruth Thackray, and indexer, Margaret Binns. And the General Secretary of the Society, our Fellow David Morgan Evans, has especially asked to be associated with these thanks, because

of his long friendship with Harry, and 'for a remembrance of good times past'.

Above all this book is a tribute from the Fellows of our Society to Her Majesty Queen Elizabeth, The Queen Mother, in this year of her hundredth birthday. It is a token of our gratitude, of our affection and respect, and of our congratulations.

SIMON JERVIS
PRESIDENT, THE SOCIETY OF ANTIQUARIES OF LONDON
JUNE 2000

ix

PREFACE

Glamis Castle, the home of Michael, 18th Earl of Strathmore and Kinghorne, Viscount Lyon and Lord Glamis, Tannadyce, Sidlaw and Strathdichtie in Scotland, Baron Bowes of Streatlam Castle, Co. Durham, and Earl of Strathmore and Kinghorne in the United Kingdom, has been the principal seat of his family since the 1370s. In that time, although the family has borne four names – Lyon, Bowes, Lyon Bowes and Bowes Lyon – the castle has always passed in the male line. Glamis was the childhood home of Her Majesty Queen Elizabeth, The Queen Mother, and the combination of history, architectural splendour and royal associations – the two first Lyon lairds of Glamis married a daughter and granddaughter of Robert II, King of Scotland – have captured the imagination of successive generations of visitors.

The present building shows the transition from palace house and artillery work to a strong tower, from a royal palace to a prodigy house – the culmination of the high baronial manner – and from a baroque palace to an enormous late Victorian country house of little comfort and less convenience. The great L-tower has always been too massive to demolish, and successive lairds of Glamis, making a virtue of necessity, have made it the centre of all later developments.

So splendid is the castle that some writers have accounted for its magnificence by attributing it to Inigo Jones – as unlikely an attribution as can ever have been made. Glamis has also profited from some extraordinarily, if unconsciously, successful public relations work on its behalf through Shakespeare's *Macbeth*.

Unless otherwise stated, the quotations and references are from or to papers, accounts, books and drawings in the Glamis archives. Although inventorized by the Scottish Record Office (now the National Archives of Scotland), the collection is housed at the castle, and there is neither the staff nor the facilities to provide any form of a service for 'information retrieval'. Previous experience has shown that the publication of documentary references has led to an increase in the number of casual enquiries. It is thus at the request of the Trustees that full details of the references have been omitted.

Acknowledgements

My thanks must in the first place go to the late Earl of Strathmore and the Trustees of the Glamis Estates for allowing me to start this study, and to the present Earl of Strathmore for allowing it to be completed. Without unfettered access to the castle and to the archives, the task would not have been possible.

The list of those whose help and encouragement I amply appreciate is long: Dr Michael Apted and Mr John Dunbar, who suggested that the study should be undertaken in the first place; the Society of Antiquaries of London for an initial research grant and to Mr David Morgan Evans, the General Secretary of the Society; the late Mrs Joan Auld; Mr Geoffrey Stell and Mr John Borland of the Royal Commission on the Ancient and Historical Monuments of Scotland, who have made the Commission's plans available for publication; Mr C J Burnett, Ross Herald, who has allowed his notes on the heraldry at the castle to be published here (Appendix A); Mr Terry Ball for his reconstruction drawings; Mr Peter Bellamy for his work on the early inventories; Sir Howard Colvin; Mr Christopher Gray; Mr Michael Broadbent of Christie's; Miss Judith Scott; Lord Arbuthnott; the late Judge William Hughes, whose notes to me on the Strathmore Case were written only shortly before his death; and again to Mr John Dunbar for permission to reproduce his note on the Slezer copper plate.

To all members of the staff at Glamis, but particularly to Lt-Colonel Patrick Cardwell Moore, Mr Peter Ord, Mr Bert Tosh, Mrs Irene Mudie and Miss Joan Paterson, who typed the text from a manuscript, always elegant but too frequently illegible. From Mary, Countess of Strathmore, I have received endless encouragement and kindness even when we disagreed fundamentally on 'one Will Shakespeare'. Nothing can equal the warmth of hospitality that I have received from Patrick and Virginia Cardwell Moore, whose house has become a home over the years.

Finally my thanks to all those persons – family, friends and colleagues – who have become hardened to the use of the name of 'Glamis' as an excuse for not doing something else.

HARRY GORDON SLADE
LONDON 2000

Editorial Notes

Unless otherwise stated, all quotations and references to manuscript sources are either from or to papers, accounts, books and drawings housed in the Glamis archives. For the reasons given in the Preface, full details of the references have been omitted.

The headings, spellings and punctuation of the inventories, extracts and partial transcriptions are as presented by the author. Free translations of Latin quotations have been provided where appropriate.

CHAPTER 1
THE FAMILY AND THE CASTLE

Sir John de Lyon
A Norman Knight descended from the Patrician family of Leoni at Rome came over with the Conqueror in 1066. His son Sir Roger de Lyon was in high favour with King Edgar son of Malcolm Canmore with which Monarch he left England, settled in Scotland and for good service against Donald Bane the usurper got a Charter of the lands in Perthshire subsequently named by him Glen Lyon. From him is lineally descended the above.

On this point, however improbable, four early manuscript histories of the Lyon family agreed, 'for', as Dickens caustically observed, 'it is a remarkable fact in genealogy that no De Any ones ever came over with anybody else'. In more recent years the late Sir Ian Moncrieff in his division of Scottish genealogy into two lines, the Galley (or Norse) and the Lyon (or Celtic), puts the Lyon family in the latter and gives it a possible descent from a Sir Lamand – or Lamont – *fl.* 1238. Now it must be a matter of choice whether one wishes to be descended from *The Decline and Fall of the Roman Empire*, from a man who entered Scotland in the tail of an English army, from a line of Norse kings with forebears rejoicing in such names as 'Ill-Ruler', 'Tree-Hewer', the 'Stingy' and the 'Fart', or from an Irish High King burnt to death while dead drunk, in spite of having been 'personally baptized by St Patrick', but fortunately the choice does not have to be made. The mists of antiquity descend with awful abruptness upon these interesting personages, and do not lift until the middle of the fourteenth century, when the first historical Lyon leaps on to the

stage. 'Leaps' is perhaps too strong a word; at some time before 1367 a John Lyon in the service of David II was holding the posts of Auditor, Chamberlain and Clerk of the Privy Seal to the King of Scots, and had acquired the lands of Fordell and Forgandenny. In 1368 he was possessed of lands in the Garioch, granted to him by the king. That he enjoyed no power derived from great territorial possessions or powerful family connections may have recommended John Lyon to a monarch who was frequently the victim of the ambitions of his overmighty subjects. Clearly he owed everything to the royal favour, and, if he were powerful, his power derived from his position as a member of the king's *familia*. In this, he set the pattern for his house for the next nine generations. His descendants grew rich in serving the Crown in all the great offices of state, but never so overly powerful as to arouse the jealous enmity of their peers; loyal to the house of Stuart as long as such loyalty was reasonable, but never, when that loyalty was no longer reasonable, rebellious – merely a little distant and withdrawn. On the whole, they eschewed violence. None perished on the scaffold, and, apart from the clutch of obligatory deaths at Flodden, only the 5th Earl died on the battlefield – at Sheriffmuir.

John Lyon did not lose royal favour at the death of David II. The king was succeeded by his nephew, Robert II, and John Lyon, already described as 'of Forteviot', was appointed Keeper of the Privy Seal. In the early 1370s he was granted the Thaneage of Glamis, a grant confirmed in the following year. He was knighted and appointed Chamberlain of Scotland in 1377, possibly to enhance his position as husband of the king's widowed daughter,

1

the Princess Jean (or Joan, or Joanna); the marriage was formally recognized in 1378–9. This lady, the widow of Sir John Keith, was the third of the king's daughters by Elizabeth Mure, and could just have been born after her parents' marriage – Robert II's marital arrangements were unorthodox in the extreme. Sir John Lyon was killed by Sir James Lindsay of Crawford in 1382, and was succeeded by his only child, John, a minor. This Sir John – he was knighted in 1404 – did nothing very spectacular and does not seem to have held any high office. He probably built the oldest remaining part of the castle – the south-east wing – a handsome and, for Scotland, fairly advanced building, which would fit well with the years 1383–1435. What might have proved more alarming for his descendants was that, by his marriage, they were put in a position of considerable risk. His wife – his cousin at one remove – was Elizabeth Graham, daughter of Euphemia, Countess of Strathearn, and consequently great-granddaughter of Robert II. Their son, Patrick Lyon, was descended from Robert II through each of his parents, and from both of the king's marriages.

Robert II's two marriages had produced two royal lines, one descended from Elizabeth Mure, the other from Euphemia Ross. The Mure line, which bore the Crown, was naturally suspicious of the younger but undoubtedly legitimate Ross line. On his return from captivity in England in 1424 James I struck at his most dangerous rival in his own line, his cousin Murdoch, Duke of Albany, who, together with his sons Walter and Alexander, was executed in 1425 on charges which may have been false and were certainly convenient. The murder of James I in 1437 enabled Queen Joan Beaufort to destroy the male line descending from Euphemia Ross by executing Robert II's son, Walter, Earl of Atholl, and grandson, Sir Robert Stewart.

At the time of his accession James II was only six, and the nearest male heir, although in the female line, was Malise, Earl of Menteith, brother of Elizabeth Graham, who had married John Lyon, and Euphemia Graham, wife of Archibald, 3rd Earl of Douglas. Malise was, fortunately for himself, in England, hostage for the unpaid ransom of James I. The Earl of Douglas had not only married a descendant of the Ross line, but was also descended from Robert II through his marriage to Margaret, sister of James I and of Joan Lyon. Earl William's claim was therefore as strong – or as weak – as

1.1   The principal front (© Crown Copyright/RCAHMS)

2

that of Patrick Lyon, both being doubly descended in the same degree from Robert II. Earl William died in 1439, avoiding the fate of his two sons, who were murdered almost in the presence of the young king at the infamous 'Black Dinner' in Edinburgh Castle on 24 November 1440. With these murders the male representatives of three of the lines descending from Robert II had been eliminated, and the Strathearn line had been effectively sidelined since the Earl of Menteith was a hostage in England. This left only the Lyon line untouched.

Patrick Lyon, who succeeded his father in 1435, was to marry his eldest son Alexander to Agnes Crichton, daughter of Sir William Crichton, the Chancellor and ruler of the king and the kingdom. If Crichton had any hand in, or knowledge of, the Douglas murders – and it is difficult to see how he could not have been involved – he may have been influenced by the thought that his grandchildren would be placed on the steps of the throne. Crichton fell from power in 1445, the year that Patrick Lyon was raised to the dignity of a Lord of Parliament as Lord Glamis. Surviving the fall of his father-in-law and that of the Livingstones in 1449, the new 1st Lord Glamis continued to gather honours to

himself: Auditor of the Treasury, Master of the Household 1450–2, sworn to the Privy Council, Ambassador to England 1451–5, and again from 1456 until his death in 1459, Keeper of the royal castles of Kildrummy, Kindrochit and Balvenie, and Lord of Session 1457, he was the complete *à tout faire*, the perfect civil servant, always willing to take on a job, and a great survivor. He must have started the building of the Great Tower, influenced perhaps by the castles of his charge, and by the building activity in Aberdeenshire at the time. He died at Belhelvie in 1459, and, according to *The Scots Nobilitie*, his widow was to complete the Great Tower in 1480–4, after the death of her second husband, Lord Kennedy. Having lived through the slaughter of the male descendants of Robert II, and survived the fall of Sir William Crichton and Sir Alexander Livingstone, with both of whom he must have been closely identified, Lord Glamis could, had he been asked what he had done, have replied in the words of the Abbé Sieyès, 'J'ai vécu'.

He was succeeded by both his sons, Agnes Crichton having borne her husband no children, and they both followed closely in his footsteps. Alexander, 2nd Lord Glamis, had been appointed a Lord Auditor of

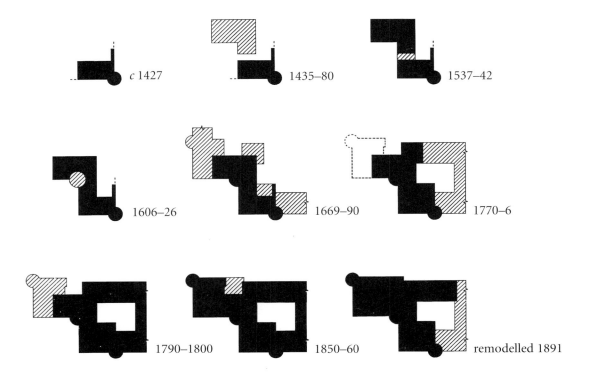

1.2 The development of the present building

Parliament and a Lord of Council at the same time as his younger brother, and he also received the Keepership that his father had held of the three north-eastern royal castles. It is a measure of the trust that both James II and James III had in their kinsmen that these three castles, which held the passes from the Highlands into Aberdeenshire, should have been left in their hands.

Following Alexander's death, in 1486, his brother John succeeded as 3rd Lord Glamis, and was appointed to the office of Justiciar in 1487. In addition, he received payment for the monies expended by his father on the northern castles. In the rebellion of 1487–8 Lord Glamis remained loyal to James III almost to the end, striving to bring about an accommodation between the two sides. When this proved fruitless, Glamis, together with the Earl Marischal and the Earls of Erroll and Huntly, withdrew to his own lands. Without their support the king's defeat was inevitable: they would not betray him, but could no longer support him – a nice distinction, but one the Stuarts often brought about by their obstinacy and untrustworthiness. There may have been family influence brought to bear on Lord Glamis to hasten his withdrawal; his son John, Master of Glamis, had married Elizabeth Gray, daughter of Lord Gray who, together with the Earl of Angus, was one of the chief leaders of the rebellion. Whatever prompted Lord Glamis's actions, it was to do him no harm. In 1489 he was appointed one of the Crown Auditors and sworn of the King's Privy Council, and in 1491 was named Ambassador to the courts of France, Castile, Leon, Aragon and Sicily.

His son, John, who succeeded his father in 1497, sired two sons, both of whom succeeded him, and died in 1500 leaving four brothers, three of whom were killed at Flodden. George, his elder son, succeeded as 5th Lord Glamis but died while still a minor; he was followed as 6th Lord Glamis by his younger brother, John. Little is known of the sixth baron save that he was a very active man, that 'he had many feuds and carried forth a great part [of them]', and that 'he had many followers wherefore commonly he was called "Cleanse the Causeway"'. Dying before his wife, he escaped the execution or exile that his marriage would almost certainly have brought him.

This dangerous marriage had been to Janet Douglas, sister-in-law of Margaret Tudor, the widow of James IV, who had taken Archibald Douglas, 6th Earl of Angus, as her second husband in 1514. Angus, although estranged from his wife, had so established his influence over the young king, James V, that by 1527 the Douglas family dominated both the administration of the country and the royal household. In 1528 the king contrived to escape to Edinburgh Castle. As the power of the Douglases lay in the control of the king's person, and as their exercise of that power had aroused the hatred and jealousy of most of the other great families, they were open to attack, and they and their connections were to suffer. A proscription of all of the name of Douglas was issued in 1528–9, and included on the list was the name of Janet, Lady Glamis.

James V was probably the least attractive, certainly the least edifying, member of his dynasty, and his policies – in Scotland at least – seem to have been based on revenge, lust and greed – qualities of which any one would have accounted for his treatment of Lady Glamis. She was a Douglas, she was reputed to be both beautiful and virtuous, and there were rich pickings to be had out of the lands and castle of Glamis. That they were not her property, but belonged to her son John, the young 7th Lord Glamis, seems to have been a legal nicety that did not bother the king. Lady Glamis, who had taken as her second husband Sir Alexander Campbell, son of the 2nd Earl of Argyll, was indicted in 1532 on a charge of poisoning her first husband. The charge was patently absurd and the Angus jury, before which she was brought, refused to countenance it. A second and equally brave jury refused to be browbeaten by the king. In 1537 a more serious charge – that of plotting to poison the king – was brought. For this she was condemned to be burnt at the stake. She suffered this fate, and at the same time her son-in-law, John, Master of Forbes, was beheaded on a charge of conspiring to shoot James V with a culverin in the course of a visit to Aberdeen 'that the Douglasses might be restor'd to their ancient possessions, titles and honours'. Her husband, Sir Alexander, who, together with her two sons, had been arrested, died in attempting to escape from Edinburgh Castle – a polite fiction for being murdered or executed – and the young Lord Glamis and his brother were detained until such time as they were old enough to be executed in their turn.

The estates were forfeit to the Crown in 1537, and their dispersal to the courtiers and others who were friends of the king began, James retaining for his own use the lands and castle of Glamis itself. In a charter of 14 September 1537, in which the king granted the lands of Nether-Coulquher to John Ros, the position of Lord Glamis is made painfully clear: 'Johannes olim dom. Glammys, filio et herede quondam Johannis dom. G., deductam pro nonnullis proditonie traditionis et lese majestatis criminibus per ipsum commissis.'[1] These were the same charges brought against the king's one-time favourite, Sir James Hamilton of Finnart. Another early grant was that made on 13 October, at Brechin, of the lands of Kinghorne to James Kirkcaldy of Grange.

From 1537 until shortly before the king's death, Glamis became another of the royal houses to which the court regularly moved, and during this time there was considerable expenditure on the castle. The visits generally took place in the autumn, and became increasingly frequent after the king's marriage in 1538 to Mary of Guise. One of the charges sometimes levelled against this much-maligned woman is that in some way she was associated with the persecution of the family and the looting of the castle – a base libel, for it had all taken place before her arrival in Scotland. The forfeiture was finally legalized in 1540 when, on 10 December, the king, with the agreement of the Three Estates, registered the forfeiture of his main enemies, Lord Glamis, Sir James Hamilton of Finnart, Sir George Douglas, the Master of Angus, and Archibald Douglas of Kilspindie.

The death of James V in 1542 brought freedom to Lord Glamis and his brother, together with the restoration of most of the estates. But freedom came too late for George Lyon, who, shortly after his release, was to die from the hardships he had suffered in prison. Lord Glamis was married on 6 February 1544 to Jean Keith, sister of the Earl Marischal, and attached himself to the pro-English and Protestant party led by the Earls of Angus and Lennox. This imposed a measure of self-sacrifice, since he had been unable to recover the lands of Kinghorne, still held by Kirkcaldy of Grange, a 'creature of Angus'. It was not until Kirkcaldy's involvement in the murder of Cardinal Beaton in 1546 that Kinghorne was recovered, a return confirmed (under the Great Seal) on 12 September 1548. After this, Lord Glamis seems to have taken little part in the political life of the kingdom, and the family tradition that he went abroad in 1548, at the time the young queen was sent to France, returning to die in 1559, may well be true.

John, 8th Lord Glamis, succeeded as a minor; he could not have been more than fifteen at his father's death. Not having been worn out by years in prison, he returned to the family tradition of serving the Crown. He first showed his loyalty in August 1562, entertaining the queen at Glamis on her journey northward to quell the rebellion of George Gordon, 4th Earl of Huntly. He continued to support her when her proposal to marry her cousin, Lord Darnley, incurred the opposition of her half-brother, the Lord James, and of the Hamiltons, who preferred their own pretensions to the throne. Her marriage to Lord Bothwell, however, strained Glamis's loyalty to breaking-point, and, although he was one of the Confederate Lords ostensibly pledged to release Queen Mary from her marriage, he was more likely to have been aiming – as they all were – at the installation of the infant James VI on the throne. With the outbreak of civil war between the Queen's Men and the King's Men following Mary's flight to England, Lord Glamis, with all of his name, supported the party that stood for the king. He survived the changes of Regency – Moray, Lennox and Mar – receiving his reward from James Douglas, 4th Earl of Morton, in 1572 when he was appointed Chancellor of Scotland for life. Lord Glamis lost both the office and his life when Morton was overthrown by the Earls of Atholl and Argyll. A few days after the coup he was conveniently killed in a brawl between his own followers and those of the Earl of Crawford. The office of Chancellor passed to Lord Argyll.

Lord Glamis had a brother, Sir Thomas Lyon of Auldbar, confusingly known as the Master of Glamis, who was equally politically minded. In spite of suffering forfeiture in 1589 for his part in the Ruthven Raid of 1587, he was back in favour in 1595 when he was appointed Treasurer, an office he held without any great loss of principles for the next eleven years.

Patrick, 9th Lord Glamis, was only three years old when his father died; his mother, Elizabeth, was the daughter of Lord Abernethy and widow of William Meldrum of Fyvie. Like his grandfather, he was said to have travelled widely in France before returning to Scotland, where he was sworn to the Privy Council and given the Captaincy of the King's Guard. An early portrait of him at Glamis – attributed to the School of Clouet – shows him to have been a remarkably handsome youth, who, given the king's predilection for handsome young men, was likely to fare well at court. His marriage to Anne Murray, daughter of the Earl of Tullibardine, took place in June 1595 and was celebrated at Linlithgow in the presence of King James VI (who had arranged it) and Queen Anne.

How soon after his wedding Lord Glamis began enlarging the castle is not certain, but he may have been moved to emulate the work that Lord Dunfermline – the Chancellor – was having done at Fyvie, the home of his mother's first husband. Structurally, if the date on the new work at Glamis is correct, it was finished in 1606, the year he was created 1st Earl of Kinghorne. His son John, 2nd Earl of Kinghorne, completed the interiors between 1615 and 1626. Succeeding to the greatest estate in Scotland (in the opinion of the English ambassador), the 2nd Earl was to die a ruined man in 1646. He kept up considerable state at Glamis which, as a number of inventories of the period show, was richly furnished, but living richly, marrying two wives – both of whom were the daughters of earls – supporting the armies of the Covenanters, building expensively and extensively, granting bonds of caution, entering into commercial ventures and incurring the wrath of Oliver Cromwell could play the devil with any inheritance. On his deathbed the earl left a plundered estate with every acre mortgaged that could be, and debts estimated at a staggering total of between £400,000 and £600,000 Scots or £33,000–£50,000 sterling. His son Patrick succeeded as 3rd Earl, at the age of three, and the estate continued to be plundered by his step-father, the Earl of Linlithgow.

Earl Patrick's childhood was impoverished, and it was not until after his mother's death in 1660, and his marriage to Helen, daughter of the Earl of Middleton, that he began, slowly, to come about. Gradually he paid off his father's debts and repaired his houses, starting with Castle Lyon, and beginning work on Glamis in 1668–9, moving there in 1670. The story of his shifts and struggles is set out in his *Book of Record* (*see* Chapter 14). Politically, Earl Patrick seems to have been a moderate in an age of faction, and he continued his family's tradition of service to the Crown, being sworn to the Privy Council in 1682, and appointed an Extraordinary Lord of Session in 1686. This last was largely an honorary post, but it carried a pension of £300 sterling and was, in part, compensation for the losses he had incurred during Argyll's rebellion of the previous year when he had been buying supplies for the government. Like most of the nobility he would have stood by King James VII and II at the time of the invasion of the Prince of Orange, and seems to have wished to assemble, in concert with other peers, such of the militia as he controlled to stand in defence of the Crown. James's own behaviour made this impossible, and with his flight to France the Stuart cause was lost. Wisely, Earl Patrick carried the address of the Privy Council to London, and made his peace with the new king. In spite of his opposition to the Presbyterian party of Lord Melville, Earl Patrick swallowed his principles and, in 1690, took the oath of allegiance to the new monarchs.

Earl Patrick's other achievement was to start his life as 3rd Earl of Kinghorne and finish it as 3rd Earl of Strathmore. The creation had limited the Earldom of Kinghorne to the heirs-male of the 1st Earl. In 1670 Earl Patrick obtained a new charter allowing him to name his successor in default of male issue. Why he should have done this, since he already had a son, is not clear, unless he was concerned at the lack of other male kinsmen. He and his father were only sons, and his only close cousins, descending from a great-uncle, were the Lyons of Brigton. Five years later, and with three sons to his credit, he obtained a further charter, and since 1677 the proper designation of succeeding earls has been Earl of Strathmore and Kinghorne, Viscount Lyon, Lord Glamis, Tannadyce, Sidlaw and Strathdichtie. The Earldom of Strathmore takes precedence over that of Kinghorne, and the eldest son generally takes the courtesy title of Lord Glamis rather than that of Viscount Lyon. In the peerage of the United Kingdom the family also enjoys the titles of Baron of Streatlam, first granted to John, 10th Earl, and then revived for Claude, 13th Earl, and that of Earl of Strathmore and Kinghorne, granted to his son, also Claude, 14th Earl, on the occasion of the coronation of George VI.

This advance in honours coincided with the political decline of the family. John, 4th Earl, who was born in 1663, is distinguished for little other than marrying a daughter of the house of Stanhope, the first of a succession of countesses of English blood (not until 1926 was an heir to be born of a Scottish mother), and for fathering seven sons, four of whom succeeded in turn as Earl of Strathmore, and the Lady Mary Lyon, one of his three daughters, who was to live until 1780, by which time she had witnessed the destruction of much of her grandfather's work at the castle. Never again were any of the great offices of state held by any of the name of Lyon, as the family's political interest dwindled into contesting the Forfar elections with the adherents of Lord Panmure. These contests became so expensive that the parties agreed to stand at alternate elections in order to save some of the costs.[2]

Two sons, both known as Lord Glamis, died before their father, and it was the third son, John, who succeeded as 5th Earl in 1712. He was to hold the title for only three years, foolishly involving himself in the first Jacobite rebellion of 1715. He was probably influenced by his uncle, Patrick Lyon of Auchterhouse, MP for Angus. Lord Strathmore raised a regiment – Strathmore's Battalion – of 250 men; his second-in-command was Walkinshaw of Barrowfield, whose daughter, Clementine, was later to become a mistress of the Young Pretender. The young earl was not happy in his command; in crossing the Forth, he and his men were driven on to the Isle of May. There, his Angus Lowlanders fought Lord Drummond's Highlanders, and by the time Mar's army had reached Kelso, Lord Strathmore was without his troops, who had not made it south. The battalion had rejoined Mar's forces before

Sheriffmuir, but was detached from the main army to guard Perth, and it is not clear how many men were at Sheriffmuir fighting with their colonel. He fell defending the colours, and with him fell his uncle, Patrick Lyon.

His death on the battlefield was a blessing for his family, although it may not have been seen as such at the time. He was dead before he could have suffered by the Acts of Attainder brought in against those alive or captured at the end of the rebellion, so it was possible for

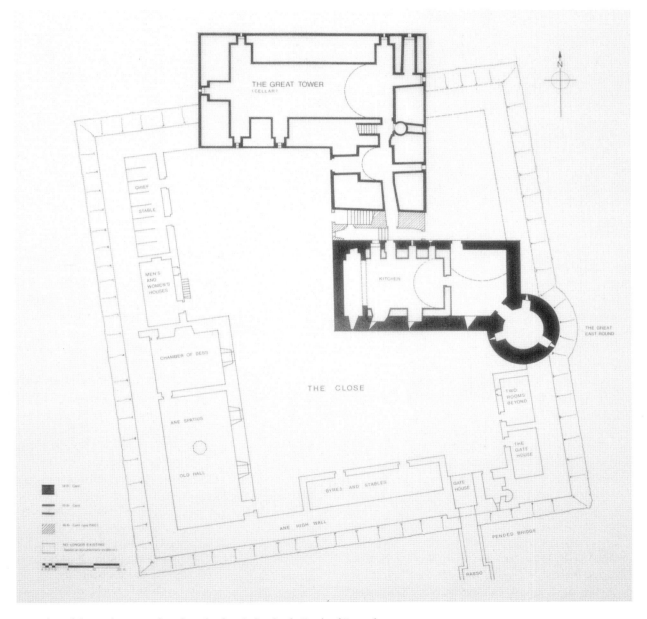

1.4 Plan of the castle c *1560, based on the description in the* Book of Record

the estates and title to pass to his younger brother, Charles, a boy of sixteen. Since he was a minor, the new earl could not be held responsible for the actions of those in whose charge he was, and who did all that was in their power to compromise his position.

The Pretender (or the Chevalier, or James VIII) had finally arrived in Scotland, landing at Peterhead on 15 December 1715. Moving south, he reached Glamis on 4 January 1716; he spent two nights there, touching for the King's Evil and displaying all the gloomy piety of his father. A romantic gloss is always put on this visit, with eighty beds made up for the prince and his companions, and all the implications of a royal court. The reality must have been slightly different with a funeral barely over, and camp beds everywhere amidst all the confusion of a defeated army. Moving on, the Pretender dined at Castle Lyon on 7 January, arriving at Scone the following day. The rebels continued at Perth until 30 January, during which time the villages and houses between the burgh and Dunblane were fired, the order for this savagery having been 'Given at our Court at Scoon, the 17th day of January in the fifteenth day of our reign 1715/16'. The Pretender left Perth on the morning of 1 February and three days later took ship at Montrose for France.

Although Glamis was to figure in the itineraries of both commanders in the course of the second Jacobite rebellion, the family had learned a lesson, and took part in no further treasonable correspondence.

Of Charles, 6th Earl, who succeeded his Jacobite brother and married Lady Susan Cochrane, there is little known save the manner of his death in 1728. He had been in Forfar attending a funeral when he became involved in a scuffle with John Lyon of Brigton and James Carnegie of Finavon. There was some dispute as to whose sword ran the earl through, but the privilege is usually allowed to Finavon's, he being less closely connected with the family than Brigton. The widowed countess enlivened the family history by being the subject of a lawsuit brought against her by George Forbes, her former factor and sometime Master of Horse to the Pretender in 1743. He was claiming certain rents due to him – *jus mariti* – by virtue of an alleged marriage, which she strenuously denied.

The 7th Lord Strathmore and his wife – a Miss Mary Oliphant, who died five months after their marriage – were totally undistinguished, and it was not until the accession in 1735 of Thomas, 8th Earl, the last of the four brothers, that a measure of interest returns to the chronicle. He married Jean Nicholson, daughter and heiress of James Nicholson of Rainton, Co. Durham, beginning the family's long connection with the north of England. Earl Thomas was a man of vision, although none of his visions was to be realized. Had they been, and had they survived, Glamis would have been an even more remarkable place than it is. In a survey of the policies, which the earl commissioned from Thomas Winter in 1746, is a proposal for replacing part of the avenue with a series of cascades and basins; from the same time dates a design for an enormous stable and office court to replace Earl Patrick's service court, which always had the appearance of something run up as an afterthought.

Earl Thomas showed no inclination to become involved in the '45, and seems to have spent most of 1745 and 1746 out of the way of all temptation in Co. Durham. The Young Pretender may have stopped at Glamis on his retreat after Falkirk, and his cousin, the Duke of Cumberland, who was there for one night in February 1746, is said to have slept in the bed that had been used by the Old Pretender – not necessarily an act of spite, since both princes would have slept in the State Bed in the State Bedroom. If it had been the bed slept in by the Old Pretender, the story of its breaking up on the orders of the earl because it had been profaned by Hanoverian slumbers is hardly likely to be true: after all, State Beds were expensive.

Countess Susan, who had escaped from the entanglement with George Forbes, remained a cause of concern until her death in 1754. Her jointure was a drain on the estate, and she was a life rentrix of Castle Lyon. Fortunately, the dowager died within eighteen months of her brother-in-law, and the estate was not burdened with two jointures.

The accession of John, 9th Earl of Strathmore, in 1753 was to open perhaps the most devastating chapter in the history of the castle, and one that was to close overshadowed by the likelihood of a total eclipse both of the house and of the family. Sixteen years of age at the time of his father's death, Earl John was to enjoy a minority of five years during which there was an accumulation of the revenues of the estate, an accumulation which seems to have given him a false idea of his spending powers. By 1763 he was having designs prepared for the enlargement of the castle, and his marriage to Mary Eleanor Bowes in 1767 spurred him on to further plans for the improvement of Glamis and its policies.

Mary Eleanor was the most notable heiress of the day, having inherited a fortune of £600,000 and the two great estates of Streatlam and Gibside from her father, and with a further fortune in prospect from her mother. Of this fortune Lord Strathmore was to see little; he does not even seem to have enjoyed the spending of the income. In spite of five children, the marriage was not a happy one, husband and wife being totally unsuited to each other. Lady Strathmore was a woman of considerable intellectual gifts – she was reckoned among the first amateur botanists of her day – but of small intelligence save in the matter of protecting her fortune, of vicious character and a fool where men were concerned. Her future sufferings she brought on herself by her own unbridled behaviour.

Between 1769 and 1776 the earl concentrated his effort on the improvements he was hoping to effect at Glamis. When he sailed for Lisbon in the latter year, in the hope of repairing his shattered health, he left behind him a partly demolished castle, a park that was largely a quagmire and a young family only partially protected from the inattention of their mother. He died at sea on 7 March, and within six months Lady Strathmore had made a second and totally disastrous marriage, becoming Mrs Stoney Bowes.

With the death of the earl came the unravelling of his affairs, and the full extent of the disaster was revealed. The curators were Thomas Lyon – a distant kinsman of the young heir – James Menzies and David Erskine of Edinburgh; the task facing them was a daunting one, the debts enormous. The English debts amounted to £76,000, the Scottish to £65,000; £50,000 was secured to the younger children and £2,000 was owed as arrears of interest on Countess Jean's portion for the last twenty years – a total of £193,000, or four times the debts left by the 2nd Earl in 1645. In addition, the sum of £8,072 had to be found out of the income from the estate to provide for the interest on the debts and for certain annuities.

In Scotland, in the case of a minor succeeding, it was the practice to bring all moveables to public roup, with the exception of portraits, armorial china, silver and linen and, sometimes, books – reservations which may have owed more to custom than to law – and these were generally bought in by family and friends. On this occasion, the sale was a necessity. The first things to go were the contents of the London house, since these were not covered by Scottish law. The pictures were removed to Christie's premises in Pall Mall, followed by the furniture valued at £314, and the bullion and plate which sold for £221 13s 2d. The curators hoped to save the old castle of Glamis and an income of £1,000 for the earl, but even this was not certain. Castle Lyon, bought in 1614 for

£2,200, was sold for £40,000; luckily it had not been secured on a life-rent to either of the dowagers. The sale of further lands reduced the debt to £30,000. To fund this and the various annuities was an income of £2,700, of which £500 was secured on the English estates for the maintenance of the younger children. From the balance of £2,200, interest on the debts and the annuities took £2,172, so that only £28 was left for the maintenance and education of the heir. The very real fear was that the estate would be totally exhausted, and all the properties would be in danger.

It was suggested that Countess Jean – who had received little of her Scottish annuity for years – might sell her English lands in return for a secured annuity (secured on what is not made clear), and leave her Scottish annuity in abeyance until after the death of Countess Eleanor, when her grandson would be able to pay it. If this were not done, then it was feared that Glamis would have to go. This wildly imaginative suggestion did not have to be put to the test, since Countess Jean died in 1778. The estate in Scotland was freed of the payment of the jointure, and her English estates fell to the earl, considerably relieving his difficulties.

Even if she had been inclined to help – which she was not – Countess Eleanor was debarred from doing so by her marriage to the adventurer Stoney Bowes. From long before the day of her wedding her properties had been the principal interest of her husband, and in spite of the deeds which she had executed and which put them beyond his reach, both she and they were entangled in a net of legalities from which there was no escape until the final divorce in 1789.

For the next thirteen years the castle lay semi-derelict, its only inhabitant being old Lady Mary Lyon, daughter of the 4th Earl. She lived there until her death in 1780, writing sadly on one occasion to the curators to ask if the charge of providing meat for Barbara Archer, who was employed in airing the rooms and taking care of the uninhabited parts of the castle, might not be borne by them.

In 1790 the earl came of age, was reconciled with his mother – previously she had detested him – purchased her interests in the English estates and began the work of repairing the neglect of the past years. Building work started again, and the castle was put into repair; a new west wing was added – although not completed internally – the roof-line altered, the policies improved and the avenue replanted. However, the castle never became lived in; the earl preferred London and his English estates, going to Glamis only for short periods in the late summer and early autumn. The rooms were modestly furnished and the servants on board wages.

John, 10th Earl of Strathmore, resembled his mother in his character far more than he did his father. He was an almost archetypal nobleman of Regency romance, whether in shooting William Lancaster, a highwayman who held up his poste-chaise on Finchley Common, or in his very public liaison with the beautiful Lady Tyrconnel. Born a Delaval of Seaton Delaval, wife of an impoverished and singularly complaisant Irish peer, she remained his mistress for ten years, until her death at Gibside in 1800. Countess Eleanor also died that year, her health possibly undermined from the hurt she received in 1793, when her coach was overset near Guildford; she had ordered her coachman to pass the Portsmouth diligence at full gallop. It was another nine years before her son settled down.

When Lord Strathmore first met Mary Millner is not certain, but it seems to have been some time in 1809. Her father has been variously described as a schoolmaster, a market gardener or a journeyman gardener from Staindrop, a village close to Streatlam Castle. After the birth of John Strathmore Bowes in 1811, Mary Millner lived openly with the earl as mistress of his household and mother of his acknowledged son. In all but name they were husband and wife, and Mary Millner, if Augustus Hare's story of a false marriage is true, may well have believed herself to have been so. In an age when moral consciousness and class distinction went hand in hand, no obloquy was attached to Mary Millner, so others too may have believed in the marriage. That she did not sit at the head of the earl's table when he had company may have owed more to her social inadequacies than to anything else. That the earl did not share this view of a secret marriage is shown in the settlements he made, securing everything which he could to his son, and excluding, as far as lay in his power, his legitimate male relations from any enjoyment from the estates of which he could not deprive them.

On Sunday 2 July 1820 Lord Strathmore, who was clearly dying, was carried in a sedan chair from his bedroom to St George's, Hanover Square, where he was married to Mary Millner by the Dean of Carlisle. The following day he was dead. The marriage was legal, the dean having taken care there should be no doubt about this, especially as the archbishop had had so many doubts of his own that he refused to issue a special licence. The future of the titles and estates now turned on the question of the earl's domicile. If it were in Scotland, then John Strathmore Bowes under Scots law would inherit everything except his father's English barony, since he was now legitimatized by his parents' marriage. If, however, the earl was domiciled in England, the law took a different view: John Strathmore Bowes had been born a bastard, and no subsequent act on the part of his parents could alter that fact. The question had to be tested through the courts for the position of the heirs to be established. The final judgement pronounced by Lord Eldon was that the earl's domicile had been in England, and therefore the earl's only surviving brother, Thomas Lyon Bowes, succeeded to the titles and settled estates as 11th Earl of Strathmore. Lord Eldon has been criticized for this decision, but it is difficult to see what other he could have reached. Curiously, in an almost identical case – Munro versus Munro – which came before the courts a few years later, a different conclusion was reached.

The titles were about all that came to Earl Thomas. Foreseeing correctly the likely conclusion of such a case, the 10th Earl, after securing the bulk of the English estates – the great Bowes inheritance – to his son, ensured that his male relations would reap as little as possible enjoyment or benefit from the Scottish properties. In a particularly vindictive settlement in 1815, the 10th Earl settled that these should go with the Earldom of Strathmore, but with the express provision that neither his brother Thomas, nor his cousins John Lyon of Hetton or Charles Lyon, both of whom were in the line of succession, should benefit at all. In addition, he placed the Glamis estate in a Trust that was to remain in force for a period of thirty years after his death. Lest this should not be sufficient protection, the Trustees were empowered to extend this Trust indefinitely, should John or Charles Lyon succeed to the titles and the estates under the entail. There is no known reason for this degree of animus on the 10th Earl's part, but it could well have arisen from personal slights offered to Mary Millner, now the dowager countess. It did not extend to any heirs who might be born to his brother, so his nephew, born in 1801, was not intended to be a victim of this rancour.

Thomas Lyon Bowes, 11th Earl of Strathmore, hardly figures in the history of the castle. Marrying three times and fathering one son and two daughters, he died in the shabby grandeur of the debtors' sanctuary of Holyrood House, where for a time he was the friend and neighbour of the exiled Bourbons. His third wife outlived him, ending her life there also. When Lady Glamis heard that the old Lady Strathmore was *in extremis*, she travelled immediately to Edinburgh to secure the pictures and valuables of the family, which would otherwise have been seized by the late earl's creditors. These she had packed and sent away to St Paul's Walden (in Hertfordshire) before the dowager was dead.

Thomas George, Lord Glamis, had died at Honfleur in 1834, before his father the 11th Earl, but not before running heavily and hopelessly into debt. Lady Glamis, whose own estates had been burdened by his extravagances, was left with four young children in circumstances so reduced that at times they almost amounted to starvation. From this state she was rescued largely through the efforts of a loyal friend, Alexander Gibbon. Even then, her life was not made easier by the extravagance of her elder son, Thomas George, who, on the death of his grandfather in 1846, became 12th Earl, and who had already burdened the Shadwell Estate, which should have supported her, with numerous encumbrances.

It was now that the Trustees, acting honourably and in good faith, but blindly, as Trustees often do, made a serious mistake. In 1850, by the terms of the 10th Earl's settlement, the Glamis Trust was due to end, but as Charles Lyon was still alive, it could have been extended. Neither the 12th Earl nor his brother was married, and it would still have been possible for Charles Lyon to inherit under the entail. In spite of this, and in spite of the evidence of his extravagance, the Trustees brought the Trust to an end, and put the young earl in possession of a largely unencumbered estate. They may have thought that his approaching marriage might have quietened him, but in this they were to be proved wrong. His wife, Charlotte Barrington, daughter of Viscount Barrington, a cold and beautiful woman, was fast where he was rackety. Described by Lady Airlie as 'perfect from the crown of her head to the soles of her feet', she was never happy in the north. Lord Strathmore did much to improve the castle for her, providing, in addition to a splendid new dining room, 'four large and beautiful appointed bathrooms, a great novelty in those days, and two great vans arrived from Maples shop in London, filled with furniture of beautiful workmanship, but totally unsuited to the old castle'. Lady Airlie tells how on her visits to Glamis she would find the countess 'installed in her boudoir entirely furnished in black Austrian bentwood chairs, all upholstered in pale blue satin, Lady Strathmore herself being dressed in pink silk

brocade, smoking cigars and dispensing tea to her friends from a silver gilt tea service'. Added to this, she scandalized the inhabitants of Glamis by coursing hares on the Sabbath! Small wonder that Lord Airlie informed his wife 'that her visits to Glamis did not improve her'.

Countess Charlotte died of Roman fever in Florence in 1854, and for the next ten years Lord Strathmore's course of living was calculated to ruin any fortune. Under the evil influence of a man named Webb – one of those hangers-on dear to Victorian novelists – who encouraged his habit of reckless betting, and possibly from a desire to emulate the successes of his cousin, John Bowes, on the turf, he dissipated his own and his expected inheritance. When he died in 1865 he was a ruined man. The stroke that finally killed him may have been hastened by the impending crash. Glamis, which had been freed from all debt during the thirty-year Trust, was now burdened with liabilities of more than £250,000. To obtain the means to meet these calls it was necessary to alter the family settlements, and this brought about another lawsuit, this time between the 13th Earl and his infant sons. Once again, the troubles of Glamis were of immense benefit to the lawyers. It is worth noting that, apart from the two lawsuits, it needed no less than seven private Acts of Parliament and one public Act to resolve the affairs of the family during the nineteenth century.

With the succession of Claude, the 13th Earl, the family name changed again. Before 1767 it had been Lyon; under the terms of her father's will, Mary Eleanor's husband had to take the name of Bowes alone; the 11th Earl changed it to Lyon Bowes; it now became Bowes Lyon, the name borne today.[3] With the change of name came a change of tone. For the first time since the death of the 4th Earl, in 1712, propriety, responsibility, piety and domesticity reigned at the castle. In fact, life at Glamis under Earl Claude reflected all that was best in Victorian society, his diaries showing that it was neither stiff nor dull. Even the visit of Mr Gladstone in September 1884, which, apart from the great man's private detective, needed the presence of six policemen by day and three by night, passed off lightly.

All his life the 13th Earl struggled to repair the damage brought about by the reckless extravagance of his brother and father. By the deaths of his mother, Lady Glamis, in 1881, and of John Bowes, with whom he had always been on good terms, in 1885, the earl's financial position was eased considerably. Towards the end of his life he was able to embark on much-needed improvements at the castle, and by the time of his death the estates were largely free of difficulties.

His son, Claude, 14th Earl, married a descendant of the great Anglo-Dutch house of Cavendish Bentinck, and their lives followed the pattern set by the 13th Earl. His family was large and united to an unusual extent, and particularly distinguished in the person of the youngest daughter, the Lady Elizabeth, who, in 1923, married Prince George, Duke of York, the second son of George V. In the course of time she became queen, and then queen mother, and with her Glamis will always be closely identified.

CHAPTER 2
GLAMIS CASTLE: THE EARLY YEARS, 1379–1480

1379–1404

The early history of the castle of Glamis, like that of the family that has lived there for the past six hundred years, is obscure, and the legendary instruction to 'Build the Castle in a bog/Where it will neither shack nor shog' can hardly be said to inculcate sound building practice. The site, low-lying and, before later drainage work was undertaken, damp, was defensible and, it could be argued, since it commands a wide area of the low country below the glens of Angus, of some strategic importance. This would have counted in its favour, and judging by the weight of the later buildings erected, the site may have been chosen because it had a natural bottom of rock or gravel. The surrounding country would have abounded in waterfowl and game of all sorts, and there is no reason to doubt that the tradition of there having been a royal hunting lodge there is founded on fact, although there is not a shred of evidence to support the story.

The royal house of Scotland has been associated with the castle since the earliest times, and to hold the Thaneage of Glamis was generally reckoned a mark of royal favour. When the chronicler Fordoun tells that King Malcolm, grandfather of that Duncan killed by Macbeth, was ambushed near Glamis and died, three days later, of his wounds, the implication is that he died at the castle. *Scotichronicon* is more certain: 'In vico Glammez rapuit mors libera regem'.[1] Of these earliest buildings no vestige remains above ground, nor is it certain that any can be found below, either here or anywhere else in the neighbourhood: neither are there any

signs of the buildings that succeeded them in the course of the next 300 years. By the middle of the fourteenth century it could be expected that there would be a stone building of some sort on the site, probably a simple hall house, not unlike Rait: a hall and chamber over cellars, with subsidiary buildings of timber and clay, enclosed by banks and a timber stockade. The stone building would have served as the royal apartments, while the lesser timber-built ones would have provided for the higher officers, the kitchens and, probably, the stables. As a hunting lodge, the living quarters of the other attendants would have been of a much more temporary nature.

At the time that Sir John was first granted Glamis it was unlikely that he would have wanted a more permanent home than was already there. His own appointments, if not his wife's close connection with the king, her father, would have involved them in the peripatetic life of the royal court. Even the acknowledgement of their marriage in 1379, probably brought about by the birth of their son, would not necessarily have changed this pattern. What was good enough for Robert II was likely to prove good enough for his children.

1404–1435

Sir John Lyon was killed in 1382 and succeeded by his son, John, as second laird of Glamis. It is to this son that the earliest part of the castle now standing must be credited. This part, the south-east wing with the round tower, the Great Round – and a short adjoining stretch of curtain wall – must date from the years between 1404 and 1435. The choice of these dates is influenced in part by family considerations, and in part by the architectural evidence.

Sir John Lyon (II) was knighted in 1404, when he was twenty-five and probably the year in which he married his cousin, Elizabeth Graham. Unlike his father or his son after him, Sir John did not hold any office of importance in the royal household, and by 1425 he may have seen that, for one of his descent, too close an association with his royal cousins could be unhealthy. In any case, the need to put down roots somewhere in the country, and to establish a territorial base would be a natural thing to do: of all the lands pertaining to the family, those of Glamis were the richest.

Given that there were family reasons for a programme of new building work at Glamis in the years 1404–35, is there architectural evidence to support this view? There are clearly two buildings of the fifteenth century at Glamis: the south-east wing and the Great Tower. According to the family histories, the latter was started by Patrick, 1st Lord Glamis – that is, after 1435

– and completed after his death in 1459 by his widow. This date is supported by the parallels between the Great Tower and Castle Huntly, built for Lord Gray around 1452. As there is nothing to suggest that the south-east wing is later than 1459 it must be the earlier of the two buildings.

In plan, the wing consists of a rectangular block, measuring 59 ft 6 in. (18.13m) by 30 ft 6 in. (9.29m), with a round tower, always known as the Great Round, of 25 ft (7.62m) diameter at the south-east corner. To the north of the east gable is a 20-ft (6.10m) length of curtain wall, now incorporated into a later building. This curtain wall, the south and east faces of the wing, and the Great Round rise from a massive battered plinth; there is no evidence for there having been such a plinth on the west or north faces of the wing. This would suggest that the plinth occurred only on the external faces of a range occupying the south-east corner of a large courtyard, enclosed by a stone curtain wall, and on the external face of the curtain wall as well. The depth

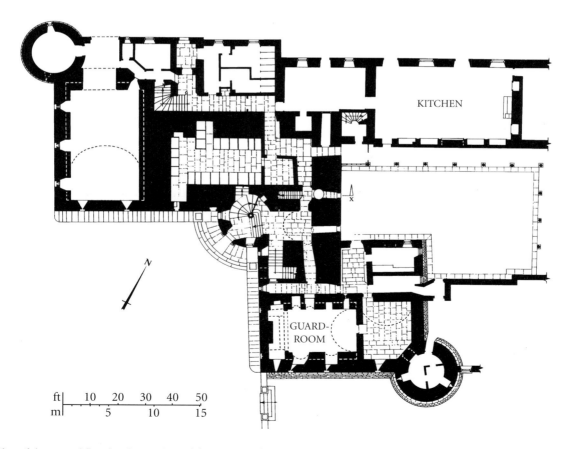

2.1 Plan of the ground floor (© Crown Copyright/RCAHMS)

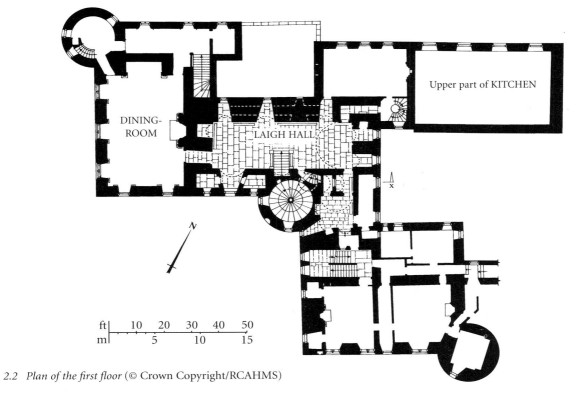

2.2 Plan of the first floor (© Crown Copyright/RCAHMS)

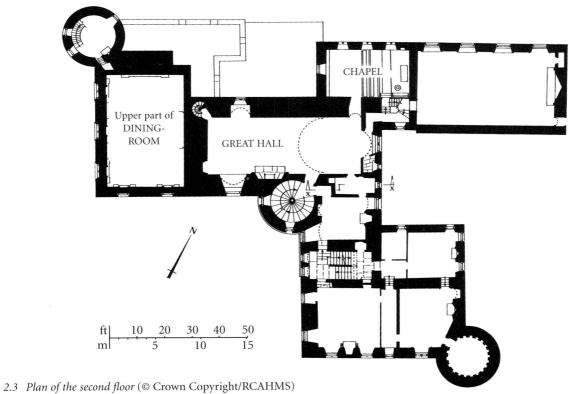

2.3 Plan of the second floor (© Crown Copyright/RCAHMS)

and extent of the plinth has never been established, and the excavation necessary for this is unlikely to be carried out because of the damage it would do to the garden. From later descriptions it seems that the ditch immediately surrounding the castle was water-filled: a sloping plinth rising directly from the water is, architecturally, a most satisfying feature.

In the course of time this wing has been subjected to repeated alterations, but it is still possible to arrive at a fairly clear idea of the original internal arrangements. When built, there were three barrel-vaulted cellars in the main block and one in the Great Round, which was entered from the easternmost cellar in the main part of the wing. This in turn was entered from the courtyard by way of a round-headed doorway, as was the middle cellar, although this doorway is now blocked. The doorway from the courtyard to the western cellar has been altered, and both the western and middle cellars were thrown into one and given a new vault in the sixteenth century. There was no internal staircase from the cellars to the first floor, so access must have been by way of an external stair. On the upper floor there are the remains of a newel stair in the wall thickness at the junction of

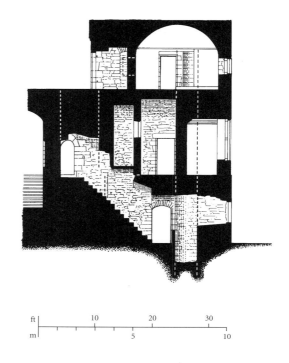

2.4 *Section, showing remains of medieval stairs (x–x on Figure 2.1) (© Crown Copyright/RCAHMS)*

2.5 *Plan of the ground floor: the original layout of the south-east wing or 'palace house', c 1430*

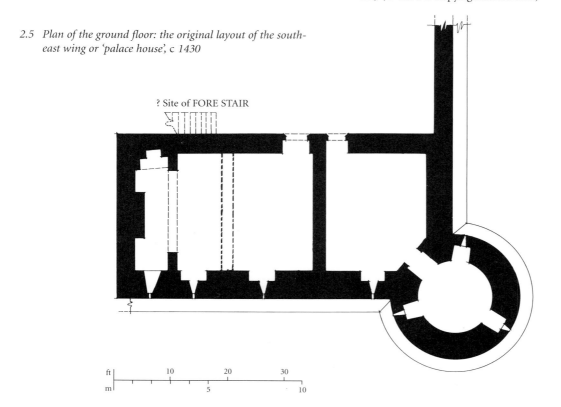

the east gable with the Round, but this would not have been continued down to the cellars.

The upper floors have suffered from later alterations even more than the ground floor, and the present cross-partitions are all part of these alterations. In the original building any cross-partition would have risen above one of the cellar walls. If there were such a cross-wall, it would have been over the wall between the east and middle cellars, producing a 'palace-house' plan, that is, a plan where the rooms on the principal floor were arranged in the sequence of hall – outer chamber – inner chamber, as at Druminnor (*c* 1440) or Strathbogie (*c* 1450), in contrast to the 'hall-house' plan of hall chamber, as at Rait (*c* 1310) or Arbuthnott (*c* 1420). With the 'palace' plan it was usual for there to be an additional floor of similar accommodation, but this has been arranged slightly differently at Glamis. When such a plan was adopted it was usual for the private stair to rise at the junction of the hall and the outer chamber. At Glamis it is placed between the inner and outer chambers. This could indicate that the whole of the main wing was given over to the hall, so that Glamis was a two-floored 'hall house' rather than a 'palace house' (which would have produced an unusually large hall) or that the hall rose the full height of the two chamber floors. Either of these solutions would have been unusual. The internal dimensions of the first floor, as far as can be judged, were 50 ft (15.24m) by 22 ft (6.71m), the length being based on what was probable before the building of the huge chimney in the west gable; this length is only 6 ft (1.83m) short of that of the hall of the Great Tower. In either a 'hall' or 'palace house' such a hall would have been of unusual size: the most likely arrangement seems to have been that of hall–outer chamber–inner chamber on the first floor, with the location of the staircase explained by the hall rising through two floors.

The position of the hall fireplace can be established. On the north wall, and partly hidden by the upper flight of the staircase between the south-east wing and the Great Tower, is a blocked opening. It has neither worked head nor worked jambs, and does not seem ever to have had them. Such openings can be found elsewhere; a particularly fine set exists at Caerlaverock Castle, and one at Tillycairn was accounted for by W Douglas Simpson as an opening left while building operations were in hand, to facilitate the movement of timbers and other heavy building materials.[2] The correct explanation for these blocked openings, which are to be found at the backs of large fireplaces, is that they are indeed a form of fireback.

Before iron firebacks or baskets came into general use, the stonework at the back of the fireplace suffered badly from the action of the fire, and was more easily replaced if a whole section of wall could be removed rather than if the individual stones had to be taken out and replaced.

In spite of the frequent alterations and refacings that have taken place in the course of time, one feature, or rather several examples of the same feature, has survived down the years. This is that ubiquitous element in early artillery fortifications, the inverted keyhole gun-loop. There are two, with the remains of a third – now replaced by a doorway – in the cellar of the Great Round, and there were three more, one in each of the cellars, all on the south front of the 'palace house'.

Loops of this type had appeared towards the end of the fourteenth century in the south-east of England at, among other places, Cooling Castle and the West Gate, Canterbury, in the years 1379–81. The dating of such loops in Scotland has been a matter of some debate, and, until recently, it was considered that the earliest examples were those at Ravenscraig Castle in Fife. Built by James II for his wife, Mary of Gueldres, and designed by the master mason Henry Merlion, it can be securely dated to the years 1460–3. The difference of eighty years between the first appearance of these loops in England and their appearance in Scotland is always explained as 'time-lag', Scotland being so far behind her southern neighbour in all matters. This theory is hardly tenable: such 'time-lag' as there was involved the time it took for an idea to be carried, either by letter or person, from south to north. There is no reason to suppose that at this social level, the level of courts and magnates, it should have existed. Society at its highest level was cosmopolitan; gunpowder, and consequently artillery and guns, were known in Scotland, and even poor and backward nations then, as now, devoted considerable time and money to acquiring the latest methods of waging war. It has not been suggested that, because Scotland was poor, and distant from Rome or Avignon, its church suffered a 'time-lag' in its knowledge of, or reaction to, the crises that were convulsing the Church at this time. The year 1460 cannot mark the date these loops first appeared in Scotland.

It has been suggested that the inverted keyhole loops in the artillery work at Threave Castle, Stewartry, are earlier than those at Ravenscraig. This suggestion was first made with extreme caution by Stewart Cruden in 1960, when he even more cautiously suggested that similar loops in the outer curtain at Craigmillar might be as early as 1427.[3] His view was that the loops at Threave could not date from the years 1455–1513, when Threave was held by the Crown, since there is no record of expenditure on such a scale in the *Exchequer Rolls*. The likely period for the work was *c* 1445–54, when the Douglas power was being re-established, a move which led James II to murder the 8th Earl of Douglas with his own hand. By the same reasoning it could be argued that the work dated from the years 1437–40 before the death of the 5th Earl and the murder of the young 6th Earl.

The dating of Craigmillar is much more problematical, since it is based on the evidence of a dated tablet, recorded by Nisbet but now vanished.[4] If Craigmillar is left out of the reckoning, it can be seen that this type of loop is found at two buildings with royal or quasi-royal owners – the Douglases always being at risk from their close cousinship with the Crown. At Glamis the loops appear in a castle, the owner of which is a cousin by blood and by marriage to the king; they are not just a piece of fashionable decoration to show that Sir John

Lyon belonged to the gun-loop building classes, but are integral parts of a very serious and carefully planned artillery work.

Sir John's son, Patrick Lyon, was sent to England in 1424, as hostage for payment of James I's ransom. He was probably about twenty at the time, and was to remain in England for three years. During that time he would have seen many things and buildings different from those he knew at home, and on his return may have persuaded his father to rebuild the existing castle, incorporating some of the changes and advances brought about by the increasing use of gunpowder and artillery. If this view is correct, and it is certainly not an unreasonable one, then the loops at Glamis are the earliest identified so far in Scotland.

The planning of the south-east wing – at least at the level of the ground floor – suggests that it was designed with defence by and against artillery in mind. With the exception of the cellar in the Great Round, which could have no independent access, the cellars are entered directly from the courtyard and are not intercommuni-

2.6   Reconstruction of the castle as it appeared c 1430 (reconstruction by author; realization by Terry Ball FSA; © Terry Ball and Strathmore Estates)

cating or served by a common passage; this makes them particularly adapted to a defensive purpose, while not inhibiting their use for domestic storage. That they are not intercommunicating is not necessarily significant. The loop embrasures, although much altered, had, judging by those in the Round, straight instead of splayed sides. In the Round two of the loops are positioned to cover, with flanking fire, the east and south walls of the building and the enclosure, those in the south wall of the main block covering the wet ditch and the land beyond. This indicates that any bank on the opposite side of the ditch must have been lowered to allow for an adequate field of fire. No loops survive in the remaining short length of the east curtain, but these could have been destroyed and their embrasures used for later window openings. It is also relevant that the south and east walls – the external and defensive walls – are 5 ft (1.52m) thick, in contrast to the north, or courtyard, wall which is only 3 ft 6 in. (1.07m) in thickness. If this interpretation and dating is correct, then Sir John Lyon's building of 1427–35 is one of the earliest structures so far

identified in Scotland designed from the outset with artillery warfare as a primary consideration.

Of the original fenestration on the two upper floors, the only remaining evidence may be the two small square windows, which today light the two transverse corridors on each floor. This raises a problem if the suggestion that the hall rose through two floors is accepted. The lower window would have lit the dais, but the upper window would have been superfluous unless it lit a gallery above the dais.

The position of the south-east wing, with its short length of surviving curtain wall and artillery loops in the south face, suggests that at this period it formed a frontal defence of the type seen at Doune and Balvenie.[5]

1450–1480

Tradition and the manuscript histories of the family have it that Patrick, 1st Lord Glamis, began the building of the Great Tower, which was left unfinished at his death in 1459, and completed by his widow some time

2.7   The Great Round: the splayed base and an inverted keyhole loop

before her death in 1484. There is nothing in the building itself to contradict this tradition, and much to support it; in addition, there is a neighbouring castle to Glamis built at about the same time with which there are close parallels, so close in fact that both are likely to have been the work of the same master mason. Castle Huntly lies on Tayside some 15 miles (25km) from Glamis and was built by Lord Gray who was granted a licence for this in 1452 (although whether this was a *post-* or *ante*-licence is not certain, since such grants could often be retrospective). However, it is likely that Glamis and Castle Huntly were built at much the same time.[6] Both are L-towers, Castle Huntly measuring some 63 ft (19.20m) by 40 ft (12.19m) in the tower and 21 ft (6.40m) by 18 ft (5.49m) in the jamb or wing, and Glamis 72 ft (21.95m) by 30 ft (9.14m) in the tower and 29 ft (8.84m) by 21 ft (6.40m) in the jamb. The accommodation is arranged on three floors in the towers and four in the jambs; in addition, because of the fall in the ground, Castle Huntly has a cellar, or pit, beneath the jamb. There are cellars on the ground floor, a vaulted laigh (ie, lower) hall on the first floor, and vaulted great hall on the second floor, equal in height to two floors in the jamb. The original entrance at Castle Huntly was in the re-entrant by way of a doorway into the ground-floor cellar of the jamb. From this cellar, which has no vault, a wooden stair or ladder gave access to the laigh hall, and a newel stair in the thickness of the wall at the junction of the tower and jamb led to the upper floors. At a later date a straight-flight mural stair was introduced to provide an easier means of access between the ground and first floors.

How closely Glamis resembled Castle Huntly in the arrangement of the entrance and access to the first floor is not certain. The destruction consequent upon the building of the great stair in the re-entrant, which destroyed much of the wall between the tower and the jamb, has removed nearly all the evidence. It is possible that the entrance into the tower was by way of a doorway into the cellar of the jamb, but even that is not certain. The cellar was greatly altered when the great stair was built, although the vault seems to have been part of the original build. The doorway into the well-room may be a later opening. It would certainly be illogical for the well to be easily accessible from the entrance, since this would have proved a serious weakness had the entry been forced. The well-shaft rose as high as the great hall, serving the floors of the tower, recalling the much earlier surviving example of this

arrangement at Rochester Castle (and in Scotland at the fourteenth-century Alloa Tower). The well must have been dug at the very latest before the foundations of the Great Tower were set, and may have been in existence for some time. The need to incorporate it in the new building would explain the building of the Great Tower so close to the early hall house.

Access to the first floor could have been managed in two different ways: *either* a direct external stair or ladder, *or* a ladder from the ground floor of the jamb to the laigh hall, as at Castle Huntly. The first is possible and was found at Castle Fraser (*c* 1454) and the considerably earlier Tower of Drum. The second would depend on the cellar vault in the jamb being an insertion, and there is no evidence for this.

Set in the wall thickness at the junction of the main walls of the tower and jamb are the fragmentary remains of a newel staircase. This was entered from the laigh hall through a doorway, half of which still survives today, opening off an embrasure, which was destroyed when the stairs from the laigh hall to the great stair were formed in 1606. This doorway did not open directly on to the stair, which it would have blocked, but into a small lobby. The door was secured from within the staircase. From this point it ascended to the great hall, where it has been destroyed by the present large doorway between that room and the great stair, and it probably continued to the upper floor of the jamb. This stair was built of well-dressed ashlar, and in the part that survives are the remains of an opening with a chamfered jamb. This may have given access to a mural closet or to an entrance to a loft over part of the laigh hall, a not-unusual arrangement and one for which there is ample headroom. From the level of the laigh hall the newel stair descended to a point where it met the head of a straight-flighted stair leading down to the well-room. Here, there is the chamfered jamb of one side of a doorway opening directly on to the newel stair, and secured on the inner side, the stair rising in a right-hand turn, and presumably descending no further. To the right of this jamb, and built with it, is the angle of an ingo which may have led to the doorway at the head of a lower flight leading to the jamb cellar. The cellar of the tower seems to have been reached from the door at the foot of the well-room stair, although this has been much rebuilt. The only other stair in the medieval tower is the small newel stair in the north-west corner of the great hall, which is built of the same finely wrought ashlar.

The first floor of the tower is devoted to the laigh hall, a room so large that there were fireplaces at each end. Traces of the moulded jambs survive, but these could be later remodellings. To the side of each fireplace was a window with stone seats on the ingoes, but only that in the east wall survives intact. The north wall has been considerably altered, and a passage, now blocked, was cut in its thickness in the seventeenth century: it is here that the blocked openings have given rise to the stories of secret chambers filled with skeletons and ghostly card-players. Sadly, the unblocked passage is shown on the eighteenth-century plans.

The south side has suffered as well. Two closets, or 'writing-rooms', have been dug out of the wall thickness on either side of the window embrasure, and an immense hole cut, first in the seventeenth and then in the eighteenth centuries, to allow for the flight of steps from the great stair.

The great hall, like the laigh hall, was so large that a fireplace was provided at each end, as well as the huge fireplace in the south wall. This is an exceptionally generous provision, and may be medieval in origin, although all have been remodelled to some extent, and the one in the north-east corner largely vanished in Earl Patrick's alterations of c 1670. The fenestration is now almost entirely of the early seventeenth century, although it is likely that its original pattern followed that in the laigh hall. The height of the great hall – twice that of the laigh hall – would allow for a loft over the lower end reached from the stair.

Externally, the Great Tower of the fifteenth century is almost entirely lost in the later additions and refacings, but it is still possible to distinguish the change in the masonry that marks the upper floors added c 1606. Typical of the tower's fifteenth-century date is the heavy chamfered offset, which marks the first floor, and the remains of the corbel table on the north face, which once supported the parapet but now carries the outer wall of the galleries.

Reasons for building are often various, and it is difficult to account for the building of the Great Tower at Glamis as anything other than an oversized example of conspicuous expenditure, which, given Lord Glamis's connection with the royal house and James II's suspicious and sanguinary nature, could have proved dangerous. Lord Glamis's tenure of the castle, 1435–59, coincided with his cousin's reign, 1436–60, yet he never seems to have been at risk. Although it so closely resembles Castle Huntly, it is more likely that Glamis served as the model for Lord Gray's castle and therefore dates from the years before Lord Glamis was appointed Keeper of the three northern castles of Kindrochit, Kildrummy and Balvenie.

The tower is typical of many erected in the second half of the fifteenth century, massive and inconvenient, lacking the convenience of the 'palace houses' or the later 'tower houses'. Heavy stone vaults and hugely thick walls led to an extraordinary disproportion between space and structure, and to chambers and closets which too often gave the impression of being quarried out of the rock face rather than being built of masonry. The accommodation, providing three huge vaulted apartments, three or possibly four chambers in the jamb, with perhaps a cap house above, is not generous in relation to the effort involved. Nor is the siting of the tower easily explained: separated by only 10 ft (3.05m) from the 'palace house', and seriously obstructing it on its courtyard side, the position of the tower is so perverse that there must be a reason for it. None suggests itself other than the need to incorporate an existing well in the new building, and this may reflect Lord Glamis's wariness where his cousin's intentions were concerned. A tower with a secure water supply must be a more secure proposition than one without.

A building, which has disappeared and which was possibly of this period but more likely to belong to the following century, is recorded by Earl Patrick in his *Book of Record*. He mentions that there was standing within the courtyard 'a spacious old hall, and off it the thing which they called the chamber of Dess'. Halls separated from the main buildings or towers of their castles are beginning to be recognized outside England. A small one has been found at Smailholm,[7] one with a purely ceremonial function has been identified at Peel Castle,[8] there was one at Old Cromarty Castle,[9] and no doubt others will come to light. The presence of a large hall with a chamber of dais in the courtyard suggests a formal rather than a domestic use, but this is an area of study in which more work needs to be done.

CHAPTER 3

THE ROYAL OCCUPATION, 1537–1542

At the time of James V's seizure of Glamis the castle consisted of two main buildings, the 'palace house', with the Great Round, and close to it – so close that they were only 10 ft (3.05m) apart – the Great Tower. Surrounding these was a courtyard containing the kitchens, stables, other domestic buildings and lodgings necessary to a great household, and possibly the mysterious 'spatious old hall' and 'chamber of Dess'. These were all enclosed by a curtain wall pierced by a gatehouse, which was approached across a drawbridge. Surrounding the curtain was a great water-filled ditch fed by the Glamis Burn, beyond which were two further ditches without running water. It is not known whether these were meant to be wet or dry, but by 1660 they had become damp and stagnant.

Although with the completion of the Great Tower Glamis had become an establishment on the grandest scale – the words 'home' or 'house' being hardly applicable – it was grand in a particularly medieval way, a Scottish medieval way at that. It was hardly adapted to the scale or style proper to the housing of the court. Any great nobleman's castle would suffice for an occasional royal visit made in the course of a progress, a pilgrimage or a hunting trip, but for housing the full court on even a semi-permanent basis something more was needed. The Scottish court, like those of Tudor England and Valois France, was peripatetic; a considerable number of palaces, all within easy reach of each other, was necessary, and in this Scotland followed the pattern of her neighbours. If England had Whitehall, St James, Greenwich, Windsor, Nonsuch, Richmond and Hampton Court, and France could boast the Louvre, St Germain-en-Laye, Fontainebleau, Blois, Chambord and Amboise, Scotland had no reason to be ashamed of Edinburgh Castle, Holyroodhouse, Linlithgow, Falkland or Stirling – or of the newly acquired Glamis.

It is clear from the *Register of the Great Seal*, the *Exchequer Rolls*, the *Register of the Privy Council* and the *Treasurer's Accounts* that from 1537 the court was regularly at the castle, but there is a lack of evidence to show how much was spent on the necessary improvements to bring Glamis to a standard suitable to the demands of the royal household. The only entries in the *Exchequer Rolls* for building work occur in 1539: 'Et eidem in tribus librus septemdecim denarius pro reparatione pontis sublicii vulgo drawbrig, et aliis expensis negotia factis'[1] and 'pro divis expensis circa reparationem loci de Glammys particulariter examinatis super compotum de terminis compoti xlvj li. xix s. x d.,'[2] references as tantalizingly brief as those to the swans on the lake at Bakey, which were unable to fend for themselves but needed feeding, the gardeners, always in need of payment for work they had done, the fish ponds, 'Et piscatosi qui impossebat lucios in stagnae circum locum de Glammys etc',[3] and to the feed required for the king's charger, a splendid beast rejoicing in the name of 'Broune Armstrong'.

For five years, from 1537 until the king's death in 1542, Glamis was in use as a palace. These were the great years of James's building works: the palace in Stirling Castle; the south front at Falkland, following on his earlier work at Holyrood; and Linlithgow. It is difficult to believe that one so given to building would not have made some alterations to this assemblage of disparate buildings at Glamis, making them conform to the pattern of palace life as lived in the second quarter of the sixteenth century. If the king did make these alterations, they are clearly visible in the present building; if he did not, then Glamis has a series of quite inexplicable architectural coincidences.

The evidence of the other palaces in Scotland demonstrates what was necessary in any self-respecting royal residence: a great hall, a chapel, the king's suite and the queen's suite. These were the basic and essential elements. To them could be added any number of ancillary buildings necessary for serving and accommodating the court, according to need or to the suitability of the site.

Of these elements the one for which there is no evidence at all is the chapel. There was hardly room for it in the two main blocks, and Earl Patrick makes no mention of it in his description of the castle as it was in 1660. This does not prove that there was no chapel. It could have vanished, demolished to make way for some of the later buildings in the courtyard.

The great hall has vanished as well, but there is strong evidence for its existence. The great hall of a palace was generally a large and magnificent apartment, which was given over to the public life of the king and was not necessarily close to the privy apartments. At Linlithgow, Holyrood and Falkland it took up one entire side of the quadrangle; at Stirling and Edinburgh it was a separate building. This seems to have been the case at Glamis, where Earl Patrick speaks of 'the walls and ruines of a spatious old hall and off it the thing whc they called the chamber of Dess', which was built in the south-west corner of the courtyard. At Linlithgow is a 'charmer of Dease', or Lyon Chalmer, behind the dais of the great hall, a withdrawing-room to which the party at the high table could retire. If such a room was necessary at Linlithgow, where the great hall and privy apartments were under the same roof, although not immediately adjacent, it was much more necessary at Glamis where the great hall was a separate building.

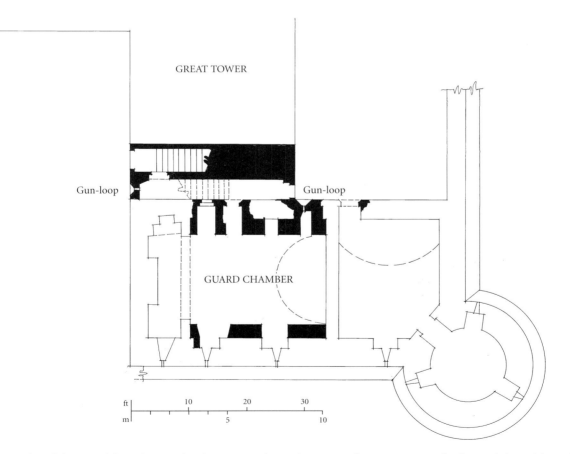

3.1 Plan of the ground floor, showing the alterations to the south-east wing for its use as a royal palace and the positions of the Craignethan-type gun-loops

The privy apartments – the king's and queen's suites – consisted of three rooms: the guard hall, the presence chamber and the bedchamber, which were normally arranged on two floors, although at Stirling they were planned on the same level around an internal court. There would sometimes be a closet beyond the bedchamber, and it was usual for there to be direct communication between the two bedchambers. This arrangement corresponds closely to the old 'palace-house' plan of hall–outer chamber–inner chamber; the use remained the same but the nomenclature was changed. It is still changing and the Historic Scotland guide to Stirling Castle of 1995 uses the terms 'King's Outer Hall' and 'Outer Hall', while the expression 'Guard Hall' may well lead to confusion with the terms 'Guard Room' or 'Guard Chamber'. The underlying principle was the same, however, whatever terminology was used, and that was 'good, better, best', with a diminishing right of access the closer one approached, until the bed and the *chaise-percé* barred all comers.

In the south-east wing at Glamis, the old 'palace house', this plan – three rooms in sequence with a staircase between the two inner chambers – already existed, but the access was restricted and inconvenient: there were no galleries or halls adjoining and the whole was crowded by the Great Tower only 10 ft (3.05m) distant. This was an unpromising situation, but capable of solution, and it was solved with considerable ingenuity. A staircase was built in the space between the Great Tower and the 'palace house', the lower floor of which was largely remodelled, and doorways were driven through the south wall of the jamb so that the laigh hall and the great hall became additional and larger halls associated with the royal apartments. The alterations were carefully thought out: the planning works, and there is no hint of bodging. Of architectural detail of the period, little survives save for five loops of the Craignethan type built in with the new work or blocking an earlier door.[4]

The first essential was improved access, and this was achieved by building the staircase between the Great Tower and the 'palace house'. This was dogleg in plan and formed the principal entrance to the combined buildings by way of the doorway at the stair foot, which opened on to the courtyard. The doorway originally had a richly moulded surround, but this was 'cloured' (knocked) back in the late seventeenth century when the doorway was blocked. The stair rose around a solid core wall with half-landings, and two flights to each floor. Immediately to the right of the doorway is a wide-mouthed gun-loop for a handgun. Internally, the loop is served by an embrasure at the end of a short passage formed under the lowest return flight of the staircase, and entered through a doorway at the stair foot to the right of the entrance. This passage also gives access to the cellar in the base of the jamb by way of a passage cut through the wall, which is 10 ft (3.05m) thick at this point, and to the cellar of the 'palace house'.

The cellarage was almost entirely reorganized. The wall between the west and mid-cellars was taken down, and the vaults – which had run north–south – were removed. A new inner wall was built against the existing north and south walls to support a barrel vault – covering the greatly enlarged apartment – which ran east–west. A massive segmental arch occupied the western end of the cellar fronting an enormous fireplace, the lum of which filled most of the western gable. A doorway was slapped through the wall between the mid- and east cellars, and the doorways in the north wall which gave access to the courtyard from the two eastern cellars were built up. That to the eastern cellar has since been replaced, but in the blocking of the mid-cellar doorway is a gun-loop of the same pattern as that beside the entrance to the staircase, and it is likely that this would have been repeated in the blocking of the other doorway.

If the doorway into the cellar of the jamb was also built up at this time, the entrance to the palace complex was limited to a single door at the stair foot, and thus security was easily controlled. This would explain the provision of the single large hall in place of the two separate cellars. This hall has been described as 'the old kitchen', a tradition which is of very recent origin. It is a tradition which would be acceptable were it not for the following:

(i)   its size is out of proportion to the building in which it is found;

(ii)   it is directly under the king's apartments;

(iii)   there is no evidence of any of the drains, sinks or sluices that are usually associated with kitchens; and

(iv)   its other likely function is now clear.

All four points, so obvious now, were lost to view when the room housed the boilers for heating the castle – boilers large enough to power a Dreadnought. Since their removal, and the restoration of the room to its secondary period, our understanding of it is much clearer. Its purpose must have been that of a guardroom, or

3.2 Blocked entrance to palace stairs and flanking gun-loop

3.3 Craignethan-type gun-loop on the palace stair (© Crown Copyright/RCAHMS)

rather a hall of the men-at-arms – the French expression 'La Salle des Gens d'Armes' probably gives the flavour of it more accurately.

The plan of the two upper floors of the 'palace house' conforms to the new arrangement of the ground floor, that is, a large room with two smaller rooms within or beyond, the private or guard hall, presence chamber and bedchamber, although at Glamis this may have not been adhered to. Here the sequence may have been presence chamber, privy chamber and bedchamber. The reasoning behind this thinking is that the guard halls for both the king and the queen may have been in the chambers on the first and second floors of the jamb. Doorways had been slapped through the south wall of the jamb on each floor, giving access from the staircase to both the laigh hall and the great hall in the Great Tower, and the jamb chambers had ceased to function as chambers, serving instead as ante-rooms between the two halls and the royal apartments; this probably meant that they also served as guard halls. If this is a correct understanding of the plan, there must have been some alteration to the access to the laigh hall: it would have been sensible to remove any external stair that may have been in existence. Any solution allowing an approach to the upper floor that was not controlled by the single entrance and the main guardroom would have been unsatisfactory, and the probability that the new staircase alone served the upper floors seems reasonable.

In the next two centuries there seems to have been a considerable amount of rebuilding, and much of the detail – the fireplaces and heavy roll mouldings – may date from then. It seems clear that the fireplace in the western room on the first floor, which has been slapped into the guardroom chimney, must be a later alteration. Probably of the period of the royal occupation of this wing is the stone seat immediately within the doorway of what is now the Queen Mother's sitting-room, a seat for the use of a page. Needless to say, the ghost of a small boy is said to have been seen here.

The normal practice was for the king's rooms to be on the floor below those of the queen, and it is ironic that this usage has been reverted to at Glamis.

3.4 *Reconstruction of the castle after its conversion to a palace during Mary Stuart's visit in August 1562 (reconstruction by author; realization by Terry Ball FSA; © Terry Ball and Strathmore Estates)*

It is difficult to trace any work of this period on the exteriors, but there is some evidence to suggest that the windows were slightly narrower than the present ones. This is most noticeable above two of the first-floor windows on the south elevation where there are relieving arches, which suggest earlier and narrower openings. The present windows on this floor are of the seventeenth-century pattern found on the north elevation of the Great Tower.

If none of the foregoing arguments is true – and it must be admitted that they are largely circumstantial and based on parallels drawn from the other palaces built for James V – it is difficult to account for this part of Glamis. It can hardly be earlier than 1528, unless the 6th Lord Glamis had ideas considerably above his station and, to a certain extent, in advance of his time. The years 1528–37 – during the minority of the 7th Lord Glamis, the persecution and execution of his mother and the seizure of the estates – were no time to be building. The appearance of gun-loops of the Craignethan type and the general planning point to the period 1537–42, and nothing in the known life of the 7th Lord after 1542 suggests that he was a builder. On a basis of probability it must be accepted that, unless other evidence emerges, there was a considerable programme of work in the last five years of the reign, necessary in order to adapt the castle for the use of the court.

Who the mason was is not known. It has been suggested that the influence of the Master of Works, Sir James Hamilton, can be detected in the distinctive form of the gun-loops in this part of the castle, and of the loops already discussed this may be true. However, the suggestion was made relative to the false loops in the parapets of both wings, which date from the 1790–1800 rebuilding.[5] Nevertheless, the influence of Finnart should not be discounted, but it was the influence of a highly placed official and not of a master mason. Given the nature of the work, the presence of the very distinctive loops and the client, it is likely that the alterations at Glamis were a product of the royal works.

CHAPTER 4
THE WORK OF THE 1ST AND 2ND EARLS OF KINGHORNE, 1600–1626

The remodelling of Glamis between 1600 and 1626 by the 1st and 2nd Earls of Kinghorne marks its transition from a medieval castle and sub-Renaissance palace to a great house in the high and original style of Scottish Baronial. To this it owes its height, its magnificent frontispiece and its fantastic roof-line. Succeeding generations have tried to make it baroque, Gothick or Balmoral Baronial, but with only limited success. In spite of every attempt at improvement, the castle remains the apotheosis of Scotland's most distinctive and highly developed architectural style. Almost lost under the weight of ridicule directed at its nineteenth-century version by critics who failed to distinguish between the originals and the copies, it is in danger once again of losing out to the taste for this same later version running so strongly among those architectural historians whose scholarship is too often influenced by fashion, and by an over-generous supply of documentation.

The finest examples of this style are really enormous pieces of sculpture set down in the landscape – a view put forward many years ago by the late Sir Sacheverell Sitwell[1] – and are almost entirely confined to the north east of Scotland, in that part of the country which lies between the Don and the Deveron. The eleven pre-eminent castles of this school to survive in the north east are Castle Fraser, Cluny (in part, but heavily disguised), Craigston, Craigievar, Crathes, Drum, Fyvie, Huntly, Lickleyhead, Midmar and Udny. There are many lesser examples throughout the area but these eleven display that curious and almost indefinable quality which distinguishes architecture from building. With the exception of Craigston, they are all buildings

which were enlarged and improved upon in this fashion, great towers which have been magnificently adorned; Craigston alone was built between 1600 and 1620. Only in the wings of Castle Fraser (1633) and the mansion at Drum (1627) is there a foretaste of the low, open houses that were to come in the second half of the century. To this group must be added one outlier – Glamis. On the exterior is the date 1606 and on the

4.1 Patrick Lyon, 9th Lord Glamis, later 1st Earl of Kinghorne, 1583: School of Clouet (© Strathmore Estates)

28

plasterwork of the hall ceiling the date 1621. It is thus a contemporary of all the Aberdeen group; there is nothing quite like it outside that group and it contains a number of features both of detail and of planning which can be paralleled in a number of the Aberdeenshire castles. In the circumstances, it seems not unreasonable to suggest that the same designer who was at work at Glamis was at work in Aberdeenshire.

The most important family of masons working in castle building in the north east was that of Bell. Virtually nothing is known of its individual members, but the most accomplished, John Bell, signed two of his works: Castle Fraser, with his initials and badge – a heart; and Craigston, with his badge. These are not obscure or out-of-the-way masons' marks, but set prominently on the front of each building: at Castle Fraser on the great armorial, and at Craigston on the keystone of the frontispiece.

Castle Fraser has an unusual detail in that the small rounds are of two floors rather than one. This is repeated at both Craigievar and Lickleyhead, with the upper lights at Lickleyhead copying those at Castle Fraser, which take the form of a vesica – a slightly pointed oval – more usually associated with late thirteenth-century church architecture. This combination of a two-floored round with vesica upper lights occurs nowhere else, to my knowledge, outside Aberdeen, except on the rounds of the Great Tower at Glamis, where the form was also copied at two later periods for the wall-heads of the great rounds on the wings.[2]

The planning of the two new upper floors of the Great Tower is a development of the planning of the upper floors at Craigston, just as the external gallery elevation is derived from that of Crathes. Bull-nosed door jambs are used in preference to chamfered jambs, as they are used at Craigston and in the Bell work at Castle Fraser. The contrasting use of ashlar and harled rubble on the frontispiece is similar to the treatment of the Seton Tower at Fyvie, built by Lord Kinghorne's contemporary and fellow statesman, Lord Dunfermline.

4.2   The frontispiece, 1606–26 (remodelled in 1790–1800) (Billings, vol II)

This seems enough circumstantial evidence to suggest that the work carried out in the first quarter of the seventeenth century at Glamis is work of masons of the Aberdeen school, and possibly directed by John Bell. It is perhaps worth remarking that the Lyons were not without north-eastern connections: some of the earliest grants made by the Crown to the family were of lands in the Garioch and the Thaneage of Belhelvie; the 1st Earl's mother was the daughter of Lord Saltoun of Abernethy by Elizabeth Keith, daughter of William, Earl Marischal, and was herself widow of William Meldrum of Fyvie; and in the confusion attending the collapse of the Meldrum fortunes, Lord Glamis – as he still was – had acquired interests in the lands of Fyvie, which he made over to Alexander Seton, Lord Urquhart, who was later to become the 1st Earl of Dunfermline.

This view is to a certain extent supported by Professor Cosmo Innes, who considered that 'the two leaders of the new style were their own architects and both men of excellent taste. The Lord Chancellor … produced … the lordly pile of Fyvie' and was rivalled by Lord Kinghorne [Strathmore] working on the 'rude mass of an old Scottish keep' at Glamis. He concluded: 'These two master builders were but a type of their age. Castle building was in high fashion in the beginning of the seventeenth century, and strangely fixed in Aberdeenshire as its favourite field'.[3]

One of the longest living traditions about Glamis, and indeed of many of its contemporaries, is that it is of French derivation: Lord Glamis had spent some years in France, returning to Scotland around 1600 and bringing the newest fashions in architecture with him. The same is said of Lord Huntly and Huntly Castle. What seems to escape notice is that if Glamis and Huntly, building in the first quarter of the seventeenth century, are representative of French style, then it is the style of Francis I and not Henry IV, a style of sixty years earlier, and as dated as last summer's flats. That the full Scottish

4.3 The upper floors and roof-line (1606–26) and gable-heads (remodelled in 1790–1800) (after Billings)

30

Baronial style is derived from that of the France of Francis I is possible, but it is derived at several removes.

The date 1606 which appears on the west face of the Great Tower may mark either the creation of the Earldom of Kinghorne, which took place that year, or the completion of the main structural work. The alterations were probably begun in 1603–4, shortly after Lord Glamis's return from France, but were not finished before 1621. They consisted of the addition of two new floors of chambers and galleries to the Great Tower, the complete reorganization of the circulation with the provision of a new staircase, reworking much of the stonework, providing an elaborate frontispiece and enriching the interior with plaster ceilings and overmantels in the newest fashions.

The new staircase was necessary to give access to the upper floors, and it was built on the grandest scale, rivalled only by Lord Dunfermline's staircase at Fyvie. It rises to the level of the new fourth floor, winding round a hollow newel, and is lit more than adequately by eleven windows. As far as can be judged, it was entered from a lobby formed in the cellar of the jamb, a handsomely moulded arch supporting it as it rises, an arch that would be unnecessarily elaborate if seen only by the servants. The present entrance, opening directly on to the staircase, is a later alteration. A flight of steps was cut from the staircase to provide an entry to the laigh hall. This was slightly to the right of the present entry, but its right-hand jamb survives complete, as do two other fragments of the head, built into the rebuild of *c* 1800. These all show the heavy roll moulding so characteristic of the period.

A hollow newel or central pier to a staircase is unusual but not unknown; its purpose is uncertain. The much larger example at Amboise, in the Tour des Minimes, dating from 1495, was said to be necessary for ventilation, which was probably true as horses were ridden up the ramp which took the place of stairs. At Leslie Castle, a late example of 1661, there is what appears to be a small fireplace at the stair foot with even smaller apertures in the core to disperse the heat: that, at least, is the traditional explanation, but a surer way of

4.4 *West gable, showing the datestone and initials of Patrick, Earl of Kinghorne; the round replaced a square cap c 1790–1800 (© Crown Copyright/RCAHMS)*

4.5 *Lickleyhead, Aberdeenshire: rounds similar to those of Glamis, c 1626 (© Crown Copyright/RCAHMS)*

kippering the inmates of the house is hard to imagine. Pitcairn quotes an old description of Cassillis Castle, where there was 'a fine stone stare turning about a hollow casement in which are many opens from the bottoms to the top, that by putting a lamp into it gives light to the whole turn of stairs'.[4] A similar feature existed at the now-demolished Strathmartine Lodging in Dundee. The Glamis newel openings are particularly fine with moulded frames, and, if used for this purpose, would have held a number of lamps. At present, the newel is used for housing the weights of the castle clock; as there has been a great clock at Glamis since at least 1686, the original function was of fairly short duration.

Externally, the stair tower is faced with ashlar and is richly ornamented with a frieze carrying the name of the builder and his wife and with two tiers of armorial panels. Only one tier (the eastern) is original, as can be seen from the care with which the stonework is set. The western tier and present entrance are set into the existing work, and packed with small rubble. Armorials were not placed haphazardly on a building but were set to enhance and emphasize the importance of the entrance. At Glamis, the armorials were thus placed on the side of the stair tower nearest to the main entrance at the foot of the link staircase and most visible as it was approached; and it would be on that side too that any gun-loops would be placed in order to cover the entrance. In addition to the loops above and to one side of the entrance, dating from the original build, there are pistol-loops below the window to Duncan's Hall and below one of the staircase windows, which could have been of effective use only if they were covering the entrance in the link.

The additional accommodation provided on the new upper floors was generous – two extra chambers in the jamb and one above the stair-head, three chambers on each of the upper floors and two galleries running along the north side of the Great Tower, together with various

4.6 Castle Fraser, Aberdeenshire: rounds similar to those of Glamis, c *1606–17; architect, John Bell*

closets and the now-gutted attic floor. The new floors were entered from the head of the great stair, and were linked by a well-proportioned newel stair immediately within the door stair-head. There may have been a further chamber in the jamb, since the early inventories refer to a fifth chamber in the jamb known sometimes as the 'Plaistered Chamber' and sometimes as the 'through gang chamber', which, from the context of the inventories, is clearly the chamber now known as 'King Malcolm's Room'. The fourth chamber in the jamb, sometimes known as 'Kathren's Room', opened off the stair; the third chamber was 'Auldbar's chamber called before Lord Errol's chamber'; 'Brigtoun's chamber' (the second chamber) was above Auldbar's, and there was still the 'Upmost chamber in the jamb'.

The inventory of 1648 shows that the 'Plaistered' or 'through gang chamber' was separated from the hall by the 'Greet' and 'Little' pantries. The expression 'through gang' must refer to its serving as the link between the hall and the private apartments in the south-east wing. Here, the sequence of rooms on the second floor was 'the Sylit Hall', 'My Lady's Chamber' and the 'Chamber within the Hall'. 'Sylit' seems to be an unknown word, but I suggest it means that the hall's roof timbers were ceiled with plaster; this would agree with the 3rd Earl's description of the third storey being 'cumsylled above wch sort of sylling is commonly a nest for ratts'. In other words, it was what would now be termed a coomb ceiling, where the ceiling rises into the roof space following the line of the roof timbers. As anyone who has lived under such a ceiling knows, the space above is quickly filled with platoons of rats and regiments of starlings, all wearing tackety boots. In the same inventory the first-floor rooms are designated 'The Purpure Chamber', 'The Scarlet Chamber' and 'The Chamber within the Scarlet Chamber'. The inventories of 1626 and 1627 describe the first of these rooms as the 'Pethement Chamber' and the 'Western Pethement Chamber'. This again is a term that is elusive, but its most likely meaning is 'paved' or 'pavement' chamber. Since the floors of these rooms are laid above the stone vaults of the ground-floor cellars, they could well have been of stone set in patterns, as was the case at Tolquhoun and Castle Fraser. At the latter James Lieper was 'put to the horn' in 1626 for failing to complete just such a floor.

The decoration of the interiors seems to have been started before his death in 1615 by the 1st Earl. The chimney-piece and overmantel in the great hall is certainly his work. The plaster is carved rather than moulded, the surround to the panel containing the Royal Arms (with the twining but not entwined thistles and roses) is handled freely and the caryatids are vigorous and of quite remarkable vulgarity. It has only to be compared with the later overmantels at Muchalls and Craigievar to see how primitive it is. The key to its early date lies in the decoration of the frieze where the lions of Lyon alternate with the mullets of Murray – the countess being Anne Murray, daughter of John, 1st Earl of Tullibardine.

The quality of the plasterwork of the ceilings both in the hall and 'King Malcolm's Room' is of a very different order, but this is not unusual for Scotland at this period. An English plasterer from York, John Johnstoun, was working in Edinburgh in 1617, and a little later that year moulds were sent to the plasterer at Kellie Castle. The work at Kellie, with strapwork enrichment, heads and lion masks, was put up in 1617 for Thomas, Viscount Fentoun, and is not unlike that in 'King Malcolm's Room', which dates from 1620. Another fine early ceiling was installed at Pinkie House for Lord Dunfermline, and a not dissimilar one is to be seen at Winton Castle. Also

4.7 *The staircase with the stairs to the lower hall; the original jamb is to the right of the present entrance* (© Crown Copyright/RCAHMS)

at Winton is a ceiling heavy with pendants very like those in the great hall at Glamis. They are supposedly the work of John White, possibly a relation of Alexander White, who worked for Thomas Dalyell at the House of Binns. Here the plasterwork is dated to 1630, and in three rooms there are elaborate pendants. The Binns ceilings are identical in some details with those at Auchterhouse, near Dundee. The seat of the Earl and Countess of Buchan, this house was being remodelled before 1628. Mary, Countess of Buchan in her own right, had in 1617 married James Erskine, second son of John, Earl of Mar, and brother of Margaret Erskine, Countess of Kinghorne.

The ceiling of the great hall at Glamis, with its three pendants, its portrait medallions of David and Joshua (twice each) and Hector and Alexander, and its heraldic motifs, is perhaps the finest in the series, followed closely by the ceilings at Muchalls and Craigievar, where the same moulds have been used, and which are presumably the work of the same plasterers. As the names of John White at Winton and Alexander White at the Binns suggest a family of craftsmen associated with ceilings of similar motifs, which in turn are linked both by family connections and design similarities (spaced at convenient geographical and chronological intervals) with other ceilings for which no craftsmen are named, it is reasonable to suggest that they are all by the same hands. The Whites may have come from England originally – the tradition is that all plasterers were English, just as all masons were French – but this is not necessarily so. The moulds for the medallions are almost certainly from south of the border, but they could have been imported. By the 1680s the next generation of the family, Robert White of Edinburgh, was providing ceilings for the 4th Earl of Dunfermline at Fyvie and for Lord Arbuthnott at Arbuthnott.

No other work of this period survives within the castle. The ceilings of the new upper floors were probably

4.8 The great hall with the plasterwork of 1621

boarded and painted in the manner of Crathes and other houses of the period. If any of this survives, it will be in the ceilings of the fourth floor behind the later lath and plaster. The ceilings of the fifth floor were either destroyed in the fire of 1916, or removed in the subsequent repairs, although most of the original floor beams survive on both floors. Where the original door openings and fireplaces can be seen, the jambs are bull-nosed, as would be expected in Bell work, and the doors were hung on the usual heavy iron pins.

The plan, with three chambers opening off long galleries on each floor, is possibly derived from, but better handled than, that at Craigston which was built in 1604–7. Unfortunately, the galleries have been divided up to provide bathrooms and closets, although it would not be a difficult task to return them to their original form. The lower gallery has windows with deep external splays to house the shutter, the pins for which still remain. There are similar windows on the first floor of the south-east wing. This type of window is rare and seems to have its origin in the windows of the great hall at Stirling Castle.

The rebuilding of the attics after the fire has left little evidence of how this floor was planned. All that can be said with any certainty is that there were fireplaces in both east and west gables, and one in the attic above the jamb: the inventories of the period give no clue.

From an archaeological point of view the saddest loss was the roof structure. The stone gables conceal the fact that there is no ridge, and that the flats lie above and upon the upper ties. On a roof of this size this form of construction is unstable, as at this period ridge-pieces and purlins were rare, and it was only the sarking, if used, that stopped the trusses from racking. If there were partitions at this level, they may have been tied into the trusses.

The lead flats, surrounded by an ornamental iron railing, were for taking the air and for viewing the agreeable prospects of the surrounding countryside. Craigievar, Craigston, Castle Fraser and Midmar all have flat-topped towers, sometimes provided with stone seats, or, as at Craigston, with retiring rooms. The leads at Glamis are only a larger version of the gazebo, which seems such a feature of houses associated with the Bell family.

The splendour that had been brought to Glamis – and the inventories show that it was very splendid – did not outlive the death of the 2nd Earl by many years. When his son returned to the castle in 1670 the old hall in the courtyard was in ruins, many of the service buildings had been destroyed by the English soldiers garrisoned at Glamis, the south-east wing was no better than a ruin, and the only rooms with glass still in their windows were those above the great staircase. Another period of building was about to begin.

CHAPTER 5
EARL PATRICK AND THE RECASTING OF GLAMIS, 1669–1695

The building work of Patrick, 3rd Earl of Strathmore and Kinghorne, has been covered in great detail by Dr Michael Apted in a paper published in the *Antiquaries Journal*. He has also dealt exhaustively with the earl's patronage of Arnold Quellin in the same journal, and with the work of Jacob de Wet and the paintings in the chapel.[1] What follows is a footnote to what he has written.

5.1 Patrick Lyon, 3rd Earl of Strathmore and Kinghorne, and his three sons, 1683: Jacob de Wet (© Strathmore Estates)

Earl Patrick did not move back to Glamis with his family until 1670. Although it is usually thought that work did not start on the alterations until some time after that, this is not correct. Two agreements, one dated 25 May, the other 14 August 1669, have recently come to light. These were between the earl and Alexander Nisbet, showing that Lord Strathmore – as he was to become – already had a very clear idea of what he wanted. The first dealt with alterations to be made to the south-east wing: the Great Round was to be raised 8 ft (2.44m), and its new upper stage to be given oval windows matching those in the rounds of the Great Tower, the windows of the upper floor of the wing were to be heightened to match those on the first floor, and two windows were to be struck out in the Pavement Hall 'one upon evry side of the chimney (which is to be [...?] to the middle of the room according to a former [...?])'. The second agreement was for building a new wing against the west gable of the Great Tower terminating in a bastion at its northern end. The whole was to be equal

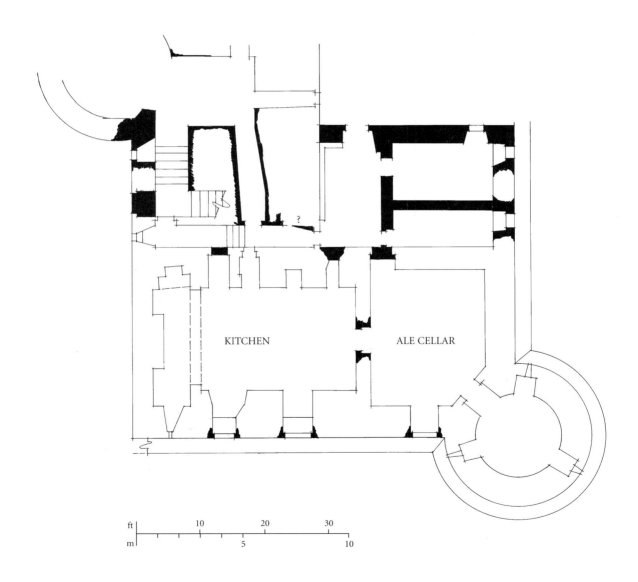

5.2 Ground-floor plan of the south-east wing: the 3rd Earl's remodelling and additions

in breadth, length and roundness to the south-east wing – 'now standing upon the end of the great jam'. A range of office houses was to be built. Nisbet was also to start a scale-and-platt stair – 'the back turnpike in the bottom betwixt the great tower and the new building'. There were to be external stairs to the upper floors of the office houses. For the first contract Nisbet was to receive '250 merks Scots and four bols of meal', the earl providing all the materials; for the second, Nisbet was to receive £1,000 (Scots) paid in three stages as the work progressed. The earl was to provide all materials 'in season' and the services of four workmen 'for services in the time of the laying' – that is, unskilled labour to dig the founds – and Nisbet was to keep five masons on site until the work was completed. Furthermore, the earl bound himself to deliver, whenever Nisbet demanded them for the hastening of the work, 'two chaldors good and sufficient farm meal'. Both agreements make it clear that the new work was to conform as closely as possible to the old work.

The contract for the new west wing specified only that the work should be 'one storie high' – possibly the earl was fearful of incurring expenditure he could not meet – but there may have been further work of which there is no record. In the contract of 1679 between the earl and Nisbet for continuing with the west wing there was a considerable amount of demolition of, and alterations to, the work already done, and much more detailed specifications of the staircase and the chapel tower. Building work was pushed ahead, and the new work was ready for roofing in January 1681, when a contract for the leadwork was drawn up between the earl and George Scott, plumber. In November 1681 attention shifted to the building in the angle between the link stairs and the south-east wing. A contract was given to Andrew Wright for timber- and plasterwork; he seems to have been dilatory in earlier work, the earl complaining that he had 'been some what tedious as to ye tym he has taken in doeing of it'.

By 1682 the main structural work was finished, and Nisbet was concentrating his efforts on alterations and adjustment to work he had already done, and to quarrying into the medieval walls and vaults to provide closets, chimneys, doorways and a prison. Additionally, four

5.3   *Copper-plate engraving of John Slezer's drawing of Glamis Castle, 1686* (© Crown Copyright/RCAHMS)

banker masons, David Lindsay, David Watson, John Devine (?) and William Whitehead, had been working on the chimneys and had apparently charged too much. On the agreement is a note: 'This thing you may well doe it upon But to your old Master that has givne you many years constant work quitte this odd seven pounds' – a first note of trouble to come.

In May of the same year Andrew Wright was contracted to plaster and panel much of the interior but was warned that some of the finest work would be reserved for the Dutch carver and, by implication, he must be prepared for an abatement in the money he had expected to earn. Wright cannot have been without considerable skill, since among the works for which he was responsible were twenty-four picture-frames.

In January 1683 came the inevitable explosion. Alexander Nisbet had put in an account for extras and his lordship was not best pleased:

Sanders Nisbet, as to your pretended additional work it shal receave this answear wtout passion

First I must tell you that I admyre wtwhat impudence you charge me wt an additional work or is it your ignorance or out of a cheating design you pretend to this. Out you not lykwayes to set down what you was obligded to doe and is not done or to be done because that which you call addition is in place of it . . .

But Sanders ther are a great many things to be done which are not as yet done and must be done.

It is the old story as true today as it was then: embark on alterations to an old building without professional advice and there will be tears before bedtime. In the course of this quarrel, Lord Strathmore twice uses the expression 'Munthulie': 'Munthulie was designed no lower than it is'; and 'The 8th article about the round light is Munthulie and pray you any hyer to admit it'.

5.4 John Slezer's published (and mis-captioned) drawing of 'Glamms House'; it is in fact Dalkeith Castle, Midlothian (© Crown Copyright/RCAHMS)

Presumably his lordship wanted a pithier expression than 'a montrous farrago of presumptuous nonsense', which was what he meant.

The accounts between the two men were discharged on 31 January 1683, and Lord Strathmore entered into a new agreement with David Lindsay and David Watson for the completion of all the outstanding work, and much else besides.

The structure of the house completed, Lord Strathmore turned to its decoration, and for his more spectacular embellishments he employed craftsmen from abroad – from Holland in particular. Jacob de Wet, apart from the panels which still survive in the chapel, provided scenes from Ovid's *Metamorphosis* for the dining-room ceiling, a painting of Icarus for the principal bedchamber together with five chimney-pieces and fourteen door-pieces for rooms in the new wing. Carving was beyond the range of Andrew Wright's skills, so the chimney- and door-pieces left to the Dutch carver were probably the work of Jan van Santvoort. None of them has survived, but Van Santvoort was responsible for the superb frame to the portrait of the earl and his

three sons, which hangs in the great hall. He is also likely to have made the two handsome lions that flank the fireplace in the same room. These are shown in Billings's engraving, by which time little table-tops had been attached to their crowns; a later age has removed these tops but provided heraldic modesty pieces instead.

A third Dutchman associated with Glamis is John Slezer who was employed by Lord Strathmore to make a perspective view of the castle (*see* Appendix B for John Dunbar's account of this drawing). This did not appear in *Theatrum Scotiae*, where a plate entitled 'Glammis' is actually a view of Dalkeith Castle before its rebuilding. However, in recent years the copper plate – the only original one to survive – has been discovered at the castle. When it was made is not certain; the engraving of the view is dated 1686, and it has been suggested that the plate may not have been engraved until after that date. Lord Strathmore's reference to it in his *Book of Record* suggests that Slezer was at Glamis some time in the late 1670s, and this is borne out by another account recently found in the charter room. This is dated 3 March 1679, and is for additional work ordered to be done by the

5.5 Detail from Jacob de Wet's portrait of the 3rd Earl, 1683 (see Figure 5.1), clearly taken from Slezer's drawing. In both, the position of the doorway in the stair link is shown incorrectly (© Strathmore Estates)

masons David Lindsay, David Watson and John Whitehead, at the instance of 'my Lord and Mr. Slether'. Much of it refers to the Great Round of the west wing, where a considerable amount of rebuilding appears to have been necessary.

From this it would seem that John Slezer was acting as a building manager or clerk of works to Lord Strathmore, a role he also undertook *c* 1677–9 at Thirlestane for the Duke of Lauderdale. This raises the question of what architectural influences may have been brought to bear on Earl Patrick. His admission is that he was his own architect, and that in this he was to blame. In spite of his hint that he employed Slezer in some advisory capacity, he found himself in a pickle in the end. Nisbet was not the only man in his employment with whom he was to quarrel. His employment of De Wet ended in acrimony, and it seems that for all his good qualities, Earl Patrick was, at least where buildings were concerned, ignorant, suspicious, parsimonious and

changeable. The decision of the 9th Earl to demolish the work of his predecessor may not have been entirely because of changing taste; perhaps it was inconvenient, badly planned and even jerry-built.

The pre-eminent architect of the day was Sir William Bruce. Lord Strathmore had a number of business and legal dealings with him, and was to employ De Wet and Van Santvoort, who had worked for Bruce at Holyrood and Kinross, and Slezer who had worked under Bruce at Thirlestane. It is unlikely that the earl would have employed these men without discussing their abilities or the work they were to do with their most important employer. He may well have taken Bruce's advice on some of what he intended to do. The internal arrangements of the castle, even in the new wing, have the appearance of being cobbled together, and would have hardly met the great man's approval, but he may have had something to do with the external effect that was achieved. Lord Strathmore did 'covet

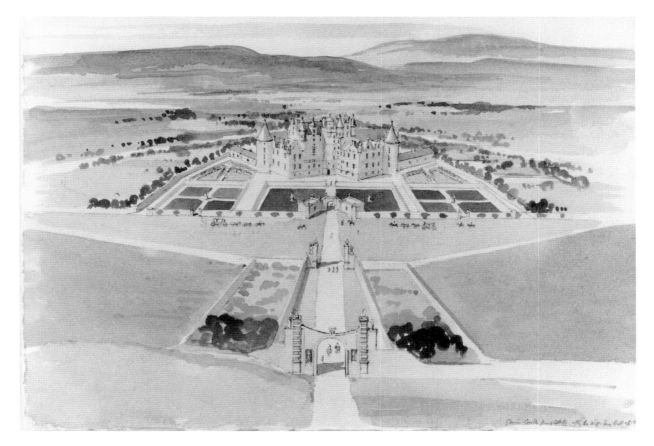

5.6 *Reconstruction of the castle and its policies, as completed by the 3rd Earl (see also Figure 13.1) (reconstruction after Jacob de Wet by Terry Ball FSA; © Terry Ball and Strathmore Estates)*

extremely to order my building so as the frontispiece might have a resemblance on both sides' and this of course was what Bruce was to achieve at Holyrood. By moving the entrance from the link building to the great stair tower and by laying out the avenue at forty-five degrees to the Great Tower and the jamb, Lord Strathmore was able to introduce the monumental axis that dominates the castle. It is now difficult to realize that the castle was not conceived as a symmetrical composition from the outset.

The documents that survive represent only a small part of what must once have been written, and there is no surviving evidence for one ingenious piece of work, which cannot have been easy to accomplish. In all the planning no thought was given to the fact that there was no direct communication between the private apartments in the south-east wing and the public and state rooms – the dining- and drawing-rooms and bed-chamber – in the new west wing, without going up and down several flights of stairs, or crossing the latter meat or servants' hall, in what had once been the laigh hall. This was overcome by digging out a passage in the thickness of the north wall, and partitioning off the west end of the laigh hall, thus linking the passage with Duncan's Hall and the private apartments.

Certain other points in the documents that have survived are worth noticing. In the agreement of 1683 between the earl and the masons David Lindsay and David Watson, mention is made of two kitchens, the new and the old. The new kitchen was always to be in the west wing, adjacent to the 'new great stare' and therefore reasonably convenient to the dining room, but this is the first reference to the 'old kitchen':

> More the beakhouse, the sloghter house and lardner and the low roume at the back entrie of the east quar-ter of the house are to be layd with ston upon edge with deu reguaird to the passadge or gutter wch voids the watter from the old kitchine so as to ffit them with

> ane ragine of the thickness of ane deall wch is to cover the same and to lift up at pleasure.

While this could be clearer, it suggests that by 1683 there was an older kitchen somewhere in the south-east or east wings. This need not have been in the vaulted cellars, and the term 'old' may be only relative, referring to a kitchen formed in 1670 when the earl's first work, after the setting out of the west wing, was to provide the necessary accommodation for his family.

By the time of his death in 1695 Earl Patrick had transformed the medieval and baronial – and largely ruinous – castle which he had inherited into the sem-blance of a baroque mansion of the largest sort. This was from necessity rather than choice: '[T]here is no man more against these old fashions of tours and castles than I am'. He would have agreed with a later writer, James Anderson, who said: 'But where law is established and the plough successfully managed the ruins of old castles are only the monuments of the ferocity of our ancestors, which a more polished age has no pleasure in repairing'.[2] It would have taken a siege train to demolish Glamis, and it was cheaper to repair than to rebuild.

Of the surviving work of Earl Patrick, the most important is the development of the symmetrical front, which has controlled every subsequent plan for altering the castle; the next important is the chapel with its paint-ings. The interiors of the room beneath the chapel, the closet formed in the east wall of Duncan's Hall, and the private apartments on the first floor of the south-east wing also remain. With their heavy cornices, pilasters and panelling they have been painted white and give a very pale impression of what they once were. From the accounts it is clear that the rooms were rich with painted panels above the doors, carved chimney-pieces and door-frames, and marbelized wood fires burning in highly polished brass and steel grates, and glowing tapestries from Mortlake on many of the walls: perhaps it is these rooms that are the real ghosts of Glamis.

CHAPTER 6
THE HERALDRY

Glamis boasts what is probably the finest surviving display of heraldic panels on any private house in Scotland. Fourteen panels ([1] to [14] in Figure 6.1), containing the arms of eight Lords Glamis and the first five Earls of Strathmore and Kinghorne, are arranged in two vertical tiers on the great stair tower, and in a horizontal band across the south and west elevations of the Great Tower and the link building. In addition, a set of the Royal Arms of Scotland [15] is above the main entrance, five panels ([16] to [20]) bearing the arms of Lyon or Murray are on the upper parts of the Great Tower, and there are two further panels ([21] and [22]; *see* Appendix A) with the initials PEK.DAM (Patrick, Earl of Kinghorne, Dame Anne Murray, the builders of the upper floors of the tower) and a single datestone of 1606 ([23] in Appendix A; *see* Figures 4.3 and 4.4). A horizontal band of lettering

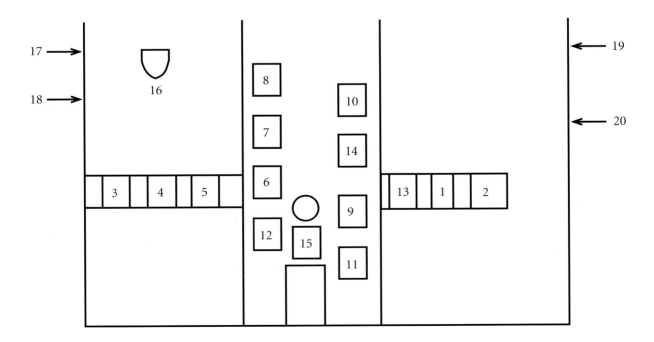

6.1 Key to the numbering of the heraldic panels

on the stair tower declares that it was built by Patrick, Earl of Kinghorne, and his wife, Anne.

Charles Burnett, Ross Herald, to whom I am much indebted for Appendix A, suggests that the panels, based on the stylistic evidence, fall into four periods: the earliest period includes the arms of the first five Lords Glamis, together with the arms of Lyon above the south window of the hall; the second includes the arms of the last three barons and the first three earls; the third, the arms of the 4th and 5th Earls; while the work of the fourth period consists of the arms of Lyon and Murray high on the upper stages of the Great Tower. From this it might be adduced that the carving of the armorials is chronological, and that each panel had been put in its place by the lord whose arms it depicts – a conclusion which appears so reasonable and simple, so clear and logical. But then there is little at Glamis that is reasonable, simple or logical. Closer examination introduces a suggestion of splendid confusion, but, unfortunately, the stylistic evidence of the carving is irrelevant.

The red Angus freestone, of which the panels are made, lends itself to elaborate carving, being soft and easily worked. It does not weather well, however, and begins to decay as soon as it is exposed to the elements. There are no means of knowing how often in their history the panels have needed to be reset or replaced – as they do at the present time. This presents no problem, as the panels are independent of their frames, and can easily be removed. It is therefore from the building itself, rather than heraldry, that an explanation must come.

The present pattern of the panels is similar to that which existed by 1683, when De Wet painted the castle in the background to his portrait of Earl Patrick and his three sons. It is shown on Slezer's engraving of 1686, on White's and Elphinstone's surveys of 1746, and on Sandby's drawing of the same year. Billings's drawing of *c* 1844 shows the alterations made between 1790 and 1820 by the 10th Earl.

The differences are important: before the demolition of the west wing by the 9th Earl in the 1770s and the refacing of the south-east wing by his son, there were at least four additional armorial panels: two at each end of the horizontal band which extended across the gable walls of both wings. As the west wing was built by the 3rd Earl, the band and panels there must have been his work, but he may have extended and copied an earlier scheme, already in existence on the Great Tower and the south-east wing.

6.2   *The entrance, the Royal Arms [15] and niche for the bust of the 3rd Earl: it is clear that these have all been inserted into the original ashlar*

6.3   *Arms of Patrick Lyon, 1st Earl of Kinghorne, and Anne Murray, Countess of Kinghorne [9]: part of the original design of the heraldic frontispiece, 1606–26 (© Crown Copyright/RCAHMS)*

The other important difference between the earlier drawings and that of Billings is the introduction of the Royal Arms [15] above the entrance. In all the pre-1790 views the entrance doorway is shown with a full entablature – architrave, frieze and cornice; now it has only an architrave. Above it was a shield bearing the arms of Lyon. To insert the Royal Arms without destroying the circular recess containing the bust of the 3rd Earl, the frieze and entablature of the doorway – itself an insertion – had to be sacrificed, and the surrounding masonry clumsily patched.

It is likely that the earliest surviving heraldry on the building, although it may have been recut at a later period, is that on the panels showing the arms of Lyon and Murray [16, 17, 18, 19, 20]. The frames for these panels are built in with the surrounding masonry. Of the same period are the two initialled pediments above the south and east windows of the hall. These too are the work of Earl Patrick and Countess Anne, but they have been built *into* the earlier existing masonry. These panels, apart from that on the stair tower containing the arms of the 1st Earl and his wife, are the only ones which relate correctly to that part of the castle on which they are found.

The horizontal band with the arms of the first five barons [1, 2, 3, 4, 5] and of the 4th Earl [13] is a puzzle.

As has already been said, it originally contained four more panels, two of which certainly date from the time of the 3rd Earl. It is possible that this entire band may have been his work – a means of introducing a horizontal emphasis to tie the disparate elements together. It can be argued equally cogently, however, that it was an existing feature that he extended across his new wing for the same reason. In that case, it cannot be earlier than 1535 – the earliest likely date of the building of the stair link – nor later than 1590, when the building of the stair tower must have been in hand, if not in mind. The oddity in this band is the introduction of the arms of the 4th Earl in 1695 [13] and of his wife, Lady Elizabeth Stanhope. This is the only panel to be dated, the date being in the elaborately carved mantling above the panel.

The remaining panels are so inconsistent in their sequence that a degree of rearrangement must be accepted. This does not affect the frames within which they are set, and which reflect two separate building

6.4 *Arms of John Lyon, 2nd Earl of Kinghorne, and Margaret Erskine, Countess of Kinghorne [10]: part of the original design of the heraldic frontispiece, 1606–26* (© Crown Copyright/RCAHMS)

6.5 *Arms of John, 6th Lord Glamis, and Janet Douglas [6]: inserted frame and panel forming part of the 3rd Earl's remodelling of the frontispiece in the late seventeenth century* (© Crown Copyright/RCAHMS)

programmes. These panels are all concentrated on the stair tower, and, with the exception of the Royal Arms, are arranged in two vertical tiers, each of four frames.

When it was built, the finely wrought ashlar of the stair tower was intended to be seen against the harled, rubble-built walls of the Great Tower. The frames of the right-hand (eastern) tier are all, with the exception of panel 11, carefully built in with the surrounding ashlar. The arms of the 1st Earl and his wife [9] – the builders of the tower – are incorporated into the band bearing the building inscription. The two panels above [10, 14] are set with equal care. The lowest panel in this tier, the arms of the 2nd Earl and his second wife, Elizabeth Maule [11], is clearly an insertion into the existing ashlar, but great pains have been taken to match the frame into the surrounding stonework.

The same cannot be said of the four remaining panels [6, 7, 8, 12] which form the left-hand (western) tier. These have all been inserted into the surrounding ashlar with no attempt at piecing in, and the frames packed roughly with small stones. This is the work of the 3rd Earl and relates to the entrance being moved from the link building to the stair tower, where it was set on the new axis. The placing of the arms of the 1st and 2nd Earls had been in relation to the original entrance in the link. Once the entrance was moved, and the new door was set centrally to the new elevation, there was an imbalance, and to correct this it became necessary to introduce a second tier of armorial panels. By doing this, Earl Patrick achieved the axial and symmetrical front that he so much wanted. However, no attempt was made to match the stones of the new features with the ashlar of the tower. The fine stone detail was partly lost: this can only mean that it was his intention to harl the stair tower and to lose its strong vertical emphasis that broke his elevation, relying rather on the balance of the new front and the tincture of the arms to achieve the dignity and splendour that he wanted. This was not done in his lifetime, but in that of his son, which is why the castle appears unharled in the De Wet painting.

The provenance of the Royal Arms, now placed above the entrance, cannot be determined. They are so very different in character from any other work on the exterior of the castle that they may have been brought from elsewhere. This is a view shared by Charles Burnett, who is inclined to date them to the years between 1620 and 1650. 'Elsewhere' could of course mean from one of the other buildings demolished on the site by the 3rd Earl, or salvaged from Castle Lyon, and left unused until the repairs of the 1790s.

CHAPTER 7
THE CHAPEL, 1679–1891

The importance of the painted decoration of the chapel has been long recognized, and the paintings have in the past received more attention than any other part of the castle. This has been directed at them as subjects of art history, their derivation and the engravings upon which they are based. Little consideration has been given to their relationship to the chapel itself, and none to the chapel as a building in its own right with a history and purpose that may have affected the paintings.

In the first of Earl Patrick's proposals for new buildings at the castle – those of 1669 – no mention is made of the chapel block; it does not figure in any document before 1679. In a contract of that year, dated 31 January, drawn up between Earl Patrick and his mason Alexander Nisbet, the second section begins: 'For the intended chapel it is to be founded wt ane equall breedth wt the back staire case', so presumably it was intended that work should begin in the spring of the same year. The third section described the work that was to be done:

The 3rd story is to enter off the Hall be making the little window open upon the north syde and end of the hall yrof into a door of a competent largeness to enter wt two leaves, wch story is to consist of ane chimley, two ovalls, three windows to the north, the soles of wch are to be so far from the gesting as to admit of lyning as far as a mans head can reach from the floor sitting on in an equall seat. The other two windows are to be of such as is ordinary but ther three on the north to be made fitt only for glass and no brod. The hight of this

work and of the stairs case is to be alyke. And it is to be finished in gavelle and toofalls all wt hewen great stones and chimney heads of a competent hight above the roof.

This description of the work is remarkably accurate. It is clear that the chapel is to have round or oval windows in the east and west walls; the windows in the north wall were to be glazed and without shutters, while the two windows in the inner room were to be 'such as is ordinary' – that is, with fixed glazing in the upper parts and shutters in the lower.

By the time the chapel came to be decorated there was a change of plan. De Wet's painting of the Crucifixion was intended as the altarpiece, and this led to the blocking of the east window. Elphinstone is not as helpful here as he might have been. His plan shows the seven windows as in the specification, but, in the view from the north east, the only window shown in the east wall is that of the inner room. The specification also mentions a 'chimley' – a fireplace – on this floor. On elevation, Elphinstone shows a stack to a flue between the western and central windows on the north, but shows no corresponding fireplace on the plan. This apparent omission is due to the plane of the plan being taken through the windows.

The masons were still working on the chapel when on 29 August 1681 a contract was agreed with George Scott, plumber, for the lead work of the roof. The earl was to supply the lead in caiks already cast. This was to be obtained in rolls 20 ft (6.10m) long and shipped from Rotterdam to Dundee. In an agreement of 2 May 1682 Alexander Nisbet was to 'dig through the north east corner of the House of Glammis at the end of the great hall a stair to go up to the platforme over the Chappeal'. This had been overlooked in the first contract; it must have been a turn-stair in the thickness of the wall. The lower part was destroyed when the new entry to the library was made for the 9th Earl, but the upper part probably still survives buried in the wall. In an account of 1683 it is shown to have cost £266 13s 0d (Scots) and two bolls of meal.

The chapel also figured in the earl's quarrel with Nisbet over bad workmanship and overcharging. It was still unfinished in 1683, when the earl agreed with David Lindsay and David Watson, paving and banker masons, for the completion of the chimney-heads, parapets and staircase, as well as for the paving of the ingang from the great hall. The chapel was probably finished and ready for fitting out by the end of 1685, and the panelled ceiling and wainscot must have been put in by the beginning of 1688; on 18 January a contract was signed between Lord Strathmore and Jacob de Wet for the painted panels and ceilings throughout the castle, of which the work in the chapel was to form a part. For this, De Wet was to receive £90 sterling, of which the sum of £35 was for the chapel paintings. These consisted of fifteen large panels in the ceiling depicting scenes from the life of Christ, surrounded by subsidiary panels painted with angels, and sixteen paintings for the panelling of Christ and the twelve apostles in the chapel, with St Paul, St Stephen and Charles the Martyr in the inner room. In addition, there was an altarpiece of the Crucifixion and a door-piece of the Ascension. These last four have disappeared but in their place are two door-pieces, the Nativity and the Last Supper, and one, larger than any of the others, showing Christ as *Salvator mundi* ('Saviour of the world'). None of these appears in the original contract, and *Salvator mundi*, which appears to have been cut down, may not be by De Wet.[1]

The present arrangement appears, certainly as far as the south wall is concerned, to be the result of a degree of rearrangement. On the east wall are spaces for five panels, but there are only three *in situ*: the Crucifixion above the altar, flanked by fabric hangings, with St Peter beyond on the south and St John on the north. The panels behind the hangings and the lower wainscot are painted with a diapered fleur-de-lis pattern, probably dating from the 1865 refitting, and matching the old

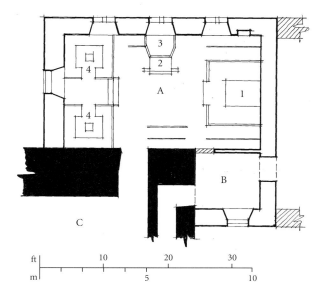

A	Chapel	1	Altar
B	Inner room	2	Reading desk
	(present staircase)	3	Pulpit
C	Hall	4	Family pews

7.1 Plan of the chapel before 1866

7.2 Ceiling panel of the Baptism of Christ in the chapel: Jacob de Wet

sanctuary carpet. On the south wall are St Andrew and St Thomas, with a panel, which appears to have been a door-piece, of the Last Supper below. Beyond the door giving on to the library stair, and not filling the space available in the wainscot, is St James Minor, with, below, Christ appearing to Mary in the Garden. Above the main door is a door-piece of the Nativity, and the last panel on this side is St Philip. On either side of the west window are St James the Major and St Bartholomew, with *Salvator mundi* in the lower wainscot below the window. On the west wall are five panels: St Judas; St Thadeus; St Matthew; St Simon; and St Mathias.

It is possible that in the original scheme the spaces on either side of the altarpiece were either plain panels or painted with the Commandments, or the Creed and Lord's Prayer. The specification also required that each picture should have its name above, and a scroll beneath containing the text attached to the original plates from which the paintings were derived. Both St Andrew and St Thomas are separated from them, and no description or text attaches to either the Crucifixion or Christ in the

Garden. These may be deliberate changes, or they may be the result of later alterations.

Clearly these alterations have brought changes in the arrangement of the wainscot on the south wall, because of the raising of the floor level at the east end, on the west wall by the lowering of the floor level, and on the north wall by the removal of the pulpit and the blocking of the fireplace. It is equally clear that the placing of panels in the lower tiers of the wainscot is at variance with the original layout of the chapel, where they would either have been covered by benches or at serious risk of damage. This is most obviously demonstrated by *Salvator mundi* which would have been largely covered by the higher floor level at the west end, and which, in any case, is a picture meant to be 'looked up to' and not 'down on'. From the contract, which specifies that 'The 3d Earle is to cause prime the roofe of the Chappel and such pannels of the side walls qron the abmen. pictures are to be drawn', it is clear that De Wet painted *in situ*. The Nativity, which fills the space above the entrance door, may have been substituted for the Ascension after the

7.3   The chapel as it appears today (refitted by the 13th Earl, 1865–6)

contract was signed, and the Last Supper may not be in fact a door-piece, but a chimney-piece. The rearrangement of the panels probably took place during the alterations of 1865.

The chapel figures in only one of the many surviving inventories of the contents of Glamis. This is the one taken in 1712, on the death of the 4th Earl. In it are listed 'A large bible, Twelve large common prayer books, Eight of a lesser vollum, Ffive little ones, Ffourtein cushens, The pulpit, Ten gilden sconces, Two large broads with black frames, A pulpit goun, and in the closet Six Kean chairs and a table'. This suggests that the furniture of the chapel was fixed, except, curiously, the pulpit. Among the fittings may have been the three tables made for the chapel by Andrew Wright (and paid for in 1688), probably the communion table and the two small tables in the private pews. The 'broads with black frames' may be hatchments.

No mention is made of an organ: there was certainly no room for one to be permanently in the chapel, but a portable chamber organ could have been brought in from time to time. Such an organ is mentioned by Defoe in 1719 ('a most nobly painted ceiling of the chapel where is an organ for the service after the manner of the Church of England')[2] and by Macky in 1723 ('The Hall is adorn'd with Family-pictures, and behind the Hall is a handsome Chapel with an Organ for the Church of England service').[3] There was an organ at Glamis as early as 1648, when a 'pair of organs' is referred to in an inventory of that year as being in the hall. In 1688 Andrew Wright was paid £6 for 'His blocking of some timbers to ye carving of the organ and mending of a panel which was broken by the carriage'. This may refer to the great organ which, according to the inventory of 1712, was in the great hall, and which seems to have been the subject of dispute between the factor, John Leslie, and the organ builder, James Bristowe, in 1739. The organ had ten stops and the estimate for its repair came to £30 sterling. It had been sent to Montrose, and the factor was asking for additional work to be done to it within the original estimate. James Bristowe objected: while some of the extra work could be done for £8, that sum would not cover the cost of beautifying the front with gilding and gold leaf; it was not going to be done at this expense; it was not part of his work, and a further £15 would be necessary. The organ is not mentioned thereafter, and it may not have been returned to the castle. It does not figure in the inventory of 1768.

Apart from the De Wet panels nothing of the seventeenth-century interior of the chapel remains, and indeed very little survives at all in Scotland of the liturgical arrangements of the second period of Episcopacy. Fortunately, a plan exists showing the chapel as it was at the beginning of the nineteenth century. It was drawn on 5 October 1800 by a Mr John Sime, at that time an apprentice solicitor and amateur of architecture. He later took holy orders and built a pulpit in his drawing-room in Edinburgh New Town. The sketch is in his scrapbook, now held by the National Monuments Record of Scotland. This shows that the communion table was set lengthways – that is, with its long axis lying east–west against the east wall. This allowed the celebrant to take the north-side position, as enjoined in the rubric. The table was fenced on three sides by a heavy communion rail in the English manner. There was no attempt at forming a raised sanctuary, and the rails were flanked by benches. In the middle of the north wall and set below the central window was the pulpit, in front of which was a three-seater bench and desk, the middle seat of which was given greater prominence than the others. This one would have been for the minister, the others for the reader and the clerk or precentor. The west end was raised three steps above the general floor level. Here, a small landing was flanked by two separate pews, each with a central table. The liturgical arrangements were a curious hybrid of Anglican and Presbyterian fashion.

Although Sime's drawing is dated 1800, it shows a much older arrangement. It does not reflect late eighteenth-century taste, and, in any case, no work would have been done to the chapel after the death of the 8th Earl in 1753, since his son intended its destruction, and the plan probably shows the chapel as it was when De Wet provided the paintings.

The late eighteenth century was the lowest point in the chapel's history. The work put in hand by the 9th Earl saw the destruction of the vestry to make room for the library staircase; the plans show that he also intended to divide the chapel into a bedchamber and dressing-room. So low had the chapel fallen that it was used as a linen store for the roup which followed on the earl's death in 1776.

For nearly a hundred years the chapel lay neglected, and it was not until the accession of the 13th Earl in 1865 that it was to be repaired. Even this was a second choice, for until the full extent of his predecessor's debts were known, Lord Strathmore had intended a large, apsidal and fully Gothic chapel at the far end of a new south range. Nothing came of this; instead, the old chapel was refurbished, and on 29 September 1866 – the feast of St Michael and All Angels – it was rededicated by the Bishop of Brechin. An excellent account of this event appeared in the *Dundee Courier* of 1 October, which throws some useful light on the chapel and on its new fittings:

> Our readers will remember the unsightly pews which crowded the floor, and the apology for an altar that stood at the east end, hidden by a cumbrous balustrade. These have now disappeared, and in their stead are seen open seats and a well-proportioned altar, raised two steps, properly vested. . . . Nor must we omit to mention that the paintings have been all cleaned, the frames gilded, and altogether a very devotional effect has been provided, and the Catholic sentiment fully evinced.

It certainly was. The service started with the consecration of the altar, followed by a celebration of Holy Communion according to the 'venerable Scotch use', a post-communion, the *Benidicite* sung in procession, matins and litany – a rather curious sequence. The services were intoned and the Gregorian chant used. The choir consisted of 'Young ladies, friends of the families, together with a few of the household, all dressed in white, and providing a very pleasing effect'. There were ten clergymen, including the Bishop and the Dean of St Andrews, and one of them, the Revd E L Pincott – chaplain to the Earl of Kinnoul – 'presided most efficiently at the harmonium'. The combination of the harmonium with the Gregorian chant is more easily conceived than described. Besides the clergy, the congregation consisted of at least sixty members of the nobility, gentry and mere laity. After these religious exercises, which had been going on since nine o'clock in the morning, the company was invited to 'a splendid entertainment provided in the ancient dining hall, during which a band played stirring and appropriate airs'.

A considerable sum was spent in preparing the chapel for rededication, although some of the accounts were several years in paying. The general furnishings came from Cox and Son, the vestments from Gilbert James French, the communion plate from Lamberts of Coventry Street, the altar chest from Oliver Estcourt of Gloucester, and the altar cloth and frontal from Heilbronners. Together with the harmonium, the total cost recorded (although there must have been other items) was £335 4s 3d. This figure did not include the cost of the stained glass, and on this the documentary evidence is confusing. In 1868 the firm of Clayton and Bell was paid £31 6s for installing – and presumably supplying – the west window. Two years later this must have been replaced, as Lord Strathmore noted in his diary that a payment of £40 had been made to Heaton, Butler and Baine for the St Michael window.

The three cross-windows contain glass depicting the Ministry of the Angels, and were designed and installed by C E Kempe at a cost of over £115. The western window of the three had been fitted by June 1882, and the others by the August of the following year. Lord Strathmore's relationship with Kempe cannot have been restricted to business: ten years later Kempe was staying at the castle over the 1892–3 New Year holiday, not leaving until 'after shooting' on 2 January.

Although the suppliers were all well known in their own fields, the effect, apart from that of the altar frontal and the windows, is not happy. The dominant note is still struck by the De Wet paintings; it is of the seventeenth century and does not accord with the later fittings, redolent of the Ecclesiological Movement of the 1860s. This is particularly evident at the east end, where De Wet's Crucifixion is obscured by a battery of candlesticks, candles, vases, and a 'beautiful jewelled cross after the Celtic pattern seen on the old sculptured stones of the district', standing on a tabernacle-like confection.

The present arrangement of the De Wet panels must date in part from the 1865–6 restoration. What condition they were in is not clear, but obviously a considerable amount of work had to be done to them and the missing panels must have disappeared by then. The urge for destruction was directed at the Protestant fittings; the paintings were saved either by family piety, or because they accorded with the ritualistic tastes of Lord Strathmore. The restoration resulted from his own strong religious convictions; the chapel was always intended for use, not display. The Revd S Gilbert Beale was appointed chaplain on 30 July 1868, and the first full service was held three days later. Before that the family had been obliged to worship in Forfar. Daily evensong was introduced on the feast of St Andrew, 30 November 1891.

The chapel is still used for services.

Chapter 8
The Eighteenth Century

The years between the death of the 3rd Earl in 1695 and of the 10th Earl in 1820 need to be treated as a single period, an extended eighteenth century. The work of Earl Patrick left little for his son to do in the way of structural work, apart from the tidying up always necessary after a prolonged period of building activity. The rearrangement of the heraldry on the main front had left the masonry in a sad condition, and in March 1701 Earl John was to enter into a contract with John Sharres for casting and harling the castle 'with lyme on the frontispiece and round the same'. The contract made clear that both the old and the new work were to be covered, and the work was to be completed by the end of August. With this done, there was to be a radical change in the appearance of the castle. Previously the Great Tower had been given a strong vertical emphasis by the contrast between its harled walls and the red freestone ashlar of the stair tower. This emphasis was now lost, for, as the contract implied, the harl was to be applied to the whole front. There was still the contrast between the harl and the carved red stone of the window surrounds, the heraldic panels and the fantastic upper works, but the old vertical element was lost.

The death of the 4th Earl in 1712 was followed by the drawing up of an inventory of the heritable and movable property within the castle. Although only folios 13 to 20 have survived, it was drawn up in a slightly more logical order than was usually the case, and allows for a fair understanding of the manner in which the castle was ordered at the time. Sixty rooms are listed, starting on the ground floor of the new west wing. On the ground floor were the 'Major's Roum', the 'Collenel's Roum' and the 'Buillard Roum'. A small newel stair led to 'My Lady's Chamber' and the 'Closet of My Lady's Chamber' on the first floor, in the round and north end of the wing. From here the inventory followed through the 'Family Drawing Roum and Dining Roum' to the 'Low Hall', which would have been the western end of the crypt, partitioned off in Earl Patrick's alterations. Next are listed the 'Counting Roum' and the 'Bed Chamber of the Counting Roum', with its closet within, both lying below the chapel and vestry. From there the 'Low Lobby' – the vaulted room now known as 'Duncan's Hall' – led to the earl's rooms in the south-east wing. These were 'My Lord's Dressing Roum', 'My Lord's Bed Chamber', 'My Lord's Govenour's Roum', 'My Lord's Man's Roum' and the 'Trans to My Lord's Roum', and are much the same today as they were then. Why at the age of twenty-two his lordship should have needed a 'Governour' is not immediately apparent. Also in the south-east wing on the second and third floors were the 'Blow Roum', with two closets, 'The Tartan Roum', the 'Suping Roum', the 'Bedchamber of the Suping Roum', the 'Closet of the Bedchamber', the 'Old Nursery' and 'Millfield's Roum'.

The 'High Lobby' – now known as 'Malcolm's Room' – led to the 'Great Hall' and 'Chapell'; beyond the 'Great Hall' were the 'High Dining Roum', the 'Withdrawing Roum', the 'fine Bed Chamber' – which contained the state bed – and the 'Closet of the fine Bed Chamber'. This is the floor devoted to the state rooms, used, except for the chapel, on only the most formal occasions, and for guests of the highest distinction. In later years they were to receive both the Old Pretender and the Duke of Cumberland.

Apart from the 'Closet of the Withdrawing Room', added as an afterthought, folio 18 and most of folio 19 are devoted to the rooms off the staircase and on the two upper floors. These were given as the 'Turnpike' and 'Stairhead' chambers, with, on the fourth floor, the 'Purple', 'Mid' and 'Gray Roums', the 'Long Galerie' and the 'Galerie Roum'. On the floor above were the 'Chaplain's', 'Green' and 'Dark Roum' – this latter sometimes entered as the 'Mirk Roum'. No mention is made of the 'Upper Galerie', which figures in an earlier inventory – presumably because it was without furniture, but there is a 'Bell House', which contained a 'large bell and a great house clock'.

The remaining rooms listed on folios 19 and 20 are the service rooms in Earl Patrick's recently built east range, except for the 'Latter Meat Hall' and the 'Porter's Roum'. The former was in the partitioned east end of the crypt, and the latter must have been close to the entrance. The rooms listed are 'John Lyon's Roum', the 'footmens' Chamber', 'Alex Lyon's Roum', 'My Lady's Gentlewomans Roum', the 'woman house', the 'Taylors Roum', the 'Cooks Roum', the 'Butlers Roum' and the 'Gill House'. Additionally, there were three stables – 'Coach', 'Hunting' and 'Ryding' – with a dormitory above the coach stable. It is tantalizing that folios 1 to 13 are missing: they almost certainly covered the kitchens, which, if the missing sheets were consistent, would have been in the low northern extension of the west wing.

The death of the 4th Earl in 1712, followed by those of three of his sons in the next twenty-seven years, did not conduce to any very extensive building operations, and it was not until the accession of Thomas, 8th Earl of Strathmore, that anything was proposed. In the end nothing was achieved, but the designs for improving the castle and dramatically enhancing its surroundings were conceived on the grandest scale. Two of these designs survive, and there may well have been others. Considering how seriously the estate was damaged by

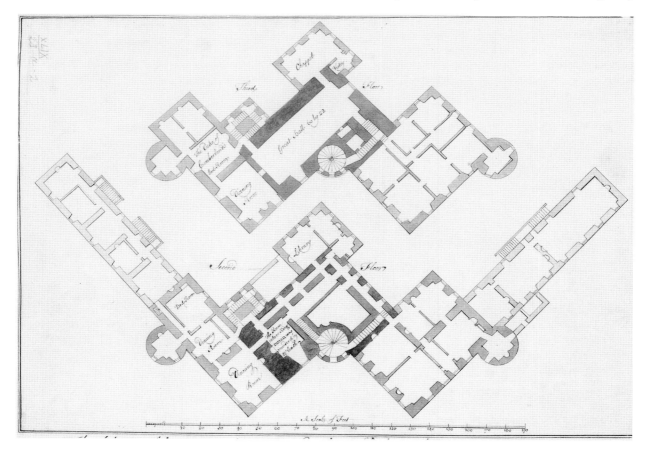

8.1 Plans of the second and third floors, John Elphinstone, 1746 (reproduced by permission of The British Library; K. Top. XLIX, folio 23.A.2)

8.2 'The Front of the Castle of Glamiss to the South', John Elphinstone, 1746 (reproduced by permission of The British Library; K. Top. XLIX, folio 23.A.5)

8.3 'The Front of the Castle of Glamiss from the South East', John Elphinstone, 1746 (reproduced by permission of The British Library; K. Top. XLIX, folio 23.A.6)

8.4 'A View of the Castle of Glamiss from the North East', John Elphinstone, 1746 (reproduced by permission of The British Library; K. Top. XLIX, folio 23.A.3)

8.5 'A View of the Castle of Glamiss to the North West', John Elphinstone, 1746 (reproduced by permission of The British Library; K. Top. XLIX, folio 23.A.4)

the cost of his son's much more modest work, the ruin consequent upon Earl Thomas's schemes, had they ever been undertaken, would have been immense. The earl had started his building career by setting himself right with his Maker, when, in 1737, he spent £19 18s 8d on repairing the roofs of the Kirk of Glamis; he certainly intended a far heavier expenditure to his own greater glory.

In 1746 Thomas Winter made a survey of the Mains of Glamis, showing the castle and its policies, together with views of the castle itself, the gates and a number of the estate buildings. It also shows an alternative proposal for the avenue from the point where it begins to slope downhill towards the castle. Had it been carried out, it would have rivalled the setting of Vaux-le-Vicomte, designed ninety years earlier by André Le Nôtre for Nicholas Fouquet.

Impressive as it is in many ways, the avenue at Glamis suffers from the situation of the castle, lying as it does at the lower end of the vista. To remedy this, Winter chose a solution both drastic and dramatic. The Barn Gate, which has since been moved to the south-west corner of the park, and which then spanned the avenue at the start of the descent, was to be demolished and replaced by a curved screen or balustrade, flanked by gateways. The avenue divided into two carriage drives, which led between new-planted lines of trees to the castle. The old avenue was to be removed and replaced

by a central feature of five basins linked by cascades and canals. The basins were of different shapes, and the fifth and largest, which was circular, occupied the area of Earl Patrick's outer court, between the formal parterres and the Gladiator Gate. Had this been carried out, the effect would have been magnificent; that it was not must be accounted as one of Scotland's losses.

Winter's reason for suggesting such a scheme was a sound one; he was not happy with the approach to the castle, writing that 'altho att present it is Very Great Being above an hundred feet Wide and a Strip of Planting of the same Breadth on Each Side. Yet in my opinion it is not by far answerable to the House, but on the contrary Eclipses it Much'. Whether the cascades and basins might have 'eclipsed it much' must be a matter for conjecture. Winter may have been influenced by John James's *The Theory and Practice of Gardening*, published in 1712, where there is a design for a some-what similar cascade.

The other proposal for work at Glamis – and equally staggering in its scale – was for a new stable and office court. The unsigned and undated drawing entitled 'Design for Offices for Glamis Supposing them to be directly behind, and to be covered from the Front, by the Body of the House' was only recently discovered in the Charter Room. It shows two straight-sided ranges, which clasp either end of the main body of the castle, linked to a semicircular stable block by pavilions and

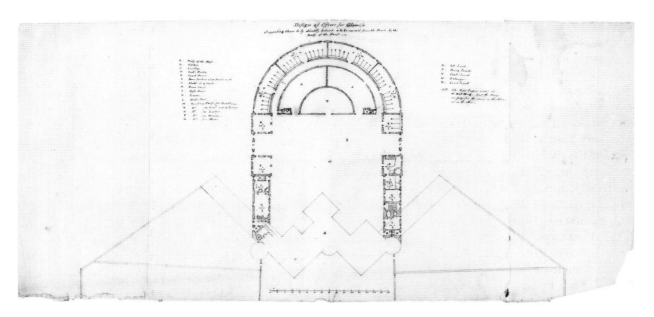

8.6 Design for a court of stables and offices, c 1746 (© Strathmore Estates)

monumental gateways, the whole measuring 260 ft by 210 ft (79.25m by 64.01m). From a note on the drawing, 'N.B. The House Keeper's rooms in the West Wing and the Dairy are proposed the same in this plan as in the other', it is clear that there were other versions of the proposed enlargement.

The accommodation that was to be provided consisted, in the west wing, of the kitchen, scullery and cook's pantry, with two coachhouses in the pavilions flanking the gateway. In the east range were the bakehouse, larder and gyle (brewing) house, with the brewhouse, and a small four-stall stable in the pavilions. The housekeeper's room and dairy must have been in the old west wing of the castle since the dairy would need to be at the level of the court.

The hemicycle was arranged concentrically with the coal yard as the core; beyond this were the dung and ash yard, a stable yard 12 ft (3.66m) wide, and then the outer ring of four stables, with standing for forty horses. Additionally, there were five 'Necessary Houses', double-seater earth closets: one for the 'Gentlemen' and one for 'Servants in Livery' at the junction of the east range with the castle, one for 'Ladys' at the junction of the west range, one for 'Men' off the ash yard, and one for 'Women' off the dung yard. Only that for the 'Ladys' was accessible from within the castle.

The design is monumental, particularly the gateways with their triple openings, and all is arranged on the most generous scale. It involved the demolition of Earl Patrick's low service ranges, but not of the flanking walls of the inner court before the front. Since it embodies none of the ideas favoured by the 9th Earl – who did not reach his majority until 1758 – it must have been prepared for his father before 1753. The architect is not known, but in correspondence Sir Howard Colvin has attributed the design – cautiously – to Robert Morris. Morris had prepared a scheme in 1742 for the stables at Blair, in a mild castle style – that is to say, near-Palladian with rather more distant medieval trimmings – and had been involved at Inveraray Castle for the Duke of Argyll since 1743, so he was not unknown to the Scots nobility.

At Inveraray, Morris was clearly influenced by Vanbrugh's sketch of c 1720 for rebuilding the castle, and he had completed Eastbury, in Dorset, to Vanbrugh's designs. Since he was well acquainted with Sir John's works, and he was working in Scotland in the 1740s, it seems not unreasonable when a design incorporating Vanbrugh-like notes comes to light that Morris's name

should be linked with it. Between 1715 and 1718 Vanbrugh had produced a plan for additions to Kensington Palace, additions that were never made. These included a stable in the form of a hemicycle with standing for forty-two horses. Circular and semicircular service courts are not unknown: Gordonstoun and Cairness are among the rare examples, which generally date from the second half of the century. Whoever designed the Glamis office court must have been aware of the Kensington drawings, and who fits the bill better than Morris?

When the 9th Earl came of age in 1759 the castle was probably in a state of disrepair, which would not have been unusual, especially if the work of the 3rd Earl had not been particularly well done. There had already been a hint of this, when, in 1742, it had been necessary to renew the ceiling in the earl's bedroom that had collapsed because of the failure of the laths and nails – the latter having been 'consumed'. This initially turned his mind to improving the castle, and the first set of proposals can be dated to 1763. An unsigned drawing, a 'Plan proposed for altering and reforming the Front of the Castle of Glammis 1763', shows the castle completely

8.7 John Lyon, 9th Earl of Strathmore and Kinghorne, 1762: Nathaniel Dance (© Strathmore Estates)

recast in a Tudor collegiate Gothick style. The general massing is intact; the basic form and the fantastical roof are still there, but all else is changed.

On the Great Tower the whole of the heraldry, save for a single panel, has been removed, the entrance has been remodelled and given a Gothick head, as has the window to the great hall, which is further improved with tracery. The oval lights in the turrets have become quatrefoils, and the fenestration in the wings has been regularized, all windows being of two lights, those on the first floor having transoms. The gabled roofs and attics on the wings have been removed, and lead flats are hidden behind a corbelled and battlemented parapet, stepped at the corners to clasp some very unlikely angle turrets. Both Great Rounds have been entirely removed.

Even as a preliminary draft the design has little to recommend it, and was soon superseded by others. It is certainly English-inspired, and almost as certainly the work of an English architect. Sometimes attributed to

Daniel Garnet, who had worked at Gibside but who had died before the date on the drawing, it is likely to be the work of John Bell of Durham, who in 1765 was helping to Gothickize Alnwick Castle. It is known from the Cellar Book that a bottle of port was brought up on 18 May 1765 for the use of a 'Mr Bell, Architect'. While this could refer to Samuel Bell of Dundee, the stylistic evidence and family's tendency to favour second-rate English practitioners argues against this.

Whoever the architect may have been, he does not seem to have worked from a knowledge of the castle, but from an older drawing – probably Slezer's – since he repeats the error shown in the doorway to the east wing. This is, in fact, in the stair link, but both Slezer and De Wet show it opening into the fireplace of the cellar. This position is not supported by any physical evidence, nor is it shown by either White or Elphinstone, both of whom position it correctly in the link. The treatment of the ironwork on the roof is also clearly based on Slezer's

8.8 Proposal for altering the castle, 1763, ?John Bell (© Strathmore Estates)

drawing, so it seems likely that Bell prepared his scheme before he ever saw Glamis.

A more elaborate and sophisticated set of proposals was prepared by John Carr of York. In this case the drawings are undated, but the Cellar Book shows that Mr Carr was at the castle on 26 March 1765, when a bottle of port was brought up for *his* use. Carr's scheme is a curious hybrid, anticipating by some years the castle style of Robert Adam and his followers, but it shows rather more respect for Glamis than Bell's does. Both designs have two things in common: hood moulds to all the windows; and the substitution of a round for the small, square cap on the north-west corner of the Great Tower – foreshadowing a later alteration – but there all resemblance stops.

The hand of Earl Patrick lies heavy on Carr's shoulders, and all the earlier work with its heraldry and gables is retained. The only noticeable changes are that the balustrades and overhanging eaves on the wings have given way to castellated parapets, and the main entrance has been raised to the first floor. This is approached by a double-flight stair, with the original entrance sheltering beneath it. Since no plans survive, it is impossible to judge how Carr intended handling the junction of the entrance with the stair; this would have been difficult and could have meant rebuilding much of the lower part of the staircase.

To the main body of the castle, which now became the centrepiece of an extended and symmetrical compo-sition, Carr added two service courts, connected to the main castle by short single-storeyed links. The links are set well back, behind the two Great Rounds, and would have been reduced to insignificance, if not to invisibility, by the buildings on either side. The drawing of the extended elevation is deceptive, since it suggests a linear rather than an articulated composition. The service courts are Palladian, tricked out with battlements, quatrefoils, crowsteps and false arches. That to the west contained the offices, that to the east the stables and coachhouses. Like Bell, Carr seems not to have visited the site, but to have based his drawings on Slezer, whom he follows in the horizontal band of heraldry, and in the positioning of the entrance to the east wing.

Instead of adopting either of these proposals Lord Strathmore was content, at least for the time being, to repair the house as it existed, and in 1765 Samuel Richardson was paid £1 10s for the brick bins, or 'bounkearts' in the wine cellars – a payment showing a sound grasp of priorities. In the same year there were payments of £31 18s to William Chisholm for joinery work and for 40 yds (36.58m) of flooring, together with a further £14 14s for work, which included a new door to the housekeeper's room and bed posts for the counting-room. William Bisset was to be paid £27 0s 7¼d for new lead, against which was to be set £14 15s 1½d for the old lead, together with a discount for ready money; Chisholm was to be allowed £6 16s for repairing the leads. An account was sent in by Hugh Duff for £7 to

8.9 Proposal for altering and extending the castle, John Carr, ?1763 (© Strathmore Estates)

cover the cost of new beds for the 'woman house', new windows at the stairhead and the mangling house, a screen for the kitchen and for the whitening of both the kitchen and the dairy.

In 1767 the founds of the ice-house in the park were dug, and 15s was paid for 'removing sand and pavement' out of the great hall, which suggests that in the interest of comfort the old stone floor was being replaced with a wooden one.

As late as 1768 no major alterations seem to have been planned. A schedule of necessary work was drawn up, including:

Painting West Wing
Painting East Wing
Firring and Theaking the easings above the leads in both wings
Mending Office Houses in Back Court
Repairs to Hunting stable and coach house
Repairs to Turrets at head of castle
Sweeping 20 vents
Repairs to roof of hunting stable and stable on W. side of N. entry
3 further chimnies

8 more chimnies
Repairs to roof of E. tower in E. wing
Another chimney
Repairs to harling 5 rods 22 yards on lower part of castle.

Much of this was work to parts of the castle which were to be demolished in the course of the next five years, and it is unlikely that it would have still been contemplated in 1768, if a major rebuilding programme was in prospect.

Lord Strathmore's marriage to Mary Eleanor Bowes on 24 February 1767 might have caused him to think of starting work, but it is not until the early 1770s that there is any sign of work being put in hand. This may have been done to please his wife's taste, but more likely to reflect the need to accommodate a young, growing and healthy family – Thomas, the fifth child, was born in 1773 – and to enjoy their proximity. This in itself is remarkable. Eighteenth-century upper-class parents did not consider it unreasonable to accommodate their offspring in rooms in the attics of their homes or even to send them away to be fostered in a convenient farmhouse. These were not solutions favoured at

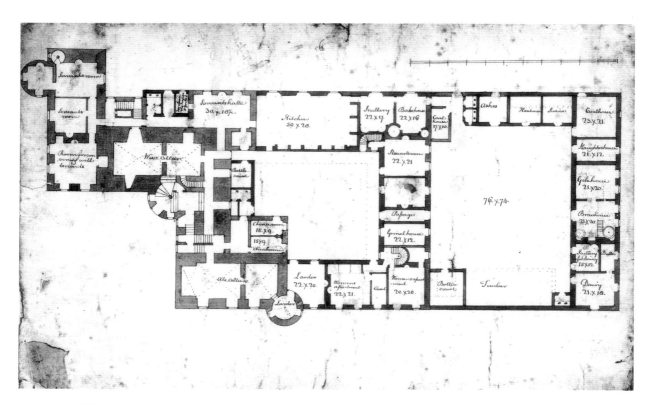

8.10 Proposal for extending the castle but retaining the existing west wing, c 1765 (© Strathmore Estates)

Glamis, where the nurseries were planned close to the parents' apartments.

The first set of proposals, which were probably prepared *c* 1769–70, survives only in one plan of the ground floor. This leaves the main part of the castle, together with the older south-east wing and Earl Patrick's west wing, unchanged, save for a small block filling the space between the staircase and chapel towers. In this are a privy, a servants' or back entry, a small room 'for cleaning knives and forks' and a passage between the staircase and the servants' hall. To the east of the old castle are two service courts, the first containing the kitchen – a huge room, measuring 50 ft by 20 ft (15.24m by 6.10m) – scullery, bakehouse, steward's room, girnel house (ie, granary), two apartments for the women servants (with a closet) and a larder. Built against the east wall of the tower, and opening into the court, are a bottle court and a two-seater privy.

The second or outer court contains the coal houses, an ash house, hen house, swine house, slaughter house, gilehouse (brewing house), brewhouse, a dairy with scullery and butter house, a second bottle court, timber stack and two three-seater privies. These courts replace the two long office wings shown in Elphinstone's views, and are clearly an attempt to rationalize the management and running of the household.

This was followed by a further set of plans, which must have been completed by the end of 1772, as work was to start the following year.[1] There is no name attached to these drawings, but a payment of £1,333 was made to 'Mr Paterson – Architect' following the earl's death in 1776, probably George Paterson of Edinburgh, father of the comparatively more famous John Paterson.

In Peter Proctor's accounts – as clerk of works he kept a separate set for the building works – is an item of £162 9s for miscellaneous expenses disbursed in, or by, March 1773, which mark the beginning of the new programme:

Work on the founds for Brewhouse and Dairy
(a pint of whiskey allowed the men by Mr. Menzies)
Cross cut and sqering timbers for scaffolding.
Digging founds for the kitchen/
Sewers and Drains,
and pumping Founds
Kitchen founds next the draw well.
Skullery founds.
dismantling many of the old garden walls.
Skreening an exposed privy.
2/- to sailors for helping up with a horse that fell into the

harbour frightened by firing of gun.
3/9 for drinks for 16 sailors who also assisted.
3/- to three porters who went down into mud to fix ropes and hammock to horse.
Slaking lime.
15 Norway Double Planks for Douchots to the library.
Library floor.
1/- for mending cart in harbour.
5/- for seaman hurt in episode

Apart from the episode of the horse and cart, this list deals almost entirely with the digging of the foundations of the two new service courts. The reference to the library, douchots and floor is puzzling. The library was to be above the kitchen, for which the founds were only just digging, and it seems early to begin laying in materials. It may refer to repairs to an existing room: there is no mention of a library in any of the previous inventories, but Elphinstone's plan marks the room beneath the chapel – sometimes known as the 'Writing Room' – as 'Library'.

The first floor of the old south-east wing had always been used as the principal private suite, and this use was continued. The new arrangement gave the main part of the medieval wing over to Lady Strathmore's dressing-room and the family bedroom. A closet occupied the Great Round, and the earl's dressing-room was in the block built by Earl Patrick, in the angle between the south-east wing and the Great Tower. A small closet led from the dressing-room to a larger closet, formed out of the window embrasures and wall thickness of Duncan's Hall – a closet originally made for Earl Patrick, and still retaining much of his decoration. Beyond the closet of the family bedroom lay the new south range of the service courts, reached by an opening cut through the wall, leading to a short corridor. Here were a privy, a room for Lady Strathmore's woman, and a suite of nurseries, three in all. Each nursery had two closets, one dark and one lit, and the last nursery, with a fired closet, led on to the housekeeper's room. These three last rooms together with the housekeeper's bed closet occupied the first floor of the cross-range separating the inner and outer service courts.

In this second scheme there is some rearrangement of the outer court. The timber store is replaced by a continuous range on the south side given over to a 'Dairy Scullery' – its earlier position having been taken by the 'Distillery' – and by 'Hens', 'Ducks' and 'Swine Houses'. The bottle court has disappeared – as has the one in the inner court – being replaced by a 'Bath House'. This is provided with a large 'Cold Bath', a 'Hot Bath' and 'Bath Closet with a water closet under'. This 'Bath Closet' seems to be in the nature of an ante-room, or lobby, and is entered from a staircase off the nursery corridor, forming a mezzanine. From this, steps lead down to the 'Hot' and 'Cold Baths'. Hot water is provided from a copper in a small room adjoining the 'Hot Bath' and serviced from the outer court.

The 'Slaughter House' has given place to a 'Store' or cellar, and the north range has been widened. This is now devoted to a 'Coal House', a room with three built beds for 'Common chaise drivers', a pend (or archway) to allow carts access to the court, another coal house and an entry to a passage, probably covered, running along the east side of the cross-range as far as the entry to the inner court. A small ash house is built in one corner, and there is a variety of privies with a total of nine seats.

The main changes proposed in this second scheme are the demolition of Earl Patrick's west wing and stair-case tower, and the building of a new wing and staircase more in keeping with modern taste, linked by service rooms to the new kitchen. In acknowledgement of the Great Round on the south-east wing there is an almost balancing bow to the west wing. On the ground floor it is proposed to provide six new fired rooms, but the plan offers no clue to their use.

On the first floor are three rooms reached from the ground floor, and from the laigh hall by the doorway that Earl Patrick had cut in the north-west corner. His partitioning of the laigh hall is reversed, and it reverts to its original form. This rearrangement renders his mural passage unnecessary and it is blocked up. This improved the structural stability of this side of the Great Tower, which may have been weakened, and has the undoubted advantage of giving rise to stories of blocked and secret chambers.

The first of the new rooms planned on this floor was a breakfast room set between the new staircase and the chapel tower. Beyond it, in the west wing, are the dining-room and drawing-room, both large, the former mea-suring 55 ft by 30 ft (16.76m by 9.14m) and the latter 40 ft by 28 ft (12.19m by 8.53m). The dining-room faces north and west, with a bowed end, the drawing-room west and south. Both rooms are high and well lit, but would have needed careful decoration and articulation of the walls and ceiling to be handsome.

In order to give these two great rooms an adequate ceiling height – 19 ft (5.79m) – part of the bedroom floor is raised five steps above the level of the great hall floor. A doorway is cut through the window in the north wall of the hall on to the landing of the stair-head, off which opens a bedchamber above the breakfast room. From the landing a broad flight of five steps leads to an upper landing from which the two state suites are reached. The larger bedchamber – that above the drawing-room – opens directly off the landing, its two dressing-rooms at its southern end. From one of these a flight of steps has been formed through the blocked window in the west wall of the great hall. Although the chamber above the dining-room is the smaller of the two, it is flanked by much larger dressing-rooms, and has the added advantage of being separated from the landing by a waiting-room. An improved plan of this suite shows the inner dressing-room as a complete octagon – a much better effect. In both proposals the waiting-room is lit from the staircase. Had all this work been carried out the chapel would have been lost, since it would have been turned into a bedchamber and dressing-room. Even as it is, the vestry is sacrificed, together with the rooms beneath it, in order to provide space for a staircase.

Once the founds were dug, work continued on the kitchen and the two service courts. By July 1774 the roof of the library was being completed, the old stables, northward of the kitchen, had been demolished, poplar wood had been ordered for the kitchen tables, and expenditure had reached £804 19s 2d. This had risen to £1,182 0s 9½d by November of the same year, when large quantities of paving stone from Beerhillock quarry had been ordered; this was presumably for the floors in the service areas. The kitchen floor was being laid in January 1775, and at the same time more of the old garden walls were taken down in order that there should be a supply of stone for the new offices. Demolition started in the west wing, where the paving of the billiard room was taken up to be saved for re-use. An interesting item was the order for 300–400 'Bolls of Shells' for the pit to the privy – an ingenious sort of soakaway.

By May expenditure had risen to £2,006 14s 11½d, demolition of the west wing was in hand, and in July stones for the founds of the same wing were being assembled. On 24 December James Menzies wrote to Lord Strathmore:

> I sit down to give you an account of what was done last summer and is proposed this. And shall begin with the building at the Castle. Most of the Roofs of

the two Courts and all the slates were put on last spring, and now all finished within with plaister etc. except some of the servants room floors to be paved. The stair nigh the kitchen doors that goes up to the Great Hall is ready for the Plaisterer who is to begin next Monday. The west wing taken down and rebuilt the Hight of the First joists with a great deep built drain lower than the foundations of the Wing which is about eight foot deep, the old walls taken down, and Rubbish in front of the Castle carried away, and ground Levelled except opposite the West wing which cannot be done till it be rebuilt.

Work continued within the castle. In February 1776 wood was ordered – 333 ft (101.49m) of gean tree – for the new stair rail, and monies spent had reached £2,840 9s 11d. The death of Lord Strathmore the following month brought the work to an abrupt halt. Nothing new

could be attempted, and that in hand was finished as expeditiously as possible. But even this – the framing of the library floor, the mould of the staircase and the protection by turf capping of the unfinished walls of the west wing – was costly, and the accounts for 1776–7 show a further expenditure of £900 16s 6d. To this had to be added the sum of £476 2s for the lead pipes bringing water into the castle, and the payment of £1,333 to the architect Paterson, producing a total not far short of £6,000 for a half-finished, partly demolished house, which might, if completed, have had some measure of convenience. If the amount paid to Paterson – nearly a quarter of the whole – seems large, it is because it represented not only his fees but work that he would have carried out as a contractor as well. Architects were still not so genteel that they were unable to be tradespeople.

The condition of the castle was now a sad one; much of it was newly built but in need of finishing, much of it

8.14 Reconstruction of the castle as it appeared 1776–90 (reconstruction by author; realization by Terry Ball FSA; © Terry Ball and Strathmore Estates)

demolished, much of it old and in need of repair, the policies a morass and little or no money to spend. Soon after the earl's death, the Trustees were faced with the need to repair the roof of the old east wing. In the *Book of Sederunt* of the Tutors is an entry that on 3 October Patrick Proctor was advised to settle all Mr Paterson's accounts, and by 1777 expenditure had virtually stopped. Old Lady Mary Lyon, daughter of the 4th Earl, who lived on at the castle until 1780, begged that the cost of the food for the woman who cleaned and aired the uninhabited parts of the castle might be a charge on the estate. This state of poverty is borne out by the sums spent between 1785 and 1788, the two largest being £4 13s 3d for repairs to the leads, rainwater heads and the iron rail at the top of the castle, and £6 19s 8d for repairs to windows; cleaning the castle annually was done by one man at a cost of £1 9s 4½d. The general condition of Glamis at this time can best be judged from James

Moore's drawing of *c* 1789, taken just before work started again, which shows the overgrown policies, the abandoned walls of the west wing, decaying stonework and an all-pervading air of decay.

The first hint of better times to come is found in a scrapbook of cuttings preserved in the Glamis charter room. An unidentified fragment of 1789 states that 'A number of workmen are at present employed in repairing Glamis Castle, the seat of Lord Strathmore, one of the most beautiful situations in Scotland!'. Lord Strathmore had reached his majority in the spring of 1790, was on terms with his mother, and money was at last to hand. For the years 1792–6 expenditure was mostly on repairs: £44 15s 10d in 1792 for a new roof to the Great Round of the east wing, and £73 1s 5½d in 1793 for repairs to lead windows and sashes. At the same time, however, work must have been in hand on the designs for the new west wing, and for the

8.15 The new west wing, 1790–1800 (© Crown Copyright/RCAHMS)

alterations necessary to make the east wing conform and preserve the balance of the front, which had been Earl Patrick's aim.

The new design, for which no drawings have yet been discovered, is curiously old-fashioned and reverts to Bell's proposals of 1763, in that the gabled roofs of the wings are lowered and given lead flats. To hide the old roof of the east wing, which was lowered to collar level, the wall-heads were raised and given battlemented parapets carried on a corbel course. This was not a happy solution, since it detracted from the elevation of the Great Round, already heightened by Earl Patrick. Round chimneys replaced the old rectangular stacks, and there was a considerable amount of refacing. This produced some curious vertical loops disguising the original openings of the cellars, and introduced horizontal loops at the wall-head. Such is the power of Glamis to create myths that it has been suggested that these loops showed the influence of Sir James Hamilton of Finnart, James V's Master of Works. At the same time, the small round was brought into line with those on the Great Tower, and what remained of the harling was stripped. This brought the east wing into conformity with the west wing, which had been given a matching Great Round.

The name of the architect of the work is not known, but five years later the earl employed Alexander Gilkie to reface the south front of Gibside in a curiously heavy handed and anachronistic style. Gilkie is said to have been recommended to Lord Strathmore by Lord Delaval, for whom Gilkie had worked at Ford Castle, but as work at Ford did not start before 1801, the recommendation may have been the other way round. It is possible that Gilkie's work at Ford was based on drawings by James Nisbet, who had died twenty years earlier, and his sources for Gibside and Glamis – if, that is, he worked there – could have been equally outdated. Colvin describes Gilkie as 'A provincial designer of no great ability whose works nevertheless have considerable naive charm',[2] which puts him firmly in line with James Thurber's 'A naive domestic Burgundy without any breeding but I think you'll be amused at its presumption'.[3]

Whoever the architect was, work must have started in 1796, as in the following year there was a payment of £283 16s 10½d for alterations to the east wing. The new west wing must have been started in 1797, as the accounts for 1798 show a payment for £305 15s 10½d for building work which included the demolition of the

9th Earl's work – accounts at Glamis being generally paid at least a year in arrears.

This new wing, although monumental in scale, did not add materially to the accommodation in the castle. The Round contained four rooms, but the main bulk of the wing only two, and there is no indication of their purpose. The ground floor, with its large carriage entrance, may have been intended as a coachhouse, but at a later date a brick vault was introduced to support the huge span of the floor above, and it seems to have become a store. The enormous room on the first floor, which rises the full height of the wing, did not become the dining-room until the time of the 12th Earl in the 1850s. Writing in 1802, Sir William Forbes describes it as 'plaistered and corniced and finished like a Drawing Room in a modern built house which has a very bad effect',[4] and he might have added that it was very badly built, as fifty years later both the floor and roof were in need of renewal. Another description, written perhaps twenty years later, notes that 'Adjoining the stone hall is the library and at the south end is a room 45 ft in length and two stories high intended to be a Drawing Room by the late Earl. Where this room now stands were the old dining and drawing rooms removed by the father of the present lord upward of fifty years ago'. Either the writer is uncertain on which floor the library was, or there was a smaller library below the chapel.

Of the 'plaistered and corniced' finish of this room nothing remains. Work continued in 1798, the accounts of 1799 showing payments of £330 17s 7½d; these may have involved a considerable amount of refurbishing, and many of the panelled doors in the castle similar to the one shown in Billings's drawing of the great hall would be covered by this. In 1799 there was also a payment of £1 15s 6d for 'five small oblong windows to the East Wing', which must include those in the new cellar lights, and a much larger sum of £292 14s for 'alterations to the top of the castle'. Apart from necessary repairs, this included the changes made to the north-west corner of the Great Tower. Until then the tower's north face had been symmetrical, with a two-storeyed cap house at either end. This arrangement compromised the symmetry of the frontispiece once Earl Patrick had changed the axis of the castle by forty-five degrees. It did not seem to trouble Earl Patrick, and neither Carr nor Bell showed any wish to change it. However, it did not suit the 10th Earl, and it was accordingly altered. Nor did the change stop there. The accounts of 1800 show the spending of a further £615 1s 8½d, part of which would have covered the completion of the work to the roof-line, which was necessary in the pursuit of symmetry, and which considerably altered the appearance of the west and south gables. Before this, the south gable had been crowned by a domed gazebo, flanked by decorative iron railings, matching the other ironwork on the roof; the west gable had been crowned by an open bartizan flanked by solid parapets concealing chimney-flues. This arrangement is shown on old drawings and paintings of the castle before 1800. By 1840 Billings shows the new arrangement. Each gable is crowned by a domed gazebo flanked by pierced stone parapets. Whether this alteration was justified must depend on whether one's view is architectural or antiquarian, but it would not be countenanced today. There was a final push to complete the work, which included finishing the new library, a new pavement in the 'Stone Hall', windows in the west wing, the new flight of steps from the main stair to the 'Stone' or 'Laigh Hall', and a great deal in the way of redecoration, doors, door-cases, shutters and cornices carried out in a soulless and mechanical fashion.

The work had taken eight years to complete and had been overseen by Patrick Brown; in 1801 his son Peter was paid £162 8s 8d for his father's trouble in superintending the alterations. The Browns, father and son, were land surveyors, but should not be confused with their more famous contemporaries George and Peter. It was not unusual in Scotland at this time, when land surveyors were expected to turn their hands to almost any aspect of estate management, to find one acting as clerk of works for the erection of estate buildings, although it was seldom that the building of mansion houses came their way. Yet it was typical that at Glamis the supervision, as well as the design, of the works at the castle should seldom be entrusted to really first-class men.

Expenditure on the new work, including Patrick Brown's fee, had come to £2,178 12s 10d, but this was not the end. Between 1804 and 1811 a further £409 16s 1d was spent, which included £110 for furniture, £43 10s to James Jopp of Montrose for a sideboard 'suitable to the Great Hall', and £117 6s to James Gartley of Aberdeen for the new clock on the stair tower.

In spite of this, the castle was little used. The earl's visits were short and increasingly infrequent, and for long periods the staff was reduced to two women servants – one sometimes dignified by the title of 'Housekeeper' – on board wages. This partial abandonment of the castle is reflected in the inventory taken in September 1820 after the death of the earl. The total value of the furniture, wines and other effects came to £935 10s 10d. Of this the most valuable item – at £189 3s 4d – was the wine in the cellar, followed by a 'Lott of old books valued at £70'. In no room were the contents worth more than £61 1s 6d, and that one was the housekeeper's.

Once again, the death of an earl found Glamis in a sad state, partly furnished and still incomplete, and with a great deal of work still necessary before it could be lived in. Behind the imposing front lay a warren of discomfort and inconvenience.

CHAPTER 9

THE INTERREGNUM AND THE DINING-ROOM, 1820–1854

The 10th Earl's settlements effectively debarred his immediate successors from embarking on any lavish building operations, although the Trustees were empowered to prevent the castle from falling into decay. This was perhaps as well, for, judging by the amount of money they were forced to expend, there may have been an element of skimping in the works carried out by both the 9th and 10th Earls. The account books show that the twenty-six years between the death of the 10th Earl and the accession of Thomas, 12th Earl, his great-nephew, £3,242 2s 11d had been spent on repairs in and about the castle, in addition to £232 9s 9d needed for repairs to the pictures in the same period. From 1846 to 1850 a further £1,634 4s 4d was spent, but there are no details of what was done. Probably it was needed for redecoration and bringing more rooms back into use; certainly, much of the interior trim dates from the first half of the century. The clue to this may lie in the inventory of linen and china made in 1844. In all previous inventories rooms had been described either by their function, the name of their occupant, the colour of their hangings, their location in the castle or by a number, but suddenly there was a change. It was the post-Walter Scott era, so they are the '1st and 2nd Tartan Rooms', the '42nd Tartan Room' (a regiment with which the family had had little connection), 'King Malcolm's Room' and, inevitably, 'Prince Charlie's Room'.

It was following his marriage in 1850 to Charlotte Maria Shute, daughter of Viscount Barrington, that the 12th Earl decided to set his mark on the castle by fitting up the enormous room in the west wing as a dining-room. He chose as his architect the Hon Thomas Liddell, second son of the 1st Lord Ravensworth. The families of Bowes Lyon, Shute and Liddell were connected; Thomas Liddell was third cousin at one remove of the earl, and uncle by both blood and marriage of the countess. An amateur architect and an amateur of architecture, he had been one of the Commissioners appointed to consider the rebuilding of the Palace of Westminster after the fire of 1834. He is also sometimes credited with the designs for Ravensworth Castle, but as he was only seven years old at the time John Nash produced the plans, he would have needed to be precocious indeed. His work at Glamis was concerned with two things: first, to bring a degree of comfort into the castle by way of cooking stoves and hot water pipes; and, second, to provide a dining-room to rival in size and splendour the great hall, now used as the drawing-room. Much of his correspondence with his clerk of works, James Anderson, survives in the charter room, and destroys one of the popular traditions of Glamis.

The dining-room – one of the most successful and complete examples of the early Victorian 'Jacobethan' style, is not a monument to Scottish taste, design or craftsmanship. There is no reason why it should not have been, but Liddell was patriotic to the point of parochialism. Himself from the north east of England – an area with which both the earl and countess had strong family connections – he preferred to rely on his fellow countrymen, and to deal with firms and craftsmen he knew. His clerk of works was from the north east; the carpenters, joiners, glaziers and plasterers were from Newcastle-upon-Tyne. Everything that could be made in that city was made there, and shipped north to Glamis. The furniture, specially made, was exhibited to appreciative Novocastrians before it ever reached the castle, and the Edinburgh firm of heating engineers already working at Glamis was replaced as quickly as possible.

How much of the detailed design was the work of Thomas Liddell is uncertain; both the sideboard and the chimney-piece seem to have been designed by James Anderson, and it is likely that the details of the ceiling and the painted windows were settled by the craftsmen who made them, once the broad lines had been agreed.

The first letter in the correspondence, which introduces Liddell, dates from April 1851 and proves that work was already in hand. The firm of Steele, George Street, Edinburgh, was involved in the provision of fittings for the kitchen, and the new heating system which was to be introduced throughout the castle. An undated sketch shows the new dining-room floor laid on joists carried on sleeper walls, which were to be built on a brick vault, the voids being filled with rubble. The floor of the west wing must have been giving trouble, because of the very great span; to rectify this, it had been necessary to insert a brick vault into the ground floor. From later letters it is clear that the new butler's pantry and service corridor had been structurally completed, and

that a new roof to the dining-room had been found necessary. Much of this work must have been finished by the end of the autumn of 1850 – the end of the building season – and probably accounts for most of the £1,639 4s 4d spent between 1846 and 1850.

By the beginning of 1851 work had advanced far enough for the question of decorations and finishes to be under consideration. The measurements of the dining-room were needed – there was a difference of 5 in. (130mm) in width between the two ends – and Lord and Lady Strathmore wanted a decorated ceiling, the timbers for which were to be of well-seasoned Memel pine. During June that year the trusses for the dining-room ceiling and roof were put up and the new heating systems installed, one for the kitchen and one for the dining-room. The heating pipes were to run beyond the armoury as far as 'the dark space below Lord and Lady Strathmore's apartments, as the warmth there will greatly add to their comfort'. A steel blade was to be substituted for the timber lintel above the sideboard recess, and the painting of the family quarterings for the dado was put in hand.

The problem of hot water had to be considered; in addition to the heating of the rooms, there were the hot closets, the supply to the butler's and service closets, and to the two hot baths for which Steele had the order. Mr Dodds of Newcastle had taken measurements for the dining-room ceiling, the manufacture of the chairs was in hand, and thought was being given to the breastwork for the chimney. At the same time, there was the problem of bringing the dining-room flue up inside the south gable of the Great Tower. Fortunately, in exploring for a position for this flue Mr Anderson (as recorded in a letter of 21 June) had found an existing one in the gable. This finished some 8 ft (2.44m) above the floor level of the dining-room, and, when plumbed, the plumb struck above the passage between the dining-room and the armoury. This inconvenience was slight compared with the enormous amount of cutting out that had been saved. The flue had originally served a fireplace in the south-west corner of the hall. In the same letter Anderson suggested that the great stair might be heated by a stove, its pipe concealed in the hollow newel. This suggestion was to surface again.

At this time Liddell's dissatisfaction with Steele must have come to a head, and he advised that the firm should be replaced by Mr Watson of Newcastle, although Steele was to be allowed to continue with the kitchen contract and some smaller works that were in

9.1 The great hall, 1820–50 (Billings, vol II)

hand. The information was conveyed to Steele in a terse note from Mr Proctor, the factor: 'Mr. Liddell has given the heating work to a Newcastle person'; one feels that Mr Proctor did not approve.

The heating of the armoury was not left to water pipes alone. A stove was to be set in one of the window embrasures, but in such a way as not to exclude the light. This was not easy as Liddell realized: 'I fear the flue for the stove in the armoury will be rather a troublesome job, but you must make what you can of it'. He clearly had great trust in Anderson's abilities, and in an age of clearly defined social distinctions and epistolary formality signed himself, unusually, 'Your friend, Thomas Liddell'.

Writing to Steele on 30 July, Anderson – who had been ill in the north country – was requesting the fittings for the warming closet and butler's pantry, as 'the family are shortly expected'. These seem to have been sent on 1 August, though what purpose they could serve with the dining-room so far from finished is not immediately obvious.

By August it had been decided there should be panels of painted armorial glass in the upper windows, and on 13 August John Brown of Newcastle was needing the sizes so that they could be made; the frames were to be provided by the firm of Barnards in the same city, and three days later Henry Watson was wanting the size of the dining-room fireplace.

In a letter of 20 September Liddell wrote to Anderson telling him of a burglary at Ravensworth Castle, and enclosing two rough sketches for a porch proposed to shelter the main entrance; both were semicircular surrounding the base of the stair tower, one open, the other closed, and both enriched with Jacobean strapwork parapets. A further sketch for the open porch arrived on 30 September, together with the suggestion that a sink and hot water would be useful in the passage behind the dining-room. There must have been times when Anderson found it difficult to keep a check on either the expenditure or his temper. He must have been sorely tried when, on 6 October, he received a letter containing instructions to introduce ventilators into the dining-

9.2 The dining-room, 1854, as it appears today

room floor, a rough sketch of a cupola to ventilate the smoking-room, and an indirect instruction: 'If Lord Strathmore would like a warm bath in the small room below next the water closet at the back of the Dining Room I have no doubt it could be managed with the hot water apparatus'. It cannot have been any easier when on 11 October he received a note from Watson (the heating engineer) to tell him that 'Mr. Ralph [the plasterer] says you are ready for the heating apparatus'.

Anderson must have submitted his sketches for the chimney-piece, as on 15 October Liddell was writing that he was pleased with the drawings, but preferred the double pilasters to be on a single pedestal – in this Liddell was not to get his way. This letter also contained a rough sketch for the firedogs, a design for new mullions, and instructions to panel the lobby between the dining-room and the armoury in oak. On 29 October Liddell let it be known that Lady Strathmore thought it best to introduce only roses into the dining-room ceiling; if this meant that she did not care for the drops, it was too late. The ceiling was finished on 1 November, and consideration was now being given to lighting the room with gas (though gas was not brought in until 1865, when the estate gasworks were built).

On 27 November Anderson heard from Liddell that the floor of the dining-room, together with the window fittings, would be sent north from Newcastle in March, and in the same letter Liddell returned to the problem of heating the staircase: 'I think the great staircase might be warmed either by hot water or hot air pipes conducted up the hollow pillar which the weights of the clock now use'. He had previously urged the removal of the clock.

At the beginning of December Anderson wrote to say that the joisting in the dining-room was ready to receive the floor, but that the ceiling was not yet ready for painting, although the heating was now on in both the dining-room and library. Liddell continued to press for the painting to start, and warned that the water in the pipes should not be allowed to boil. He was also concerned that the lead on the roof of the dining-room corridor had not been laid, which suggests that the work was slightly out of phase. There was also mention of the upper windows, which would give a great richness to the upper part of the room, and to the colour – a light, warm stone colour – to be used on the walls.

Writing from Towcester on 18 December, Liddell gave instructions that Steele was to put up the kitchen range, and this seems to have been completed by the middle of February 1852.

Painting started in the dining-room on 15 March, for which Brown and Richardson's estimate was £27, which did not include the ceiling. The drawing-room was to be distempered at a cost of £12, with the chimney-piece, which was to be painted, an extra. Brown had by now completed the quarterings for the dining-room wainscot.

John Brown, a pioneer in the revival of the art of glass painting, was well known in Newcastle as a 'house and landscape' painter. He worked on his own account but from Richardson's address. He seems to have been used by Richardson at times as a subcontractor, and clearly did not allow the profitable role of interior decorator to offend his susceptibilities as an artist.

Liddell had requested Anderson to send him the size of the upper windows as early as 10 August 1851 in order that the stained glass might be prepared. One had been completed by 2 February, when Liddell wrote that it was finished 'and beautifully done'. On 10 March he was even more forthcoming: 'Mr Brown is an intelligent man. He has painted the heraldic coats for the dining room admirably. The painted windows are very successful'. The finished windows were dispatched from Newcastle early in April.

Decoration continued throughout March and April; the dining-room and passage behind it were completed, the drawing-room chimney-piece was to be painted, and thought was given to the great staircase. The first suggestion – 25 March – was that it should be painted a warm stone colour, showing the joints and varieties in the stonework, but six days later it was decided to paint it like stone – 'an improvement on whitewash'. This makes it clear that the original treatment had been lime – or whitewash – applied directly to the stone. The painting 'like stone' led invariably to plastering, and this was confirmed 8–10 April, when it was ordered that the great stair and the stair to the private apartments were to be painted, and that the 'imitation of masonry on the staircase must be that of handsome Ashlar work'. To receive this plaster it was necessary to peck the freestone. Work started on the staircase on 5 May. Forty-four years later the plaster was removed.

Meanwhile, discussion centred on the upper windows. These were double: rectangular with clear glass, mullions and transoms externally, and an undivided square with painted armorial glass internally. Liddell, who had earlier expressed his reservations about the mullions and transoms, would have preferred the windows to be glazed externally with large sheets of plate glass, but Lord and Lady Strathmore wanted 'the antique character'. The arguments rumbled on for the next two months, but were in fact irreconcilable. By night there was no problem; at considerable inconvenience oil lamps were set within the embrasures to light the panels,[1] but by daylight the shadows cast by mullions, transoms and lead cames on the inner windows considerably lessened their effect. As far, however, as the external appearance of the castle was concerned, the earl and countess were right in their insistence on the retention of 'the antique character'.

By August the chimney-piece had been dispatched, and on the 12th of the same month Liddell was writing to Anderson about the hangings for the temporary sideboard, bidding him bear in mind that there was no blue in the carpet, and adding that Lord Strathmore wished the sideboard to be made up of old oak carvings which he had in London.

The room was now virtually finished. In September the magnificent fire grate was sent up by Watson, and sketches were being prepared for the sideboard. Two of these survive among the Glamis papers, one of which appears to be that finally adopted. Writing to Anderson on 12 February 1853, Mr Burnup reported 'We have got the sideboard partly put together, and Mr. Liddell is much pleased with your design. He has not yet fixed upon the ornaments'. This may refer to Liddell's having to make a choice between the two designs submitted by Anderson, to whom it is clear that much of the credit for the work must go.

Whoever was responsible, the final result was remarkably successful, and it depended entirely on the handling of the decoration. The proportions of the room, with the two tiers of windows, are not happy, and had the upper tier not been reduced to square openings internally, the result would have been very strange indeed.

The style chosen was carefully controlled 'Jacobethan', the three dominant elements being the ceiling, the chimney-piece and the sideboard recess. The ceiling is flat, divided into square panels with a drop at the corner of each panel. The panels are subdivided by shallow ribs with thistles and roses. The ceiling is further enriched by an elaborate frieze embellished with lions. The chimney-piece is in two tiers, each with double pilasters framing the Strathmore arms on the over-

mantel, and the splendid fire grate with its brass surround and dogs, capped by the lions of Lyon, and the fireback bearing the arms of Shute of Barrington. The pilasters are fluted and of a vaguely Roman Doric nature, and the cornice has added enrichments. The lower frieze continues round the room as the frieze of the wainscot. This is arranged in two tiers of narrow panels separated by a band of square panels containing the quarterings of the Lords of Glamis. The doors are all panelled with the wainscot, so no door-case break its run.

The sideboard recess is flanked by single pilasters similar to those on the chimney-piece. Their pedestals are formed by the lower tier of the wainscot panels. The full entablature is simpler than that of the chimney-piece.

The south and west walls are broken by two tiers of windows, ten in number, with richly carved surrounds. They flood the room with light, and, as Liddell predicted, give great richness to the upper part of the room. This richness of light and colour is enhanced by, and enhances, the contrast between the plain plastered surface of the upper walls, and the elaborate detailing of the woodwork and the ceiling.

Much of the furniture was provided at the time the room was decorated, and was designed for it; of all the pieces the sideboard was the most magnificent. Its manufacturers clearly thought very highly of the handiwork, believing that exhibiting it to the press and public might bring them some benefit. Perhaps they were right.

On 18 June 1853 one of the Newcastle journals, under the headline 'HUGE GOTHIC SIDEBOARD', informed its readers in increasingly breathless language that:

> An oak sideboard of extra-ordinary dimensions and beauty is now being made by Messrs. Wm. and Cuthbert Burnup of this town … for Lord Strathmore whose *stately* dining room in the *splendid* baronial residence of Glamis Castle now in the course of renovation and enlargement it is intended to *grace and adorn* … *extraordinary* piece of furniture … *correct* taste of the amateur artist kinsman of the noble owner … truly gothic sideboard … a credit to the town in which it was produced … visited by several persons of *distinction* … well known *urbanity* of the manufacturers.

What more is there left to say?

Chapter 10
The 13th Earl, 1865–1904

BUILDING WORK

Claude, 13th Earl of Strathmore, was the last of the great building earls, and it is to his taste that Glamis owes much of its present appearance. His brother had died on 15 September 1865, and could hardly have been in his grave before the Edinburgh firm of Brown & Wardrop was commissioned to enlarge Glamis as it had never been enlarged before. The dispatch with which the great nineteenth-century practices worked is amazing, and the first drawings of the new proposals were ready by 16 December. Further drawings, showing variations to the plan, followed on 4 January 1866. At the same time, improvements to the policies were planned, a new garden was contemplated, routine

maintenance continued apace and gas was brought into the castle. What was not realized was the extent of the 12th Earl's debts. Once this became apparent, there was an end to these grandiose schemes, and in 1870 Brown & Wardrop were paid £180 for the drawings and estimate they had prepared, and dismissed.

In fairness to Earl Claude, there was need for some alterations and improvements at the castle. It was almost a hundred years since there had been a young family at Glamis. His family was young, large and would be larger, but it should not have been impossible to find space within the existing rooms for his eleven children.

In 1873 and 1879 it was proposed to add an additional floor to the south range, but this proposal came to nothing, and another ten years were to pass before

10.1 Improvements by Brown & Wardrop, 1866 (© Strathmore Estates)

circumstances made it both possible and necessary to extend the castle once more. Work started on the south range in 1890; in 1892–3 the area south of the castle was landscaped and the Dutch Garden was created by Arthur Castings; and in 1895–6 work was being carried out on the interior of the Great Tower under James Ferguson. The recasting of the north and east ranges from 1899 to 1901 gave the castle its present form.

The earliest of the Brown & Wardrop drawings – 16 December 1865 – is a block plan of the castle showing the proposed additions. The whole of the two service courts, except for the kitchen with its adjoining scullery and bakehouse, was to be demolished, and replaced by a single court with round stair towers in three of its corners. The south range was to extend for nearly 200 ft (60.96m), terminating in an apsidal-ended chapel. A new block was to be added to the east side of the Great Tower, filling the space between Earl Patrick's addition

to the south-east wing and the eighteenth-century kitchen, and there was to be some building between the chapel tower and the west wing.

To the north of the north service range was a court-yard with pended openings in its east and west walls, with a north range devoted to a washing-house and a game larder planned on a most generous scale. Behind it was a bleaching green, and to the north east of the washing-house a covered stable court, with a turret-flanked entrance.

By 4 January two sets of plans had been provided, and to accompany these were three prospects of the castle, differing slightly from the plans, and an additional drawing showing the proposed treatment of the new chapel.

The chief difference between the two sets lies in the treatment of the south-east corner. In one, this is devoted to a large chapel on the first floor, with traceried

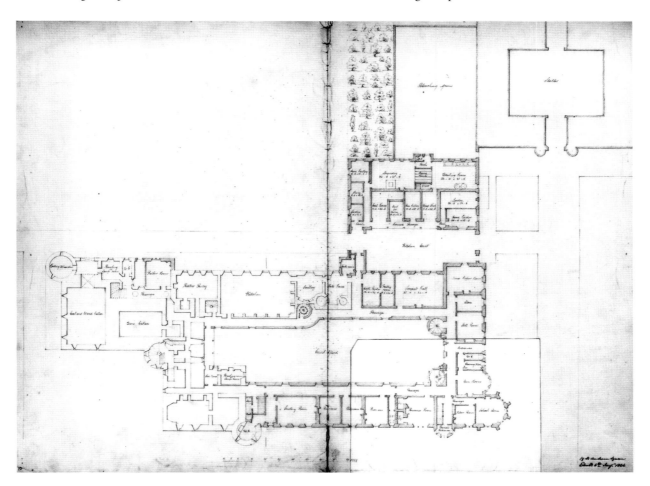

10.2 Ground-floor plan with new office court and stables, Brown & Wardrop, 1866 (© Strathmore Estates)

windows, buttresses, which suggest a vault was intended, and a three-sided apse. One elevation shows a ground-floor porch and round stair tower, but the plan shows a round tower surmounted by a cap house. The tower contains a lobby and the half-landing of an open straight-flighted timber stair, and the cap house simply contains space – an architectural solecism of the first order. Another drawing dispenses with the chapel altogether, the south-east corner finishing with either a square pavilion, or a round tower balancing the old Great Round at the corner of the south-east wing. This seems to have been the solution favoured, since it is the one shown on the large perspectives; the rededication of the old chapel in September 1866 shows that the idea of building a new chapel had been abandoned.

On the ground floor of both designs were the business-, smoking- and gun-rooms, schoolroom, tutor's room and two or three small bedrooms – probably for the boys of the family – together with additional service rooms. On the first floor were rooms for the women servants in the north range, nurseries in the east range and private apartments for Lord and Lady Strathmore in the south range. The family was beginning its retreat from the splendid discomfort of the older parts of the castle.

The private apartments, on the first floor of the south range, were separated from the rooms in the older wing – which had always been the earl's rooms, and which may now have been intended as the principal guestrooms – by an open-well staircase. These new apartments faced south across the park, and were served by a long passage running the length of the north side of the south range. This was a service passage rather than a corridor, as, except for the sitting-room, none of the rooms, which were all intercommunicating, opened off it. Central to this suite was the family bedroom: to the west, but separated from it by a water closet and lobby, were Lady Strathmore's boudoir and the lady's maid's room, while to the east, beyond a bathroom and another water closet, were the earl's dressing-room and sitting-room. At the eastern end of the passage was – figuratively, if not literally – a green baize door, beyond which lay the nursery suite. This consisted of a day and night nursery, a maid's room and nursery pantry, schoolroom and a room for the governess.

If not on the same scale, the accommodation intended for the female servants was unusually good: not skyed in the attic, but on the same floor – although at a respectful distance – from that of the family. The housekeeper and cook each had rooms of their own; the two housemaids shared a bedroom, as did the stillroom maids. A water closet, bathroom and large sitting-room were also provided, the only disadvantage being that,

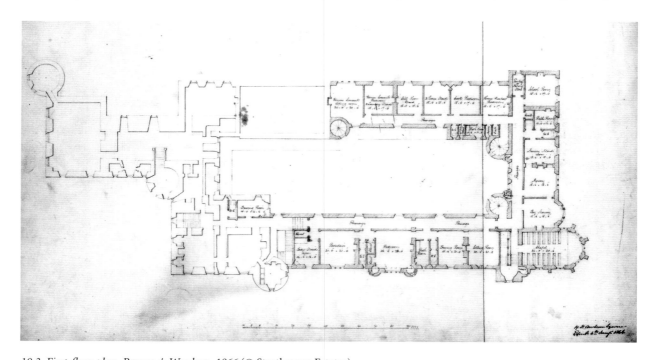

10.3 First-floor plan, Brown & Wardrop, 1866 (© Strathmore Estates)

apart from the water closet and bathroom, all these rooms faced north.

The treatment proposed for the elevations can hardly be described as distinguished: the general style – restrained collegiate with round towers wherever possible – did not compete with the old castle, but it was spread too thinly on a building which, although low, was too large, and which was echoed in a minor key by the stable court. There were too many dormer-heads and crow-stepped gables without the redeeming fantasy of the seventeenth-century work.

The least satisfactory part of the design was the treatment of the chapel tower and the 9th Earl's kitchen and library. The chapel was given a western oriel, an embattled parapet, a bell-cot at its north-east corner and, more open to criticism, new pitched roofs, each at right angles to the other, its crow-stepped gable containing a rose window. This double roof covers a single space, and deceives for no reason other than a desire for quaintness.

Equally objectionable is the library; refenestrated, with a stepped parapet and a pair of gables, it gives the impression of a double-pile, which it is not.

Brown & Wardrop produced another design for the north range in 1867. This left the library and chapel untouched, treating the elevation as a simplified version of the south front, the only concession to fantasy being the false two-floored rounds on the north-east gable, copied from those on the Great Tower. A further and simpler set of alterations and additions to the existing service courts was produced in 1869, with the aim of providing quarters for the housekeeper and two small stables. It came to nothing, and in 1870 the firm's – mostly Mr Wardrop's – connection with Glamis came to an end.

Throughout the 1870s and 1880s Lord Strathmore toyed with ideas for more building work at the castle, but it was not until 1890 that anything was put in hand. In doing this, he was probably influenced by the thought

10.4 The south-east range as recast and partly rebuilt in 1891 (© Crown Copyright/RCAHMS)

that unless he did it now – he was sixty-six – it would not be done in his lifetime. The death of John Bowes in 1885, which meant that the great Bowes inheritance had come back to the legitimate line, must have eased his financial position, and the growing number of grandchildren, the family of his eldest son, Lord Glamis, made the work necessary. This time the work was to be in the hands of three separate architects; nothing on the scale of the Brown & Wardrop designs was to be attempted, and it was to be spread over a period of ten years.

This did not mean that money had not been spent on the castle in the previous twenty-five years. Leaving aside the very large sums spent on the gardens and policies, the cost of refitting the chapel – which cannot have been far short of £600 – nearly £4,000 on furniture, and the £1,312 10s 11d accounted for by the building of the new gasworks, the monies devoted to repairs and permanent repairs at the castle had, by 1874, reached a total of £10,715 12s 11d, and all this from a heavily encumbered estate.

The drawings for the alterations to the south range were probably started in 1889, as the date of building – 1891 – is carved on one of the windows of the central feature. The addition, which is on three floors and of six bays, abuts the old south-east wing, and projects beyond the line of the old south range, which it completely dominates. In its details it is generally in sympathy with the older work, but it suffers from an extremely aggressive central feature, which overwhelms the rest of the elevation. This is a projecting double gable carried on corbels. Three widely spaced windows, each crowned by carved pediments, are surmounted by two heavily architraved windows, two crow-stepped gables and a central chimney-stack. There are two other pediments in turn and three armorial panels scattered about the elevation: it is all very odd. The intention is to combine restrained baronial exuberance with due regard to architectural economy: but exuberance is difficult to restrain and seldom sits well with economy, and the effect is rather less than baronial. More successful is the rest of the south range, where the original eighteenth-century building has been given simple crow-steps and dormerheads. Internally, the rooms and passages are spacious, comfortable and undistinguished.

The main building work had been finished by 1891, but other work continued throughout the following year with the grates and fireplaces being installed. A note in Lord Strathmore's diary records that 'Claude and I approved Ferguson's proposals for the nursery wing'.

Most of the work carried out by Arthur Castings (1891–3) belongs more properly to 'Gardens and Policies', but he does seem to have formalized the setting of the main entrance. The levels around the castle had been raised when the 3rd Earl formed his new entrance in the great stair tower. Every drawing of the front of the castle, from Slezer and De Wet to Brown & Wardrop, shows Earl Patrick's entrance at ground level, without even a single step up to the threshold. Some time between 1866 and 1887 (MacGibbon and Ross published their account of the castle in the latter year),[1] the levels were lowered and a stone apron with steps was provided. Castings remodelled this, giving it added dignity and providing two stone plinths on which are mounted the Lion of Lyon.

In January 1896 the family was comfortably installed in the new and newly arranged rooms, and attention could be turned to the older parts of the castle. This involved the restoration, or 'antiquing', of much of the interior, in the course of which a considerable amount of the decoration carried out for the 12th Earl by Thomas Liddell was removed. This is best described in two letters written by James Ferguson to the earl, who was then away from the castle.

Glamis. 13 Jany. 1896

My Lord

I have to inform your Lordship that we have commenced taking off the plaster at the Castle on Monday 5th. inst. and that work is now proceeding satisfactorily.

The walls of the writing rooms in the crypt and the walls of the main staircase up to the square of the top landing are stripped and we have commenced to repair and wash the walls of the foot of the staircase. I can now see that we will have plenty of time to do the staircase right up to the top and I have given instructions accordingly.

The only thing we have as yet discovered on the staircase is an opening about 2ft. wide and 2ft. 7ins. high just about the first turn from the bottom. This appears to have been a window and has looked into the crypt in the arched recess just over the crypt stair. I presume we may build up the back of this and form it into a recess in the stair well. Or would your Lordship prefer to have it opened through to the crypt to form a sort of borrowed light to the crypt stair. This could be done by removing the old armour and wood to which it is affixed and refacing the wall at the back of it, which I remember is very rough.

In regard to the writing rooms off the Crypt, we have made a rather awkward discovery. These rooms have been quarried out of the solid wall and the sides of them faced with small stone which, however, are fairly regular and may not look bad after they are cleaned. No attempt has been made to put in a ceiling of any sort to support the wall above; you are simply looking up into the heart of the wall which is prevented from falling merely by the cohesion of the lime and the stones. I do not anticipate any danger of the wall giving way but still small portions of it might fall at any time.

I think the best thing to do with this will be to put a flat stone ceiling and fill in the space above with concrete. We can do this by cutting a chase in the walls to support the ends of the stone slabs.

The Eastmost room is partly under the Drawing Room fireplace, and the outside wall of it is so thin that rather than run the risk of cutting it to get in the ceiling I would build a new wall about 9ins. thick on the face of the old one, to support one end of the ceiling stones. We have not yet done anything in the Drawing room. I shall be glad to have your Lordship's instructions as to the matters I have referred to.

I have the honour to be
Your Lordship's obedt. and faithful servt.
Jas. A. Ferguson

The second letter was written two weeks later:

29th Jany. 1896
My Lord

I have to acknowledge the receipt of your letter of the 20th. inst. The old window is not in the centre of the arch over the crypt stair but is about 6ins. from one side of it as indicated on the following rough sketch. I am afraid on that account that it would not look very well to be opened through.

We have finished the main stairway so that we should have plenty of time to do the old stair leading to the top of the castle as her Ladyship wishes.

In cleaning the wall of the passage leading from the Drawing Room to the Oak Room we have discovered what I think has been a window before the main stair was built (The present window in this passage has been slapped in). There is a splendid arch over it but we found that the chimney flue from the fireplace we opened up in Duncan's Hall went right through it. This evidently had been done when the stair was built also. I should be glad to know what your Lordship would like done with this. If you wish it made into a recess – which I think would look very well – and at the same time want a flue for the fireplace in Duncan's Hall the only way to get the latter will be to carry a pipe up the back of the recess as there is not sufficient thickness in the surrounding walls to permit of a new vent being slapped in.

We have to reface a considerable portion of the walls of this passage but are now well advanced with it.

I do not intend beginning to [design] the door in the Drawing Room until we are nearly finished with the rest of the work, but as soon as I have opened it up I will send your Lordship a sketch as requested.

I have the honour to be
Your Lordship's obedt. Servt.
Jas. A. Ferguson

The stripping of the plaster from the main staircase left it in the condition it is today, but the reference in the first letter to the proposed work in the drawing-room does not make clear what this work was to be. In the second letter, however, this becomes apparent. Ferguson writes of a doorway that is to be opened up, and a door that is to be designed. The door could be the huge door leading from the staircase which has replaced the panelled door shown in Billings's engraving; it is of this period, but the contract makes clear that the new door is to hang in an as-yet unopened doorway. This must be the opening to the newel stair in the north-west corner of the great hall. This is shown blocked on the eighteenth-century plans, and not shown at all by MacGibbon and Ross. It also makes sense of Lady Strathmore's wish to have something done to 'the old stair leading to the top of the castle'.

The description of the two writing-rooms, quarried out of the wall thickness on either side of the south window of the crypt, is typical of the way in which eighteenth-century builders tore into the fabric of an old building, putting their faith in the structural strength of lath and plaster. Neither is shown on Elphinstone's plan, but both appear on the plans of the 9th Earl's intended alterations.

More puzzling is the 'passage leading from the Oak Room to the Drawing Room', since there is little evidence of this today. However, on eighteenth-century plans a passage is shown on the west side of what is now known as 'Malcolm's Room'; this passage is also shown on Arthur Hamilton's drawing, which dates from after 1893, since it shows the plan of the Dutch Garden. Whether the removal of the dividing wall is part of Ferguson's process of 'antiquing' is not certain. Traces of the partition line can still be seen on the cornice on either side of Malcolm's Room, and its removal must have involved repairs to the ceiling, which must have had a very peculiar appearance, divided so unevenly.

In 1899 drawings were being prepared for the extension and completion of the east and north ranges in a truly baronial manner. Part of the north range had already received its complement of crow-steps and gables before this new batch of drawings was produced. It is a sad fact that the number and complexity of architectural drawings is in inverse ratio to the quality of the building that results from them. While the plans prepared for the 9th Earl and the later ones of Brown & Wardrop displayed a clear understanding of the workings of a great house, and of the hierarchy of its staff, these proposals were incoherent, and came dangerously close to the cry of Clive Pearson to Sir Robert Lorimer at Castle Fraser, 'can't we stuff the footman in there?'[2] Certainly, all concern for 'the morals of the maids' has disappeared. Once the domestics of opposite sexes would have been rigorously segregated; now they were on adjoining floors with a connecting staircase. Typical of the lack of thought given to the planning was the squeezing of a carriage house into the stable court, at the expense of light and air to the servants' hall.

If the plan was muddled, the elevations of 1901 were worse, and had degenerated into a species of 'villadom', more suitable to the less prosperous suburbs of one of the larger burghs. In this, Glamis is typical of the gradual decline of the architectural work in Scotland in the second half of the nineteenth century, a decline which pages of turgid prose from the pens of architectural and art historians will never raise to the level of the second-rate.

THE 13TH EARL AND THE MAD MR HENEAGE

There is an episode in the life of the 13th Earl which was unconnected with Glamis but, as Poobah in *The Mikado* put it, provides 'corroborative detail, intended to give artistic verisimilitude to an otherwise bald and unconvincing narrative'[3] – the earl's connection with Biarritz and his dealings with the mad Mr Heneage.

It is one of the received truths that the 13th Earl was a man of a religious and gloomy nature, the one being consequent on the other. That he was religious is true, that he was gloomy is more doubtful. Only a man with a keen sense of the ridiculous would have answered, leave alone preserved among the family papers, the letters of Mr Heneage, which caused no little inconvenience in the first three months of 1885.

The previously unknown fishing village of Biarritz had sprung into prominence and fashion in 1854, when Napoleon III built the Villa Eugénie for his wife, and the new watering-place became the seat of the imperial court during part of each summer. There was a large British colony, and Lord Strathmore was accustomed to spend part of each winter there. His first visit had been in 1869, and he generally stayed from January until March, first of all at various hotels, but later at his own house, the Villa Bon Air. As Jane Austen had written of Bath, and might, with equal truth, have written of Biarritz: 'It was a much safer place for a gentleman in his predicament: he "might there be important at comparatively little expense"'.[4] That was in the days before the death of John Bowes, when money was not as plentiful as it was to become later.

Mr Charles Heneage, the other principal actor in this little comedy, was the second son of George Fieschi Heneage of Hainton Hall in Lincolnshire, where the family had been settled since 1398. If not as grand, the Heneages were, in point of antiquity, quite as respectable as the Bowes Lyons. This particular member of that Lincolnshire family of respectable antiquity had been in the diplomatic service, and was then forty-four years of age.

The earl had met Mr Heneage, who frequently visited Biarritz, in 1884, if not earlier, but he can hardly have been prepared for the storm that was to burst upon him on 10 January 1885 and was to rage for the next three months. Lord Strathmore had arrived in Biarritz that morning on the overnight train from Paris, and with his rolls and coffee at the Villa Bon Air came a letter from Mr Heneage, written earlier that morning. Following his recent return from Austria, Mr Heneage had put down the name of his cousin, Miss Chalfont, for one of the subscription balls at the Hôtel Palais Biarritz, and had attended two such balls himself:

I have ascertained the so-called Palais Biarritz is a gambling Hall. Under the circumstances I require an explanation from you who are (nominally I own) responsible for the invitation issued to my cousin, Miss C.

It does not appear that when I met you and Lady Strathmore, and Lord and Lady O'Hagan[5] last year at the 'P.B.' that the locality had been used prior to that date for immoral purposes.

This was a pretty accusation to meet a travel-weary and barely breakfasted peer of particularly blameless reputation. Before he was able to reply, another letter arrived to inform Lord Strathmore that Mr Heneage was arranging a dance at the Hôtel l'Angleterre, and that he had changed the day from Wednesday to Thursday 'which could not fail to be agreeable to the Society of Biarritz'. This was followed on the 12th by a copy of a letter Mr Heneage had sent to Sir Andrew Fairbairn,[6] President of the Biarritz Ball Committee, in which he had demanded to know: 'Was the Palais Biarritz suitable as a resort for gentlemen or gentlewomen, to meet for innocent and honourable amusement or not? since it was used for gambling and worse vices'.

Lord Strathmore was not the only recipient of Mr Heneage's letters, but he was to receive copies of letters sent to others, as well as calls for help from them, including Lord Chesterfield.[7]

On the same day – 16 January – Lord Strathmore received a long and rambling letter from Mr Heneage putting the following points regarding both the Palais Biarritz and the subscription balls held there:

It is not suitable for this purpose since other vices beyond gambling have been permitted under public surveillance. … The laws of no civilised state based on religion, whether Catholic or Protestant, allow vice or virtue to alternate by contract. … Apparently these vices could be purged if Lord Strathmore would take the hotel in conjunction with the Countess. … The law requires that the Countess of Strathmore inhabit the hotel 'en bonne mere de famile' for 2½ to five years, as the French law might require. The original offence is then purged, and gentlemen and gentlewomen can meet together 'de novo' for innocent and honourable amusement.

According to the earl's diary, Mr Heneage also asked to see the Ball Committee, but the request was refused, and the following day his subscription was returned.

It should have been clear by now that on the subject of morality in general and the subscription balls in

particular, Mr Heneage was away with the fairies, and that a waste-paper basket was in order. Probably the earl was not used to dealing with, or even recognizing, obsessionally deranged minds, and he seems to have regarded the whole affair – so far – as something to be handled with a light touch. This was not how Mr Heneage saw things, and on the 14th he dashed off an indignant letter to Lord Strathmore demanding that he read a notice posted in the drawing-room of the Hôtel l'Angleterre. This was probably a copy of some verses of the same date, a copy of which, in the earl's hand, is still preserved at Glamis:

One Mr. Heneage, so they say,
A dreadful row has made to-day
    About the Ball Committee
And very naughty words has used,
And Palais Biarritz much abused
    In language which we pity.

If Mr. Heneage be so pure
He's much too good for us I'm sure,
    This Paragon of Virtue
So what could the Committee say,
Except 'You'd better stay away
    For fear the place would hurt you'!

This was hardly calculated to soothe Mr Heneage's indignation, and Lord Strathmore only made matters worse when, on the following day, he wrote to the furious moral crusader. His Lordship thanked Mr Heneage for his letter, 'since until he received it he was not aware that there was a ball at the Palais, but since he had been made aware he would profit by the information, and put his name down as a subscriber'. He also pointed out that balls took place at the casino, 'but that it did not occur to the subscribers that because there was gambling in the autumn, there was no reason why they should not dance in the winter'. A busy day, the 14th, since the ball took place that evening.

Mr Heneage, to his intense annoyance, was not being taken seriously, and the result was a long and rambling letter to Lord Strathmore. In it was this curious passage:

[He] had known a long time since that President Grevy[8] had made his arrangements to abolish 'Monaco'[9] in two or three years at the personal instance of our Queen – that neither himself, Lord Vivian,[10] Lord Aylesbury (whose daughter, Lady

Listowel, is sister-in-law to my brother)[11] could in anyway by our presence in the Palais Biarritz thwart the Queen's wishes. . . . That is the simplest view I can take of the whole matter.

He added a footnote to the copy that '[He] would esteem it a favour if it were shewn to Lady Strathmore'. This request was firmly endorsed 'N.O.!'.

The breach was not yet complete; two further letters arrived on 17 January, both on the same subject. One was to Lord Strathmore, in which he offered: 'if the Earl was getting up theatricals in aid of the unfortunate Andelusians he would be happy to act *The Follies of The Night*, which with other gentlemen, he had performed in America under Lord Lyons[12] twenty years ago'. In the second, to the countess, he offered, if there were to be a concert at the Villa Bon Air to sing, 'if Mrs. Croker, a consummate musician, can be permitted to accompany him'.[13] These entertainments were to be in aid of the victims of the recent Spanish earthquake[14] and a further ball was proposed, together with a festival to raise additional funds.

On the 19th the earl was informed that Mr Heneage had written to the Bishop of London[15] to say that he was 'not accusing Henry Bradshaw[16] of actual and moral insanity, but would drop the case against Sir Andrew Fairbairn because of the great infirmity with which he had been afflicted'. Any hope of a musical entertainment vanished when Mr Heneage declined any further acquaintance with Mrs Croker, because of Mr Croker's intrusion on his privacy – probably in an excess of pastoral zeal on the chaplain's part, and the wretched Crokers were given their *congé* with the note, 'Mr. Heneage has had quite enough of Mr. Croker's *croaking* and Mrs. Croker's *croaking* and desires that it stops'.

Mr Heneage precipitated a further row by insulting a Mrs Hughes at the *table d'hôte* at the Hôtel Continental; he was turned out of l'Angleterre on the 26th and refused admission at the Hôtel France. Two days later he was ejected from the casino for being drunk. His next letter was written on 7 February to Lady Strathmore from the Hôtel des Princes – it is surprising that by then any hotel could be found to take him in. In this, he wrote to say that the earl could not pass his medical examination, but that he could not deal with him unless he was 'certified of sound mind and understanding', which was his reason for writing to Lady Strathmore. The postscript introduced an ominous note: 'Up to the present I have only shewn you both kindness, indulgence, and forbearance, but you will be so good as to bear in mind that there is such a thing as a sense of Public Duty'. Later in the month Lord Strathmore was to be his target again. Writing on 20 February, Heneage was demanding to know: 'Why was the consul at Biarritz not ex-officio member of the *Cercle Anglais*. He will cause questions to be raised in the House of Lords, and Lord Strathmore will have to account to the Parliament and Press of the World'. 'Another idiotic letter', noted the earl.

There were more letters during March: two on the 3rd to Lady Strathmore, the first advising her 'to induce Lord Strathmore to keep clear of Saphieha[17] and not trust his toadies Fairbairn and Bradshaw, nor offend the Spanish Element as they have their success too. . . . He will get him out of consequences of recent *faux pas* at the club misnamed the *Cercle Anglais*'. The second informed her that: 'he [Mr Heneage] had seen the Proceureur of the Republic. Saphieha and company may "hang up the fiddle and the bow" for it is up with their game – for taking advantage of Lord Strathmore's weak state of health'.

The situation was clearly getting out of hand, and from a cryptic allusion in the earl's diary it seems that the patience of the authorities in Biarritz and of the proprietor of the Hôtel des Princes gave out. The next letter to Lady Strathmore, written on 8 March, was from the Hôtel St Etienne at Bayonne. It contained a threat: 'I will give you one week to leave for London on the understanding your husband is placed under Dr. Tuke (of Albermarle Street)[18] whose daughter is married to a gentleman in the Foreign Office'. On the 12th Lady Strathmore received yet another letter telling her that her husband was not of sound mind or understanding but that Mr Heneage could not help her as 'Notwithstanding my special knowledge of lunacy I have no power to sign a Certificate of Sanity or Insanity'. He was approaching the French authorities to have Lord Strathmore sent home under restraint, and Mr Croker's wife summoned as a witness at the official enquiry. What effect this outburst had on the French authorities is not clear, but it produced an indignant letter two days later from Mr Croker to Lord Strathmore 'enclosing these lunatical letters'. The Crokers had incurred Heneage's wrath at the Lawn Tennis Ground, and the difference was referred to the earl, 'Who at all events represents an old and distinguished family'. How that was to the purpose is not made clear, but it showed a very proper frame of mind on the part of the chaplain.

Meanwhile Sir Andrew Fairbairn, who had been in London since February, was making enquiries, on his own and Lord Strathmore's behalf, of his fellow legislator Edward Heneage,[19] brother-in-law of Lady Listowel, and elder brother of the cause of all the trouble. Writing from the House of Commons' Library on 18 March, Sir Andrew describes a conversation that he had had with the elder brother when the House met in February. Edward Heneage had said that he was powerless to act: 'I am afraid you will not get the elder brother to move. ... I hinted his brother might get into some scrape and be called out by the foreigners. This did not seem to affect him, and he said it might be the best thing for him and teach him a lesson'. His advice was to take no notice, as since his illness in Russia and unfortunate marriage in Austria, his brother had been subject to these attacks: 'No one suffers more from his egotistical literature than his family and the Foreign Office'. He thus ignored the point that this present outburst was inconveniencing neither his family nor the Foreign Office. Nor does it excuse the singularly complacent note struck by Edward Heneage in a letter to Fairbairn and sent on to Lord Strathmore: 'He had

been curiously free from letters the past few month'. It reiterated that there was nothing he could do, although it might help for his brother to be forced to leave Biarritz. As a further crumb of comfort he added that 'It was his younger brother's habit to deluge Ministers with letters on the topic of the disgraceful state of the lunacy laws in England. The irony was that he had been certified within the last year as competent to manage his own affairs'.

At this point the correspondence ceased. Lord Strathmore was to leave Biarritz on 28 March on the 1.51pm train, travelling straight to Paris, and reaching London at 5.30pm the following day. Nothing more is to be found of Mr Heneage in the Glamis papers. He died in 1901, three years before the earl. Perhaps he continued in his efforts at reforming the morals and manners of continental watering-places and the British aristocracy abroad with equal success. Lord Strathmore retained his connection with Biarritz until 1891, through his association with the 'Societé Anonyme de la Grande Plage de Biarritz'.

CHAPTER 11
THE TWENTIETH CENTURY

The new century opened with the completion of the north range, and the last major internal work, the installation of a new ceiling in the library, or billiard room. This was the huge, austere room above the kitchen, flooded with a north light pouring through four great windows, and built by the 9th Earl. The suggestion that it should be given a new and elaborate ceiling had first been made in 1851. Thomas Liddell hoped that Mr Dodds, who was taking measurements for the library ceiling, would not find the same discrepancies that he had found in the dining-room. In the same year a sketch – now lost – was produced for the ceiling border. Nothing came of this proposal, but in 1903 Lord Strathmore decided to commemorate his golden wedding by installing a new ceiling. It is Jacobean, but a very 'milk-and-water' Jacobean in style, with timid little nods at its more robust cousins in Malcolm's Room and the dining-room. Neither this ceiling, nor the handsome seventeenth-century chimney-piece carved with the Blakiston arms (brought from Gibside in 1920), has been able to make any impression on this huge room, which remains obstinately eighteenth century in feeling.

Glamis nearly fell victim to fire, that great scourge of country houses, on Saturday 30 August 1916. The cause of the outbreak was never discovered, although it was most likely to have been either an overheated flue setting fire to an adjoining timber, or to burning soot falling on the duckboards on the roof. The outbreak was at the top of the Great Tower, and well beyond the reach of the apparatus of the Forfar Fire Brigade. It was not until the arrival of the Dundee Fire Brigade with its much more powerful equipment, forty-five minutes after the fire

had been discovered, that it was possible to pump water from the Dean and bring the fire under control.

For a time the danger was very great, especially from burning fragments falling on to the lower roofs, and from water pouring through the castle when the lead pipes from the cisterns in the roof melted. Had it not been for the untiring efforts of the Lady Elizabeth Bowes Lyon in organizing a body of willing workers with brooms to speed the torrent down the great stair, the damage would have been immense and the seventeenth-century plaster ceilings would almost certainly have been lost.

It is difficult to get a clear account of the fire damage. Legend has added a rich gloss and the official report – if such a thing ever existed – is missing. It may be that some of the stories have become exaggerated with the passage of time, but if the actual damage was less than sometimes thought, the potential danger was enormous.

The day cannot have been one of strong wind, since a breeze at ground level is something much rougher on the castle roof; and the fire seems to have been contained, since it burnt up through the roof rather than spreading along the passages and through the rooms. It was discovered at six o'clock in the late afternoon, and by nine o'clock was completely under control. A photograph taken after the fire shows firemen standing round a large hole in the roof, and, though the damage is extensive, the scene is not one of total devastation. The limited downward extent of the fire is shown in the survival of the main seventeenth-century beams in the ceiling of the fourth floor. Nevertheless, had it not been for the

Lady Elizabeth's prompt action in summoning both fire brigades, and had the lower roofs taken light, it is difficult to see how the castle could have been saved. Even so, the damage from smoke and water must have been considerable. The *Dundee Courier* of 1 September is reticent on the extent of the fire damage, but more forthcoming on that caused by water: the dining-room's 'beautiful furniture and rich carpets and tapestries' were 'made clammy by streams of water which could not be stemmed'; damage to the panels in the chapel was attributed to water from the tanks in the roof (or perhaps to the firemen, who took 'Peculiar pains to souse/The pictures up and down the house').

Following the fire, it was estimated that the cost of repairing the damage would be £4,198 5s 1d. Until this could be done, a temporary roof was provided at a yearly cost of £255. Rebuilding did not in fact take place until 1925–6, when, together with the architect's fee, the cost came to £4,027; the temporary roof had been up for nearly ten years and cost £2,295 in the end. The new roof, designed by Mr Waterston of Kirriemuir, was a roof, neither more nor less, and although the old forms were preserved externally, internally it was nothing but a covering supported on massive steel sections above an echoing space where the attic had been. Today, this could not have happened without a careful survey of everything that had survived the fire. Indeed, given the evidence of what had not been lost, it is likely that there would have been a restoration of the damaged parts. If Waterston made a survey of the roof and attic floor, it has not survived in the Glamis records. It is possible to reconstruct the layout of the attics at the turn of the century from Hamilton's drawing, but there is no evidence of the roof construction that was used.

Following the replacement of the roof, little other than routine maintenance was done at Glamis for the next forty-two years save for the introduction of electricity in 1929. A specification for this had been drawn up in 1903, but for some reason the work had not been carried out.

In 1972 Fergus, 17th Earl of Strathmore, inherited the title, and he and his wife came to the castle. Glamis, which had always been something of a show place and needed a regiment of servants to run it, was by modern standards quite unsuitable as a house – it may be wondered if it ever was suitable for such a purpose – and a fresh attempt had to be made at forming a new home within the enormous building. Because of the traditional use of the first floor of the old south-east wing as part of the private apartments – a tradition that was not relinquished – the solution was inevitably a rambling one. The architect chosen was James Dunbar-Nasmith. By concentrating the accommodation in the 1891 wing and the cross-range between the two office courts, and by demolishing the late and intrusive carriage house, the result has not been unsuccessful.

In the end the castle has won. No building earl, even had he wished it, could have afforded the siege train necessary to demolish it. Each building earl has been faced, as Clive Pearson was faced at Castle Fraser, with a building that defied him, and each may well have said in the words of Clive Pearson to Sir Robert Lorimer:

It is in my mind that we have endeavoured to fit the Castle into what we pretend would be our necessities; whereas we ought perhaps to proceed on the basis of fitting our necessities into the Castle as she is with the very minimum amount of disturbance.[1]

The true ghosts of Glamis, the building works of Patrick, 1st Lord Glamis, and Patrick, 3rd Earl of Strathmore and Kinghorne, have never been laid.

CHAPTER 12
ROOMS, FURNITURE AND FITTINGS:
THE EVIDENCE OF THE INVENTORIES

A notable collection of inventories survives among the Glamis papers. Dating from 1626 onwards, they chart the family fortunes and throw useful light on the history of the building. They deserve to be fully transcribed and annotated.

The Compt of the haill plenisching wt in the plaice of glammis 25 October 1626
This inventory marks the completion of the building works of the 1st and 2nd Earls, listing the newly built rooms on the upper floors and at the head of the 'Great Turnpike', and referring to the 'Upmost Galrie'.

The furnishings are rich and colourful: bed hangings of red, green and yellow, of taffeta and velvet, cloth of gold and embroidered panels, worked linen and worsted, curtains of changing or shot taffeta; tapestries both printed and woven; table carpets; bedsteads, feather beds, pillows and bolsters. The usual allowance of bedsteads seems to have been two to a chamber, one low and the other standing, each with one feather bed. In the 'Mid Chamber' there was an exception – some particularly delicate creature needing no less than six feather beds.

The Inventar of sic plenishings as was left behind my lord in glamis at his outgoing in Ja' 1627 and fund in 3 Mai 1627
This follows the pattern of the previous inventory but gives more details of the furniture, including the pair of organs and of virginals in the hall. Why there should be a 'kist full of takkits' in one of the upper chambers is not made clear, nor are we told why 'My lords nyt gown'

remained unnoticed in the 'ceilled Hall' for five months. There seems to have been a measure of confusion: the low round was home to an iron toasting-stick, a black satin gown laid over with silver lace, a little covered pot and a cloak of flowered taffeta.

The 'Mid Chamber' has been reduced to two feather beds, and there is a distinction being made now between English and Scottish blankets, and the quite inferior plaids reserved for the beds of the lower servants.

Inventar of the haill bedding wtin the plaice of glamis 4 Januar. 1630
Again, reference is made to 'English' and, more specifically, 'single Scottish blankets of the English fashion'. Tablecloths (or board cloths) were of Flemish and Scottish damask, or dornick, or of some unspecified material in the servants' hall. Sheets could be of linen, common linen or Holland cloth.

Inventar of the plenishing w'in the hous of Glamis taken up befir Brigtoun and Mr. Silvester Lammie minister 10 december 1639
Frederick Lyon of Brigton was the youngest brother of the 2nd Earl, and Mr Lamie was the minister of Glamis. This inventory was taken a month after the death of Margaret Erskine, first wife of the 2nd Earl, and deals with household linens, bedding and hangings, curtains, carpets and chairs, jewel, silver and clothes, some of Lord Kinghorne's clothes and items belonging to the Earl of Erroll.

The colours are startling: the 'Great Chamber' boasted a purple cloth bed with covering and tablecloth of the same ornamented with yellow lace, which must have contrasted oddly enough with the green hangings in the room. Elsewhere, there were coverings and hangings of scarlet with blue lace, and others of red and green; Joseph might not have felt out of place at Glamis.

The Lady Margaret was well set up in jewellery: bracelets set with diamonds, pearls, sapphires, coral and cornelian; a great coral necklace and a ring set with an ape's head in agate; diamond and ruby rings left to Lady Mar, the Countess Marischal and Lady Rothes; and a 'goldin lyon sett wt diamonds and ane emband in the brest of it', the work of the goldsmith James Arnott.

Here followeth the nett and inventar of ... belonging now to Gilbert Earle of Erroll delyverit out of the hous of Glames ... daitit the xv and xvi dave of febry 1648 yeir
A long preamble shows that this was a list of all the property in the castle at the time of the 2nd Earl's death belonging to his cousin, the Earl of Erroll. It includes furniture, hangings, clothes, silver and jewellery, the earl's parliament robes (red velvet lined with white satin), together with his coronet and its black box, and a number of charter chests. That containing the writs of Esslemont had been broken open, the key having been lost, and Lord Erroll's ownership of it being disputed. The dowager Lady Kinghorne was inclined to question Lord Erroll's right to a number of the items claimed.

Inventarie of the house of Glamis taken upon the ... day of ... fourtie eight years
This inventory, like the previous one, was taken two years after the death of the 2nd Earl, when an attempt was being made to unravel his affairs, and before the castle was spoiled by the Earl of Linlithgow, the step-father of the 3rd Earl.

The furniture remains much the same; there is still a pair of organs in the hall, but instead of virginals, there is now a pair of harpsichords. In the ceiled hall there is a particularly attractive item: 'Ane aiken buird identit wt blak and whyt and the four pillers made in for of beastes'. This may be the 'blak eybain chekke' found in Brigton's chamber in 1627.

[An undated inventory without a title]
Once marked *c* 1700 (crossed out and *c* 1680 substituted), this inventory includes a reference to Lady Helen's room. As she was the daughter of the 4th Earl of Strathmore, it cannot date from before 1695, the date of his accession, nor is it likely to date later than 1712, the year of his death. It is not complete, and has been considerably corrected, but it does include the 'Low' and 'High' summer houses, the former furnished with a marble table. These are probably tea pavilions or banqueting houses within the gardens.

Among the furnishings of the dining-room are a pair of harpsichords, a picture of the 'Royal Oak' (at Boscobel or at sea?) and a Great Bible. The outer room – or stair lobby – was decorated with a pair of 'Dear-horns'. In the withdrawing-room were 'a pair of tables furnished wt twenty three men and two boxes' and a 'large Japan scrine' which may be the one which is still at the castle.

The 'Black Marble Room' – this probably refers to marbled wood – boasts a 'fine of Inlay'd-work' and a bed with purple and yellow silk hangings. The 'Outward Room' has 'a suite of green hangings all sued wt pillars and flowers, covered wt black serge, four pieces of black serge on the sides of the windows'. A similar treatment is repeated in Lady Strathmore's bedchamber, where black hangings cover 'the fine sued silk cloath coloured hangings' and where there are black window curtains and a black-covered armchair. This amplitude of black hangings tends to confirm that the inventory was taken after the 4th Earl's death (ie, 1712 or 1713).

[Inventory of the House of Glammis]
Although this inventory again bears no date, it is usually given to the year 1712. It appears to be earlier than the previous one, and may have been taken following the death of the 3rd Earl in 1695. It notes that in the dining-room is 'The frontispiece of the house and three other little pictures' which may be Slezer's drawing of the castle. A similar picture is found in the closet of Lady Strathmore's bedchamber.

Other curiosities are the 'Tartan Room', complete with a full set of tartan hangings and tablecloths – surely a very early example of interior decoration of this genre – the two fine alabaster statues and portrait of Charles I in the 'Fine Bedchamber', the chapel furnishings and quantities of 'pises of finie Imgerie Arras hangings'.

[Silver at Glamis in porter's lodge]
This brief and not very impressive list (*c* 1695) must be something of an afterthought following the inventories taken after the 3rd Earl's death.

A pair of branched candlesticks holding four candles
Three pair of Square Candlesticks

A pair of large turned Candlesticks wt Sniffers and Standishes
A pair of lesser turned Candlesticks wt Snuffers and Standishes
Two pair of Snuffers
Four Sconces
A perfuming pot wt the pan
Two cups belonging to the chappell
Two hand candlesticks wt snuffers and Standish
A writing box wt two candlesticks and ane extinguisher fixt to it
A bell

1714: Silver in the Butler's Charge at Glamis

This far more impressive list runs to 187 items, mostly marked with a coat of arms or a cipher and crown – more properly a coronet, but the inventory has it as a crown.

The oldest pieces seem to be two cheese plates with the initials 'P E K' for Patrick, Earl of Kinghorne, which date either from 1606–15 or from 1646–7. Another early set may be the 'Basone and Lower' (basin and laver or ewer). The four dozen silver trenchers would be ample for all but the largest parties, as there are only two dozen knives and one dozen spoons to three dozen forks. One large and four lesser rings are probably what are more generally known as potato rings. Unlike the list of *c* 1695, this inventory consists entirely of table silver.

On the reverse is a rather more mundane list:

Also two the butler (Charles Lyndsay)
Thirty two Choppen Bottles full of Aill
Two dozen of Choppen Bottles full of Claret Wine
Nyntion dozen of empty
One dozen of empty mutchin bottles
Twenty wine and aill glasses
Six oil and vinegar cruits
Two glass decanters
A large lym bason for punch
A lym decanter with a powther head
A large earthen jug

Inventory of Pictures within the Castle of Glammis taken 15th April 1751

Of the seventy-three pictures listed, all but two are portraits. Four of the portraits are royal: Charles I, Charles II, James VII and Queen Mary. The identities of most of the other sitters are not given. De Wet's portrait of the 3rd Earl and his three sons hangs, as it always has done, in the great hall, but there is no mention of its companion piece, the portrait of Countess Helen and her daughters. When this picture passed from the family is not known, but it may have been on the death of Countess Helen in 1708; it could then have gone either to her daughter, Grizel, who married the 3rd Earl of Airlie, or Elizabeth, who began a busy married life by taking the 2nd Earl of Aboyne as the first of her three husbands (the third was a commoner).

The two non-portraits hung in the earl's bedchamber: one was an allegory of Matrimony; the other, 'Our Saviour answering the Pharisees and Herodians concerning the Question they ask'd Him, Viz. If it was lawful to give Tribute to Caesar or not', now hangs on the library staircase.

[An inventory of household linen taken in March 1753]

Taken two months after the death of the 8th Earl, this inventory includes fourteen entries for bed linen and blankets, the most recent being 'Six pairs new ditto [servants' sheets] made 1753'. The rest of the list is made up of table linen, most of it of damask, and marked with the initials 'I.S.' for Jean Strathmore (Jean Nicholson of West Rainton). The patterns have in many cases been recorded: Hearts and Diamonds, Lidington Knot, Southern Knot, Satin Knot, Birds Eye, Bear Ear, Square Knot, Wave and Diamond, Lady Blantyre's Knot and Lady Pourie's Knot.

Added to this is a further list of sheets, blankets and table linen, which do not form part of the original inventory since some are dated 1759, 1763 and 1764. The purpose of this inventory is probably to record all the linens at the castle, which were the property of the dowager countess ahead of any future marriage of the 9th Earl.

Inventory of Arms 18 February 1754

Apart from an earlier mention of an ammunition room, located somewhat startlingly on one of the upper floors, the inventory of arms is the first reference to guns at Glamis, which were probably kept in the old gunroom off Duncan's Hall. The list – even if excessive by today's standards – is more in line with the normal contents of a country house gunroom and the needs of a gentleman travelling in his own coach than those of a castle armoury.

11 Gunns with locks (12 gunns more)
1 Blunderbuss (1 blunderbuss more)
3 pair Silver mounted pistols
2 pair Livery pistols

2 pair ruffler pistols
1 side pistol
1 loader bag and belt
5 Broadswords (1 broadsword more)
6 Small swords and six little swords for boy (2 small swords more)
2 Hangers and small sword with handle
2 Fyles and 1 … Nett 1 Rabbit Net (The netts not in the gun room)

Register of Books borrowed from the Library [1740–58]
Although the library at Glamis was not a notable one, it was a respectable working collection of legal, classical, devotional and practical books. As was the case with many great house libraries in eighteenth-century Scotland, the books were available to any respectable person in the parish who wished to borrow them on signature. In practice, this generally meant kinsfolk, factors, lawyers and ministers, but tenants and scholars were not excluded, and many poor students must have benefited from this generosity. Certain books were more popular than others: volumes of Turkish history, *The Rudiments of Honor*, Leslie's *Socinian Controversy*, Clarendon's *History of the Rebellion in England*, Bede's *Ecclesiastical History* and Lord Stair's *Institutions* were in regular demand. In April 1741 William Ker borrowed not a book, but 'a Cremona fiddle in bad repair without a Bow, marked "S" on the back with ye point of a Diamond'.

Taste in reading is difficult to judge. What is to be made of Lady Mary Lyons – a well-established spinster – who on 23 February 1740 took out 'for her own proper use' *The Holy Bible*, *The Military Discipline* of Humphrey Bland, Rabelais' *Works*, *The Rudiments of Honor*, *The Pantheos for the Use of the Dauphine*, *The Institutions* of Antone Perezius and Plutarch's *Lives*?

The last entry in the register is for 16 November 1754, when the 9th Earl – he was seventeen at the time – took out a formidable number of books for his own use:

Historia Gurnadine de Italie
The Art of Preserving Health
Chamber's Dictionary, 2 Volumes
Gregory's Astronomy
Dryden's Juvenal and Perseus
Gordon's Tacitus
Oeuvre de Boileau 2 Tomes
Broyer's Royal French and English Dictionary
Majoris Rerum Scoticorum Historia
Julius Caesar

Cyrus' Travels
Stanley's Lives of the Philosophers
Oeuvres de Vorture [?] 2 Tomes
Pensées de Pascal
Fables par Fontaine
Antoninus' Meditations in English
Jamieson on Virtue
Theocritus
Confucius
Historical Dictionary 2 Volumes
Grammaire Francoise
Gay's Fables 2 Volumes
Telemaque 2 Tomes
Patrick on Grotius
L'Histoire de Charles 12ème Roi de Suede
Sentences Morales
Antoninus' Meditations in Greek
Rennet's Roman Antiquities
Villenis' Paterculus
Persian Tales 2 Volumes
Universal History 2 Volumes
Hill's Arithmetic
Maniere de bien penser sur les ouvrages d'Espri
Horace par Monsieur Dacier in 10 Tomes
David Simple 2 Volumes
Les Revolutions de la Republique Romaine par Monsieur Virtot
Les Revolutions du Portugal par Virtot
Les Revolutions de Suede par Virtot

Whether the earl was a prodigy or was being bludgeoned by his tutors must be a matter for debate. It is difficult to think of a boy of his age tolerating such a reading list today.

Inventory of Household Furniture in Glammis Castle Decr. 1768
This inventory was made nearly two years after the 10th Earl's marriage to Mary Eleanor Bowes, and before he began his alterations and improvements. By far the most complete inventory to date, it seems to have been used as the base inventory until the earl's death.

The first section is devoted to the contents of the rooms, recorded floor by floor. Much of the furniture is that which figures in the earlier inventories, but there are some changes. There is 'A new firr Press for the ?' in Lady Mary's closet, and 'A Harpsichord with it Stand and Stampt Leather Cover' in the drawing-room – not to be confused with the old harpsichord in Lady Ann's room. The Lady Dowager's room includes a particularly delectable item: 'One toilet table. Gause toilett with silk petticoat and hood'. Twenty-four small pictures – twelve of them representing the twelve months, are listed for the drawing-room closet, together with 'A Sett of Musical Glasses'.

The great hall is meanly furnished but contains the 'Three Mettle candle branches' that Billings shows in his engraving, published nearly eighty years later.

The servants' accommodation is given in some detail but with curious omissions. While the housekeeper and 'My Lady's woman' both rate a room and a closet, the butler and coachman only a room, there is no mention of either 'My Lord's man' or the cook. There are two beds in the 'Woman's House' – which may take two persons each – and eight beds for footmen. If at the same level of use as for the women, there must have been a platoon of footmen at Glamis.

For the first time the contents of the kitchen and closets – other than furniture – are listed separately. Kitchen utensils are given under copper, ironwork, pewter, tin and wood, and the dairy figures in its own right.

In the china closet there is china with the family crest – almost certainly Lyon, as the Bowes china would have remained at Streatlam and Gibside – Staffordshire ware, 'Blew and White China', 'Dragon China', 'Tea China' some 'Blew and White', some 'Blew and Guilt', which includes coffee cups as well as '15 Gentlemen's Cups'. The silver for tea and coffee is entered under 'Tea China'.

Silver plate, which includes 'Old Plate', shows, among other items, 'Ane Epirne', 'A Silver Cross for the Middle of the Table', 'My Ladies Ink Standish', 'Two Gold Cups', 'Two Chalices' and 'Two Wine Strainers witt Stands', to which is added the note 'One of which was taken to Gibside by Mr. Marriotte 20th Dec. 1770'.

The list of linen is a running one, starting with the small amount of table and bed linen in the castle and adding to it as fresh was made. This was woven locally and then made up, a considerable amount being sent to Gibside. Some old linen is listed but excluded from the inventory if it is worn, as is the case with one 'Hagabag' tablecloth, burnt with a warming-pan, or, as with one top sheet, when used for 'burying the Fisherman'. Some was taken down for use for 'Rags for the Poor'.

In 1773 some 1,200 yards of linen of various qualities was made at Glamis to supply the castle, Gibside, the dowager countess and Lady Mary, who was in need of three pairs of sheets.

The roups that followed the death of the 9th Earl left the castle stripped of most of its contents, and it was not until after the rebuilding of the west wing at the end of the eighteenth century that there was any move forwards refurnishing it.

Inventory and Valuation of the Furniture, Wines and Other Effects in Glamis Castle and belonging to the late Earl of Strathmore Sept. 25th 1820
Judging by this inventory, the refurnishing had been of an economical nature. The total valuation is £935 10s 10d, of which £190 8s 4d is the value of the cellar, and £70 is for a 'Lott of old books'. The remainder of the plenishings are valued at £675 2s 6d – an inconsiderable sum for a house of this size. In only eight rooms are the contents worth more than £30 – those in the housekeeper's room being set at £61 1s 6d and those in Lord Strathmore's at £30 5s.

Apart from the port, claret, sherry and books, the most valuable items are the four-poster bedsteads in five of the principal bedchambers. These, together with their feather beds, bedding and curtains are set at £20 each. The least valuable item is a set of 'Tind Spoons' from the housekeeper's room at 2s.

There is nothing in this inventory to suggest that Glamis was ever the principal domicile of a wealthy man.

Inventory of Glamiss Castle 23 Novr. 1844
By the time this inventory was taken the castle was already well set up in comforts. It makes no mention of furniture, dealing only with linen, bedding, china, glass, silver and clothes. The 11th Earl lived for only two more years, and by the terms of his brother's settlement was debarred from any effective enjoyment of the estate, so the inventory may mark the end of a period of refurbishment of the castle being carried out by the Trustees. It specifically notes items bought in 1836, 1837 and 1840, but it also lists china – family, which is to say armorial, and blue – which figured in the inventory of 1768.

In a later hand it is noted that five 'coarsen' bolster slips have been made into 'pillow slips for servants'; that of sixteen damask tablecloths, 'several cut down (old) for pastry napkins'; and that of nine old breakfast tablecloths, four have been torn down for glass cloths. Of three mangling sheets, two are almost worn out, as are all the roller towels.

One of the linen presses, which cannot have been looked in for years, produced 'A Gentleman's Coat and

Vest – black', '5 pieces of Sewed work on linen very old', '2 Tartan Curtains', '4 Pairs of Gentleman's Slippers and 1 Clothes Brush' and '5 Pieces of old Tapestry'. From an old chest in the family bedroom came:

2 Black silk Coats – Breeches	Jester's Coat and
1 Tartan Coat and Breeches	Breeches
5 Coloured Silk Coats	2 Caps
7 Pairs of Coloured Silk Breeches	3 Pairs of Shoes
1 Cloth Coat	1 Pair of Clogs
1 ditto and Vest	1 Gold headed Cane
5 Summer Vests	3–4 Sewed Belts
4 Silk Vests/2 very fine	Sewed Satin Band
	and Gauze Curtain
	1 pr. Black Gauntlet
	Gloves

All the bedsteads, except for 'My Lord's', which had a 'Down Bed', are provided with feather beds, two or three mattresses, blankets, binders, bolsters and pillows. The servants also have feather beds, but their mattresses are of straw. Generally, the principal beds have white cotton counterpanes, except for 'Prince Charles's' and one of 'King Malcolm's', which are described as 'Twilted'. There are fourteen beds in thirteen bedchambers, with an additional thirteen beds for the servants.

In the inventory of 1820 the bedchambers were numbered, but by 1844 most had been given names: 'Lady Mary's Room', 'King Malcolm's Room' (with two beds), '1st and 2nd Tartan Rooms', 'Patrick and Helen's Room', and, inevitably, 'Prince Charles's Room'. Glamis was evidently succumbing to what has been described as 'Over-the-water-to-Charlie gentility nonsense'.

Inventory of Linens and Furniture in Glamis Castle 18 February 1861
This inventory was probably taken when the financial difficulties of the 12th Earl were becoming apparent, and the Trustees needed to know just what furniture, linen and other furnishings were in the castle.

Tartan is even more in evidence than before: it is used as hangings for the mahogany four-posters in the 'Green Tartan Room' and 'King Malcolm's Room', for the three window curtains in 'Miss Brown's Room', for the curtains to the two tent bedsteads in the 'Lady's Maid's Room' and for a bedstead in one of the attics. In

addition, there are three long curtains of Stewart tartan in one of the presses.

Lady Mary Lyon's chest is still used for storing linen, and the chest from the 'Family Bedroom', holding the jester's suit and the silk coats, breeches and vest, and described as an 'Old Japanned Chest', has been moved to 'Prince Charles's Room'.

The linen is what would be found in any large country house, some of it marked with the year in which it was made up; none seems to have been bought or added since the death of Countess Charlotte Maria in 1854. The patterns Shell, Flower, Diamond and Snowdrop are recorded. 'Twelve Gentlemen's Night Caps' – the same number as in 1844 – must have been held in reserve for casual overnight guests, and there is a separate entry for '2 sheets used by William Lady Glamis's Butler'.

Much of the furniture is new: marble and mahogany and birch, and, together with the new Brussels carpets and the small patterned black-and-white carpet for the bedrooms, may have arrived in the great vans from Maples of London, as described by Lady Airlie.

Lord Strathmore's room is furnished with a mixture of oak, walnut and birchwood, and the result cannot have been an altogether happy one: the half-tester bed is hung with muslin curtains; the chintz window curtains match the chintz-covered sofa; and there are both a bust and portrait of his dead wife. The bedroom china in both his and Lady Strathmore's dressing-rooms is pink and white with a gilt border. Her dressing-room seems to have been left much as it must have been in her lifetime, even to her silver- and gold-mounted whips – the latter incorporating a parasol. In spite of Lord Strathmore's having installed four bathrooms, most bedrooms – and his dressing-room – are provided with tin baths and water cans.

Later inventories are much more prosaic, throwing little light on life at the castle or the lives of its inhabitants. It is to bills and diaries that one must go to learn what was supplied for the chapel, or that the 13th Earl bought two grand pianofortes from Erard – one for the drawing-room, one for the schoolroom. It is doubtful if any inventory would now record that a top sheet had been used for 'Burying the Fisherman' – but then it is extremely unlikely that today a top sheet would be used for anything of the sort.

CHAPTER 13
THE POLICIES AND GARDENS

The policies at Glamis are among the most extensive in Scotland, enclosing some 1,080 acres (437 hectares) within today's boundaries. In the late seventeenth and early eighteenth centuries these boundaries extended much further, the surrounding hills planted with wooded enclosures, pierced with rides and walks, and dominated by the great avenue stretching from the castle to Hunter's Hill on the southern horizon. At their greatest extent, in the time of the 3rd Earl, the policies and parks spread over nearly 3,000 acres (1,214 hectares). Within these would be the formal, pleasure and kitchen gardens, their form and nature changing as fashion changed. Almost every time the castle was remodelled, the gardens followed suit.

The earliest mention of gardens, or at least of gardeners, at Glamis is found in the *Exchequer Rolls* of 1537–42, when the castle was a royal palace and the court was regularly in residence there. Unfortunately, the references are more to do with the fees paid – usually in oatmeal – to the gardeners and always with retention monies, which were released only on completion of the work, than to the work actually executed. This may be because such jobs as repairing the banks and ditches in the gardens and around the ponds were beyond their normal duties. This must certainly have been true when they were called upon to feed the swans on the Lake of Bakey, or when the fisherman (*piscator*) was paid for stocking the pools around the Place of Glamis with pike. These pools were the ones that the gardeners had just repaired.

These payments suggest that there were already gardens in existence before James V seized the castle. Their extent is not certain but they seem to have lain largely in the land between the inner and outer ditches, outside the main enclosure of the castle, and to the south. By the time Earl Patrick came into his inheritance they were wasted and decayed. His own brief description from the *Book of Record* gives a fair idea of what he found:

> The old chattered and decayed trees which surrounded the house, yet there were not many, and the most of these that were, were to the southward, a common mistake of our ancestors whereas reasonably any thickets or planting that are set about any man's house ought rather to be upon the north, northeast and northwest, neither was the planting which was here of any bounds. The whole planted ground not exceeding four aikers att most verie disproportionable to the greatness of the place with a verie low wall of dry stone scarce sufficient to hold out any beast.

One can only assume that the garden at Glamis was not the prime source of produce for the castle, nor of pleasure for its inmates. In any case, after the works carried out in the early seventeenth century they could take the prospect and the air from the leads.

When Patrick, 3rd Earl, arrived at Glamis and began setting the castle and its surroundings in order, his first task was to overcome the water-logged condition of the site which had been brought about by years of neglect, exacerbating an already unfavourable set of physical conditions:

> without the great ditch ... there were two other great ditches on without another, without any direct

conveyance there to the river – which stankt up the water so as that the place by reasons of these ditches appeared most exceedingly marish and weat and was generally condemned for it is supposed to be an unwholesome seat for a house. These ditches were the cause off and necessitate me when I built the walls of the garden bouling green kitchen gardens and back Court to put over rough pends where the ditches runn and these pends are visible to this day and I hope though the house stands low, for it stands on a plain inviround on all syds save to the south with runing water which in my apprehensions is very delightfull yet no considering man will now censure it as a marshy place or unwholesome for that cause.

With the drainage settled and the remodelling of the house well in hand, Earl Patrick was able to turn his attention to the design and layout of the policies and gardens which were to be its setting. Here, as with the castle, the work of his forebears defeated him in his search for perfect symmetry:

form'd my entry which I behooved to draw a little about from the wast else it had run directly thorrow the great victual house att the barns which my father built and I was verie loath to destroy it: very few will discover the throw in my entrie which I made as unsensible and possiblie I could. Othrs more observing have challenged me for it but were satisfied when I told them the cause, others perhaps more reserved take notice of it and doe not tell me and conclude it to be an error of ignorance but they are mistaken.

What Earl Patrick achieved and what he intended is best seen in the background of De Wet's great portrait of the earl and his three sons, and in Thomas Winter's survey of the Mains of Glamis, carried out in 1746. For an account of the achievements, it is best to return to his *Book of Record*:

There be now an entrie from the four severall airths and my house invyraned with a regular planting, the ground on both syds being of a like bigness and the fig-ure the same with a way upon either syd of the utter court to the back court where the offices are att the north gate the gardners house is apon the on syde and the washing and bleatching house on the other with a fair green lying thereto to bleach upon and a walk there is planted which goes round the whole intake

wherein when you are walking you'l behold the water runing on both syds of the planting. And upon the west side where the river is to make the way accessible from the west I have built a bridge and have cutt downe a little hill of sand which I caused carrie to such places as were weat and marish. The utter Court is a spacious green and forenent the midle thereof is the principal entrie to the south with a gate and gatehouse besyde two rounds upon each corner, the on is appointed for a Dayrie house and the other for a Still house, and the gate house consists of on roume to the gardine and another to the bowling green, the walls are lined, the roof plaistered, the floor lay'd with black and whyt stone and are verie convenient and refreshful roumes to goe in to from the gardine and Bouling green. There is in the gardin a fine dyal erected and how soon the walk and green plots are layed there will be statu's put into it, and there is a designe for a foun-tain in the Bouling green and on the great gate from the gardine and another from the bouling green to the utter court at the south end of which directly forenent the gate of the inner court, there is another great gate adorned with two gladiators, from which the avenue goes with an enclosure on each syd holdne with a plan-tation of fir trees which is ane entrie of a considerable bread and lenth leading straight up to the barns and offices there, which offices stand yet unreformed as they were, but if it pleas God that I live I intend to make them better. There are two stak yards there, the on opposite to the other, betwixt which there is a wall across to the avenue and a great gate placed therein verie pleasant to behold, what I have of further designe not yet done, time will produce the knowledge of, only upon the west syd there is a park but a great part of the wall therof is ruinous tho. latlie but done, by reason of the bosness of the stone which mulders into sand and dust and was gott upon the river syd a litle below the stone bridge, they were sought there because of the great convenience and nearness of them but all that's done is lost labour. And paralel to this another park is designed upon the east syd of the principal entrie and so be time other two parks which should invyron the whole house and would be a circumference betwixt three and four miles about, and planting secured by an inner wall, for it's better being hem'd after the manner that is don betwixt the girnal house and the warens. This if it were done, and the planting any thing growne to a hight was'd make the seat of the house verie glori-ous as invironed with a wood of no less bounds, but it

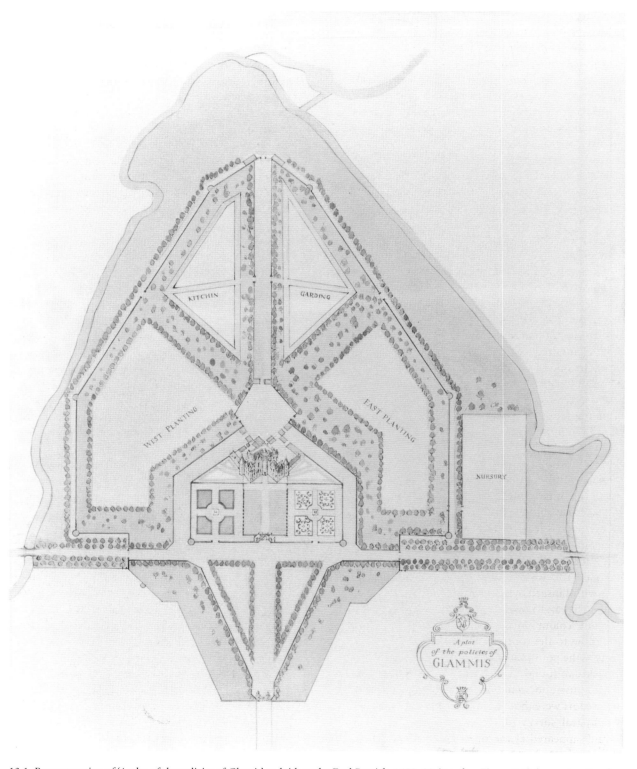

KITCHIN

GARDING

WEST PLANTING

EAST PLANTING

NURSURY

A plot
of the policies of
GLAMMIS

13.1 Reconstruction of 'A plot of the policies of Glamis' as laid out by Earl Patrick, 1670–90 (see also Figure 5.6) (reconstruction by author; realization by Terry Ball FSA; © Terry Ball and Strathmore Estates) is a work of great time and what I shall not be able to accomplish I hope may be done in the succeeding age, and this park might have four gates, on answering to each of the four severall entries to the house.

I purpose lykeways to lenthen the avenue with a double row of trees on each syd from the uttmost gate att the barns thorow the land betwixt the barns and the toune straight to the open att West hill and perhaps further.

Whether by Earl Patrick or during the succeeding age, this magnificent layout was accomplished, becoming perhaps the finest baroque garden and landscape in Scotland. By the 1760s, when it was swept away, it is said that the firs had reached a height of 100 ft (30.48m).

It is fascinating how the design encompassed and incorporated both the ornamental and useful elements in its layout. The dairy and the stillhouse were features of the outer court; the kitchen garden and bleaching green were not banished from sight, as they would have been a hundred years later, and the stackyards were linked by one of the great gates across the avenue. The 'refreshful' rooms in the gatehouse probably would have served as tea-rooms or banqueting house, and may have been the 'supper room' and 'summer dining room' referred to in the inventories.

Little of this grand design has survived: the gateways, more or less intact, have been moved and stand at the principal entrance to the park; two of the four lead statues of the Stuart kings escaped the instruction given in 1789 (recorded in the *Book of Sederunt*) that they should be sold as old lead to the best advantage. When originally put up, they were painted, as were the statues in the gardens at Castle Lyon, where, in 1718, Thomas Murray was paid £38 16s for 'Colouring and painting ... tuise over with Linseed oyle and whyt lead' the eleven statues in the Dial and Lower Gardens. This painting however was not 'colour' in the usual sense of the word, but, according to the contract of 1685, 'after the manner of brass' – the poor man's 'bronze'.

The two rounds, which Earl Patrick built for use as a dairy house and stillhouse, and the two corners of the outer court were thought to have survived. However, the geophysical survey of 1983–4 showed that they must have disappeared at the time of the alteration of 1770 and that the present rounds set on the lawns are modern – that is, probably of a period after 1800. Their original purpose is uncertain and what appears to be the re-use

of older fragments and the blocking of openings may be a deliberate archaeological joke.

The sundial, one of the largest and most elaborate in Scotland, may be Earl Patrick's work. He says 'Ther is in the garden a fine dyal erected', but this could mean that it had been erected before his time, and it may have been reset. Against this view is the fact that from the geophysical survey it appears to stand correctly at the junction of the walks in the eastern parterre. According to S R Higgs, the base and plinth are correctly orientated, and the whole was designed for the Glamis latitude of 56½°, although the lions and pineapple, supporting the dials, have been turned slightly from their original positions

13.2 The sundial at Glamis Castle, probably erected before 1660 (© Crown Copyright/RCAHMS)

which means that there were errors in the dial readings which now need to be corrected.[1] These movements can probably be traced to repairs rather than to a resetting of the whole dial in a different location. If the dial is in its original position it is certainly the work of Earl Patrick, but if it has been moved from elsewhere, then it must be the work of his father or grandfather, and date from the first half of the seventeenth century.

Of Earl John's great avenue, the spine of the whole magnificent design, nothing except the idea remains. It fell to the forces of nature in the hurricane of 1772 before man could lay it low; but its ghost remains, for it was replanted in the nineteenth century.

The grandeur and architectural splendour of the gardens at Glamis should not be allowed to disguise the fact that there was a severely practical side to them as well. Not only were the gardens meant to provide a suitable setting for the pretensions of the owner, but they were also intended to provide fruit, flowers and vegetables for the great house and for those to whom the laird might choose to give produce and garden stuffs. Any surplus would then be sold, the revenue earned going towards meeting the considerable running costs. In the second half of the eighteenth century this was being done at Drum, where the produce sold was equal to half the value of that being sent to the house. At Glamis this practice started even earlier; trees were being sold from the nurseries by 1716 when it was noted that 1,343 had been sold since Lammas and that a further sixty-three limes [lymes] were being raised.

The nature of the planting in the gardens can be gathered from the accounts for seeds. In 1711 the cost for Glamis was £57 4s, and the seeds bought in March were:

Onions, leeks, carrots, parsnips, turnips,
radish, lettuce, beetrave, cresses,
purslane, coliflower, spinnage,
cucumber, cabage, asparagus,
marjoram, turkey beans,
double clove gilly flowers,
french and african marigolds,
hotspur pease,
Kasten pease.

A second parcel of seeds contained:

Indian cresses,
Cardums benedictus,
round spinnage,

indian cresses [a second listing],
silesia lettuce,
french leek,
red Spanish onion,
white beet,
garden cresses.

An even more extensive order was placed in 1712:

Strasburg Onion	
London Leek	
Orange Carrot	Smooth Spinach
?swelling parsnips	
White turnips	
Yellow turnips	
London radishes	
Cabbage lettuce	
English Cabbage	
beetrave	
Italian cellary	
golden purslane	
green purslane	
Italian coliflower	
Sweet thyme	
Winter Savory	
Cucumber	long cucumber
Dutch Asparagus	short cucumber
Sweet Marjoram	
African Marigold	French Marigold
Double clove gilly flower	
Hotspur pease	long hotspur pease
large white rouncival pease	
Turkey beans	Kydney beans
Onions (more)	4 garden spades at £2 18s each
£34 6s	£34 14s
	£69

The seeds were obtained from Daniel Crocket, Merchant in Dundee.

Nearly a hundred years later, Strasbourg onions, orange carrots, Italian cauliflowers, London radishes, and Silesian lettuce were still in demand and being ordered for the gardens at Arbuthnott House.

The planting of trees continued. In 1720 this included 'birks' (birch), firs (9,500), alders, planes, 'giens', elms and forty-seven fruit trees, among them cherries, apples and pears in the gardens.

By the 1740s Earl Patrick's gardens no longer conformed to the accepted canons of taste, and in his survey of 1746 Thomas Winter suggested improvements in the layout of the policies. These stopped short at destroying Earl Patrick's formal parterres, but envisaged the destruction of much of the avenue. In Winter's words it was:

> A design for altering and making that part of the *Avenue* betwixt the House and the Barns for altho' at present it is very Great Being above an hundred feet Wide and a Strip of Planting of the Same Breadth on Each Side YET in my opinion it is not by far Answerable to the House But on the Contrary Eclipses It Much and were itt made by this Design Im still Desiderent that It would be near Equal to the Auspicious Front of this *Magnificent Pile*. The Water can be got in Plenty to accomplish the *Bason*, *Cascades* etc having the Command of the Burn of Glammis, And I believe that this Design would be Easy made hear having all necessary materials near at hand.

The survey contains other elements of proposed work, some of which was done, notably the planting at Crams Hill and the Hunter's Hill with their circular rides and radiating vistas, and in the serpentine walks in James Park. It is always a difficulty, when faced with surveys of this period of early improvement, to decide how much is an actual record and how much merely suggested improvement. In the case of the Winter survey of Glamis it must be accepted that it contains a large element of the latter.

Winter was the son of Thomas Winter, an English surveyor, who had arrived in Scotland in 1726 to survey the Monymusk estates for Sir Archibald Grant. The son had worked at Monymusk, where he made his first survey in 1736, and for the Duke of Gordon in 1738, but Glamis is his first known large commission. Sadly, his proposals came to nothing, apparently because there were no means of carrying them out, the 8th Earl being chronically short of money. It was at this period that honey was being sold from the gardens in considerable quantities.

A good idea of the condition of the gardens is given in a letter from James Baillie to the 8th Earl, who was then at his wife's home at Rainton (Baillie writes it Bainton) in Co. Durham. The letter is dated on the cover:

J.B. Sept ye 8th 1747
M lord
This is to aquaint your Lordship of the produce of the Gardens this Season, the Cherries on the Standards ripn'd very well and the Apricots what Apricots was one of the youn trees in the Fountain Court was good and ripn'd Earlie, and Some Very good Bonoumemagnum plums on the Same wall one of the same kind of three years since Grafted had a Very Large fruit on it all the plums of that kind is bearing very well this Season, the Oflino(?) Applies Against the walls they had a very good quantity on them and particularly in the East Angle the Largest and fair'st of that kind. If ever seen, the other kinds of Apples Against the Walls hav a Moderate quantity on them, Very few pears this Season some very Large Fargonells and Queen pippins the Espeliar of Mother Apples is bearing very well in the East Angle and the Leadentons these, the other kinds there has but few on them. The Standard Apples in the Kitchen Ground is bearing very well and the Little Orchard in the East planting a great many of the Apple trees in it is bearing Extremely well both large and well favor'd fruit, but the pears planted in the Same place is not bearing they are too much Crouded which Intercepts both Sun and Air from exhaling hurtful vapours from the trees. Your Lordship was designed when last here to Cause Remove the Lime trees that is planted on the bordure Where the Apple trees stands they have destroy'd Severall Apple trees having such quantities of Branches overdrops both trees and hedges to the great prejudice of both. The Utmost bordure in the west planting is planted latter with apple trees and the Limes on the same bordure is more Numeros than in the other Garden and the Apple trees is so overdrop by the Limes that their branches is tending so much Downwards that stops the Passage betwixt the Hedges if your Lordship were pleas'd to given orders to remove these Limes it would make room for thining the Orchard, one of the great advantage to the Gardens. The two vistas in Hunter hill is not quite open'd to the extreme ends yet there has been little Sale for timber Since harvest began, which has been very favorable Since it began, Most part of the harvest is cut down already and a great deall of the Corns Carried into the barnyards. Severals are of opinion the Corns is but small and particularly the Oats but all is very well ripn'd this year I am My Lord your most humble and Obedient Servt.
Ja: Baillie

The 9th Earl regarded the remodelling of the policies as being as important as that of the castle, and attempts to discover the authors of the designs for both are equally

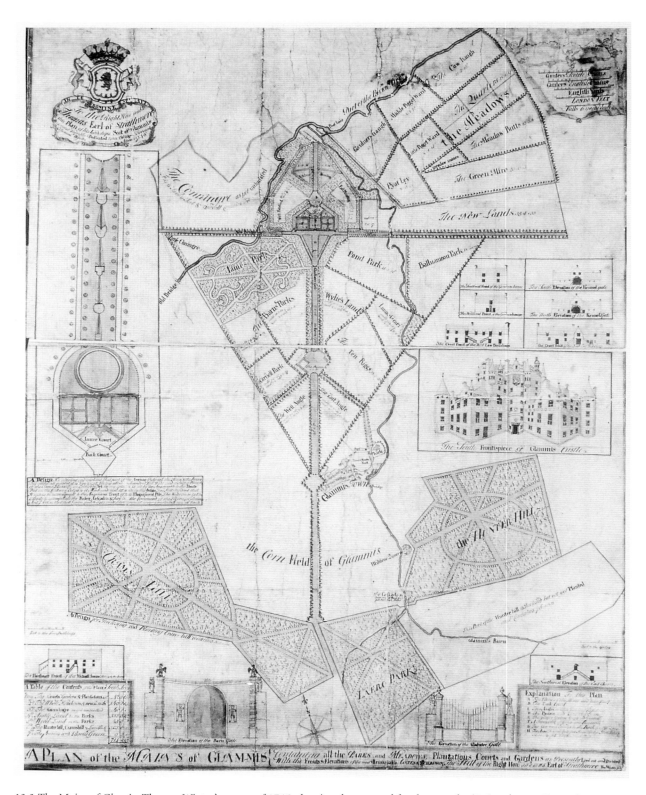

13.3 The Mains of Glamis: Thomas Winter's survey of 1746, showing the proposal for the cascades (© Strathmore Estates)

difficult. This difficulty arises from the family trait of not settling on one person but invoking two or even three practitioners at the same time.

Three plans were produced for the remodelling of the policies, and three – or perhaps four – names of eminent surveyors can be found at Glamis; but with whom the ultimate responsibility for the accepted scheme lay is not certain. The names that occur in the ledgers and account books are those of Robert Robinson, Thomas Whyte and James Abercrombie junior. A Mr Robertson also appears; he may be Mr Robinson, transformed by a slip of the pen, or he may be James Robertson. There are, in addition to the entries in the accounts, three large surveys showing proposals for replanting and remodelling the policies, two undated and unsigned and one signed by James Abercrombie and dated 1768. One of the unsigned ones also appears to be his work.

The authorship of the survey that is clearly not by Abercrombie is attributed by Alan Tait to Robert Robinson.[2] Robinson, an English disciple of Lancelot

'Capability' Brown, had been at Glamis between 9 and 13 April 1764, when there was an entry in Patrick Proctor's ledger for 'Mr. Robinson's Bill of Entertainment for taking the level and survey of the Loch of Forfar'. There was a further payment in July of the same year 'to account for work done to the Earl of Strathmore', which might have been to Robinson (as Tait suggests), but which might equally well have been to James Robertson.

Miss Deborah Turnbull suggests[3] that the unsigned survey is in the style of Thomas Whyte senior. Whyte, another Englishman and disciple of Capability Brown, was at Glamis in 1771–2 when there were two payments, £42 5s in January and £42 in October to 'WHYTE, Mr. Thos.'. These are explained in the Crop Account Book of 1774 as: 'Mr. Thos. WHYTE at two different times for coming to Gls. to give his advice about thinning the trees in the lawn and bounding the several plantings to be made'.

The payment of 1764 was not the only one made in connection with Robinson: for some reason William Lyon, the factor to Archibald Douglas at Castle Douglas

13.4 The 8th Earl's proposals for the cascades and service courts, c 1746 (reconstruction by author; realization by Terry Ball FSA; © Terry Ball and Strathmore Estates)

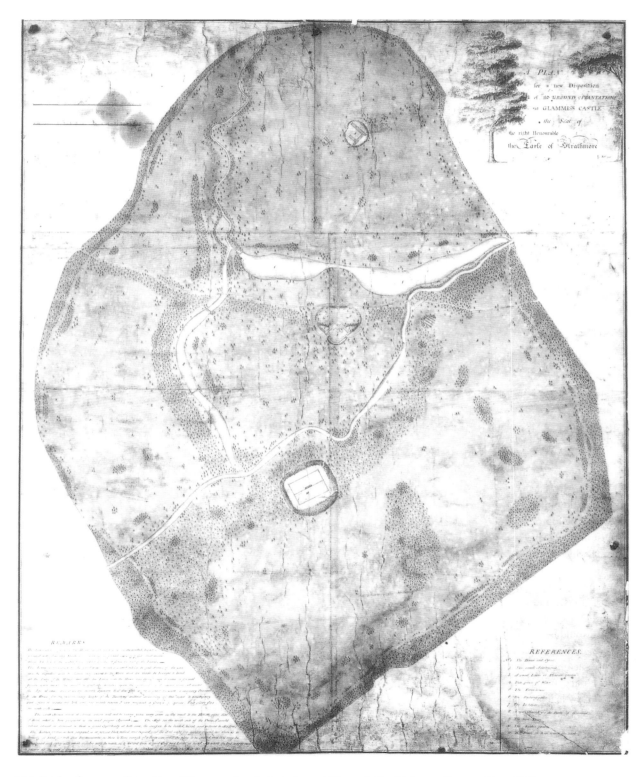

13.5 'A plan for a new disposition of the ground and plantations at Glammis Castle', James Abercrombie, c 1760
  (© Strathmore Estates)

– where Whyte was working in 1770 – was repaid £42 for a sum, or sums, of that value which he had paid to Whyte. There is no indication of what this might be for, unless it was an advance on the expenses of travelling between the two places.

What is clear is that none of these drawings is a survey of what was actually existing. Survey in eighteenth-century terms could be either a record of the site as it actually was, or a set of proposals for what it might become, and the drawings need to be read with that in mind.

At the time that Robinson had visited Glamis in 1764 Lord Strathmore had not started on his rebuilding of the castle, although he had consulted both Bell and Carr the previous year and both architects had prepared schemes for a major remodelling. It is almost certain that had these been likely to come to fruition, they would have appeared in some form on Robinson's proposals. He may well have prepared a scheme, but if so it has not been found.

James Abercrombie was conservative in his approach. Although he wished to make as much use of the water of the burns as he could, he wished to preserve the gatehouse or part of it, and he was reluctant to lose all the avenue. In fact, his design of 1768 retains the line of it, from the bridge over the water to the castle itself. His own remarks on the 1768 survey are the best guide to his thinking:

> The Lawn No. 3 in front of the House is proposed to be neatly levelled turfed and planted with flowering shrubs accompanying a gravel walk of 7 ft. that winds along the top of a sunk fence that divides it from the rest of the lawn. This lawn is occaisioned by the great gate which I cannot advise to pull down; if the Gate can be dispensed with the Lawn may extend to the Water and the roads be brought to land at Entry of the House; and although the Lawn with the House and Offices seem to make a formal figure upon paper, this would be effactually advoided upon the ground as it cannot all come under the eye at once, and it is my humble opinion that this Gate is in a great measure a necessary ornament to the House for the extraordinary height of the Building without something of this kind to accompany and soften it would not look well, for which reason I have prepared a Groupe of Spruce and Silver firs on each side.

> The south Avenue while it stands which will not be many years, may serve as the road to the House, after

that I think what is here proposed is the most proper Approach – The Moss on the north side of the Dean I would advise should be drained as there is Great Opportunity at both ends, the surface to be levelled, burnt and reduced to Meadow. The Kitchen garden as here proposed, is at present bleak, naked and exposed, and the soil unfit for garden ground, but there is a remedy at hand for both these Inconveniences, as there is Trees enough of a large size about the place to be spared and that may be transplanted with safety, with which a shelter may be made, as to the soil there is good Clay and Loam at hand with which the soil may be made to answer all the ends of Garden ground, and for several reasons I think the situation the most eligible that the place affords.

Abercrombie's plan was prepared before any major works had been started at the castle, which is shown in the form that it had been given by the 3rd Earl, hence his reference to the buildings seeming to make a formal figure upon paper. Although the design is entitled 'A PLAN for a new Disposition of the GROUND and PLANTATIONS at GLAMMISS CASTLE', much of what is shown probably represents what had already been started, some of which survives today.

Abercrombie had started work at Glamis in 1765–6 but his relationship with Peter Proctor was never an easy one. Proctor viewed all Abercrombie's accounts as impositions, if not downright robbery, and Abercrombie complained that the factor wanted twenty-five guineas' worth of work for every guinea expended, that he was noted for clipping the workmen's account and was known to refuse payment unless the bill was abated. Another complaint against Abercrombie was that he had claimed £39 for surveying the farms, when the work had been done in fact by his son, Charles. It is surprising that Abercrombie lasted as long as he did.

His two designs allow for a great shelter belt around the park, an uninspired stretch of water, narrowed to a tiny waist where crossed by a bridge, a large walled garden well north of the castle and the 3rd Earl's gatehouse floating in curious isolation on the lawn before the castle. Isolated from its contact with the baroque garden, the gatehouse would have presented a curious sight and his plea for its retention as a single feature throws some doubt on Abercrombie's taste. His work was largely associated with preparing the framework for the future improvements; he seems to have been responsible for planting the shelter belts, for the canal and ice-house in 1766, digging clay for making bricks, drainage, and work on the grounds for the nurseries. He seems not to have been employed after 1771–2, and this may have been brought about by the dispute over the employment of his son. For surveying and planning sundry parts of the estate he was paid £119 0s 8d.

The work being done increased during the years 1772–6. The undated and unsigned survey must date from not earlier than 1773–4 and may be as late as 1775–6. The evidence for this is the form in which the castle is shown. Gone is Earl Patrick's symmetrical plan with its spreading office wings – the 'formal figure upon paper'. In its place is the new layout with the large lateral service court of which Robinson could have known nothing in 1764, but of which Whyte must have been aware after 1773, since by then the plan had been prepared and the founds were being dug.

Whyte's proposals were more imaginative than Abercrombie's in his treatment of the water – it was less *arrangé* and more naturalistic in its meanderings – but it was hardly an improvement on the earlier design. The woodland ride that encircled the park in Abercrombie's plan disappears almost completely south of the castle, the enclosed garden is moved to the east of the castle, which fronts on to an open lawn with a great circular carriage sweep, and all traces of the avenue have been swept away. It is doubtful if any of Whyte's proposals were carried out; once again, the Strathmore tendency to know better than the professional seems to have asserted itself, and the earl went his own way.

Matters were speeded up or at least helped on their way in 1772, when the avenue was laid low by what was generally described as a great storm or hurricane – one of those 'Big Blows' to which north-eastern Scotland is prone – of which James Menzies wrote to Lord Strathmore briefly in February 1773.[4] The payments made in 1773 and 1779 for 'cutting and breaking the tops of the fir trees in the Avenue above the Castle' and for grubbing up their roots must refer to clearing the storm damage from the avenue, rather than to its felling, although any trees which had been left standing would then have been felled.

Work continued apace throughout the following years, and at the end of 1775 Mr Menzies was able to tell Lord Strathmore that much of the ground before the castle had been levelled, and that what remained of the old garden walls had been demolished; the walls already taken down had been re-used, the coping stones as covers for the drains and sewers, the rubble incorpo-rated into the new building and as founds for the west wing. At the same time the gateways had been taken down and rebuilt: the Satyr Gate – or Barn Gate – at the head of the main approach just to the west of Glamis village; the Gladiator Gate on the approach from the Kirriemuir road; and an old gate near the kirk. In the process, two of the gates were to have lodges added to them; there seems to have been some rearrangement of the stonework, and finials have replaced the eagles on the Barn Gate.

Two other land surveyors are recorded as working at Glamis in the 1770s – one of whom was a Robert Ainslie – but they seem mostly to have been employed in valuing and dividing parts of the estate into farms.

With the 9th Earl's death in 1776 everything was thrown into confusion and all but essential work came to an end. The cashier's accounts showed that £2,077 12s 0¼d had been spent on the policies. No further work was undertaken for fourteen years; drawings of the castle during that period show it set in a waste, almost the blasted heath of Shakespeare's creation, and in 1783 it was noted that the roof of the west round in the garden was collapsing. The great dial and two of the lead statues survived, but only just, for in 1789 the 10th earl instructed that they should be sold as old lead. It is likely that the framework of the present layout was in place with the wooded ride around the park already planted and the old gates repositioned marking the three principal entrances. The avenue was gone; it is not shown in John Ainslie's map of the Shire of Angus (surveyed in 1794), although its line on the ground must still have been visible.

In June 1802 Sir William Forbes visited the castle and sent his son an account of what he saw:

I made William drive down to the castle that [I] might see the Park. ... On the Outside the fine timber in the Park remains untouched, and the noble Old Dial is also left entire, as well as the metal Statues still keep possession of their pedestals although they are of little intrinsick merit, they give an air of antient magnifi-cence to the whole. But I perceived a piece of made water, which I do not recollect formerly, at no great distance from the Castle, of which I am at a loss to dis-cover the meaning – It is of the following fashion. [Here follows a rough sketch of a rectangle with three equally spaced circles in it. On one circle is a black dot, and the whole rectangle is contained within a further rectangle, the outline of which is broken.] The Three small round spots are 3 Islands, perfectly Circular, of a very nice Shaven Green turf, and the dot on the middle of one of them is a solitary tree, such I suppose, as had been on each of the others. The Banks are somewhat raised above the ground which surrounds it, and the whole is inclosed with a paling. I could get nobody to instruct me in the use of it, as a little Country Girl showed us thro' the Castle. It has since occurred to me that it may perhaps be a Fish Pond in which case it may desire some merit from its utility, tho' none from its beauty. For if it be meant as a piece of water merely, I never saw anything more tasteless or absurd.[5]

On the evidence it is hard to fault Sir William's judgement, for a more absurd object is hard to conceive. It is a pity that Sir William gives no indication of its size or when he was formerly at Glamis. It is certainly post-1776; it is shown to the east of the house on the survey of 1810, and appears faintly on the geophysical survey of 1983–4.

The survey of 1810 – a very utilitarian effort compared with the great eighteenth-century drawings – was made by John Blackadder and his son. It shows the great dial and the two rounds on the lawn before the castle, but no avenue or central drive; otherwise, the planting is much as it is now. Neither Abercrombie's nor Robinson's walled gardens had been built. Writing in 1835 for the *New Statistical Account* – which was not published until 1845 – the Revd James Lyon, who was 'assisted by Mr. Blackadder, civil engineer' – speaks of the principal avenue having been 'almost entirely destroyed in the course of a few hours by a hurricane in 1772' and there is nothing to suggest that the avenue had been replanted at that date. However, there is a revised version of the 1810 survey – possibly by William Blackadder – which differs only in that it shows the present park layout with the long avenue as now existing. This plan is undated but is in the same style as the original. Neither plan shows the butler's pantry and service room, so the undated one must be earlier than 1846, when the 12th Earl began his improvements. They may of course both be of the same date, showing different proposals. The replanting of the avenue seems to date between 1835 and 1846, possibly after Billings's visit in the early 1840s; the £3,242 2s 11d spent 'in and about the castle' between 1820 and 1846 might have included this work.

Beautiful as the present setting of Glamis is, the destruction of Earl Patrick's gardens must always be a matter of regret, and it outraged no one more than Sir

Walter Scott. Some thirty years after his visit in 1793 he wrote:

> Down went many a trophy of old magnificence, court-yard, ornamented enclosure, fosse, avenue, barbican, and every external muniment of battled wall and flanking tower out of which the ancient dome rising high above all its characteristic accompaniments, and seemingly girt round by its appropriate defences, which again circled each other in their different gradations ... once showed its lordly head above seven circles (if I remember aright) of defensive boundaries. ... A disciple of Kent had the cruelty to render this splendid old mansion ... more *parkish* as he was pleased to call it; to raze all those exterior defences, and bring his mean and paltry gravel walks up to the very door from which, deluded by the name, one might have imagined Lady Macbeth (with the form and features of Siddons) issuing forth to receive King Duncan.

As at least half the destruction had been wrought by Earl Patrick some hundred years earlier, the contemporary recollections of the most eminent authors may not always rest on a basis of sound historical fact.

The 11th and 12th Earls took little, if any, interest in the policies, and it was left to the 13th Earl to bring order to the gardens of the castle, a task that occupied him for the rest of his life, and was carried on by his son and daughter-in-law.

The 13th Earl must have put his plans in hand within weeks of succeeding his brother in September 1865. As early as 19 January 1866 a report on proposals for a 'Kitchen, Fruit and Forcing Garden' had been prepared by Archibald Fowler of Castle Kennedy (*see* Appendix C); at the same time designs for features in the park were being prepared by the architects Brown & Wardrop. The estimate of £655 for the bridge was considered excessive, and Andrew Ralston, the factor, was instructed to redesign it at less cost. Ralston was conscious of the delicacy of his position and pointed out the impropriety of such a course of action. In the end, the bridge was to cost £669 15s, though whether this was Wardrop's design or Ralston's is not clear. Wardrop produced drawings in September 1866 for a set of gates to the garden, estimated to cost £213 and of a monumental hideousness with lion-surmounted stone piers and heavy rococo ironwork.

Fowler's proposals fared better, though it is doubtful if Lord Strathmore would have adopted them had he known how far the expenses would outrun the estimate. The report, which was accompanied by a plan showing the position of the garden and its adjuncts, together with drawings of the fruit and plant house and all other necessary buildings, makes it clear that there was no garden at the castle. Fowler suggested that a garden of four acres would not be too large for 'supplying what may be required in an establishment such as Glamis Castle implies', and from the plans, rather than from the report, it is possible to gain a clearer view of the grandeur of his ideas. There was to be provision for a peach house, vinery, fig house, melon pits, cucumber pits, houses for pelargoniums, orchids, camellias, fine foliaged plants and mushrooms. There were also three bedrooms for the gardeners with a mess-room kitchen, and a sitting-room and bedroom for the foreman. Fowler, 'Not being in possession of all the necessary data to make an exact calculation', estimated a cost of £7,800, with an annual expenditure of £700 to £800, 'less or more as it may be ill or well kept'. To maintain it 'would require eight men and occassionaly [sic] some boys to work it. A man and horse would also be nearly constantly employed'. None of this seems to have included the 'intelligent, active and experienced gardener', who should be appointed and would need to be provided with a house. In the event, the capital cost of the garden came to nearly twice Fowler's estimate; £13,376 had been spent by 1868, and there seems to have been a further £6,066 in 1869.

This did not dampen Lord Strathmore's enthusiasm, and in 1892 Arthur Castings of Craig's Court, Charing Cross, was surveying the ground in front of the new building – the family wing of 1891 – advising and preparing drawings for a new garden. The designs seem to have been completed by February 1893 when Castings was paid. Known as the Dutch Garden for no very good reason, the design is highly derivative and owes much to Lord Strathmore's constant intervention: there were to

be piers with lions towards the forecourt; there were to be pedimented niches, as at Edzell, with recesses for flowers; the scrolls were to be based on those at Minley, as were the piers; the balls were to copy those at Coombe; the groundwork of the scrolls were to be in common yew with an outer border of light-coloured euonymus; and so on and so on. Only once did Strathmore try Castings's patience too far. Battlements were suggested, and the reply to the request was couched in terms used by all architects when faced with the desire to cast out sin but not the sinner: 'I do not think the effect of a low embattled wall as seen from the forecourt would be such as to meet with your ultimate approval as battlements low down on the ground are never satisfactory and are quite opposed to the teaching of the "fathers"'. There are no battlements!

An article in the *Gardening World* of 27 September 1897 (*see* Appendix D) gives a very good idea of the richness of the Glamis houses, typical of most of the great establishments of the period, a richness which today would be considered almost unendurably vulgar.

The last great gardening exercise at Glamis was the creation in 1907–10 by the 14th Earl and his wife of a garden in the shrubberies, 2 acres (0.8 hectare) in extent. Planned by Arthur Castings, laid out by the head gardener, Thomas Wilson (who had been noticed with approval in the *Gardening World* article), and 'evolved and designed by Countess Cecilia', it is now known as the 'Italian Garden', but at one time was the 'Autumn Garden'. Neither description is particularly accurate, Italian gardens being not generally given to large herbaceous borders: it is an 'Edwardian Garden', an extremely good one, and deserves to be recognized as such.

A commemorative plaque records that, unusually for Glamis, the work was carried out by local men 'RESIDENTS IN THE PARISH OF GLAMIS' – residents but perhaps not all natives: Hans Hansen is hardly an Angus name.

CHAPTER 14
GLAMIS: LITERATURE, LEGEND AND LETTERS

Some would have it that Shakespeare wrote *Macbeth* as a compliment to Patrick, Lord Glamis, newly created Earl of Kinghorne, and as a result of a visit to the castle while on the way to Aberdeen with his company of players. Neither story seems very likely. Shakespeare's play by Holinshed out of Fordoun and *Scotichronicon* was certainly written as a compliment, but as a compliment to the new monarch, James VI and I. It was

14.1 'An Imaginative View of Glamis Castle', Alexander Nasmyth, c 1820–30. A curiosity as, apart from the fanciful setting, it shows the castle as it was before 1777. Nasmyth can never have seen it, and must have relied on an earlier drawing, possibly Sandby's (reproduced by permission of The National Gallery of Scotland)

intended to emphasize – that is, if it had a message at all – the historical pedigree of the Stuarts (always a touchy subject) and the fact that there had been but one attempt, and that only temporarily successful, to overthrow the royal house of Scotland. None of the action of the play takes place at the castle, and Macbeth, Thane of Glamis, is a traitor and murderer – hardly a compliment to a loyal courtier, rising in royal favour, to be associated with treachery.

However, the popular mind will always associate Glamis with *Macbeth*, and has done so, certainly since 1746 when, on his survey of the castle, John Elphinstone marked one room – the 'Latter Meat Hall' – as 'The Room where King Duncan was murdered by McBeath'. The story lives on, although today 'Duncan's Hall', the legendary scene of the murder, is in another part of the castle. Shakespeare, in fact, sets the scene of the killing at Macbeth's stronghold of Inverness. This is dramatically more powerful than following the story in *Chronica Gentis Scotorum* or *Scotichronicon*, where the king was attacked by Macbeth at Bothgofnane, and then carried to Elgin where he died. It was Duncan's grandfather, Malcolm, who, at the age of eighty, may have died at Glamis from wounds received in an ambush nearby.

Probably the most important work on Glamis, a work which makes no pretence to literature and contains no hint of legend, is the *Book of Record* written between 1684 and 1689 by Patrick, 3rd Earl of Strathmore and Kinghorne. Edited by A H Millar and published as *The Glamis Book of Record* in 1890, it is invaluable both for its information about the building works at the castle, and how a young and impoverished nobleman, succeeding to a derelict house and an embarrassed estate, was able to overcome his difficulties. Written without thought of publication and totally lacking in pretension, it is a most human document.

Early in the following century – probably in 1725 – Daniel Defoe visited Glamis in the course of his journey through Great Britain. While he complains of the 'most scandalous partiality displayed by native writers towards Scotch subjects', it is difficult to see under which denomination his own account falls:

> Glamis is, indeed, one of the finest old built Palaces in Scotland, and, by far the largest; and this makes me speak of it here, because I am naming the Pretender and his Affairs, though a little out of Place; when you see it at a Distance it is so full of Turrets and lofty Buildings, Spires and Towers, some plain, others shin-

> ing with gilded Tops, that it looks not like a Town, but a City; and the noble Appearance seen through the long Vista's of the Park are so differing that it does not seem like the same Place any two Ways together.

> The great Avenue is a full half Mile, planted on either side with several Rows of Trees; when you come to the outer Gate you are surpris'd with the Beauty and the Variety of the Statues, Busts, some of Stone, some of Brass, some gilded, some plain. The Statues in Brass are four, one of King James VI, one of King Charles I, booted and spurr'd, as if going to take Horse at the Head of his Army; one of Charles II, habited *à la Hero*, which the World knows he had nothing of about him; and one of King James VII after the Pattern of that at Whitehall.

> When the Pretender lodg'd here, for the Earl of Strathmore entertain'd him in his first Passage to Perth with great Magnificence, There were told three and forty furnish'd Rooms on the first Floor of the House; some Beds, perhaps, were put up for the occasion, for they made Eighty eight Beds for them, and the whole Retinue of the Pretender was receiv'd, the House being to able to receive the Court of a real reigning Prince.

> It would be endless to go about to describe the magnificent Furniture, the Family Pictures, the Gallery, the fine Collection of Original Paintings and the nobly painted Cielings of the Chapel, where is an Organ for the service after the Manner of the Church of England. In a Word, the House is as nobly furnish'd as most Palaces in Scotland; but, as said, it was at the Brink of Destruction, for had the Earl not been Kill'd, 'tis Odds but it had been gutted by the Army, which presently spread all the Country; but it was enough, the Earl lost his life and the present Earl enjoys it peaceably.[1]

The poet Thomas Gray stayed at Glamis for some days in 1765, while making his second tour of Scotland. The 9th Earl may have met Gray during his time at Pembroke College, Cambridge University; the latter moved to Pembroke from Peterhouse, where he had been the victim of student humour of a fairly rough nature. Possibly there was a connection through Gray's friend Dr Thomas Wharton of Old Park, Co. Durham. Whatever the link, the earl thought well enough of the scholar, twenty-one years his senior, to invite him to Glamis. Gray's description of the castle, before the destruction of Earl Patrick's work in the course of the 9th Earl's improvements, is contained in a letter to Dr Wharton, and it agrees with that of Defoe:

you descend to the castle gradually from the south, through a double and triple avenue of Scotch firs 60 or 70 ft high under three gateways. This approach is a full mile long, and when you have passed the second gate the firs change to limes, and another oblique avenue goes off on either side towards the offices. The third gate delivers you into a court with a broad pavement and grass plots adorned with statues of the four Stuart Kings, bordered with old silver firs and yews alternately, and opening with an iron-palisade on either side to two square old-fashioned parterres surrounded by stone fruit walls.[2]

Like Defoe, Gray was struck by the fantastic appearance of the castle in a distant view:

rising proudly out of what seems a great and thick wood of tall trees, with a cluster of hanging towers on top. ... The house from the height of it, the greatness of its mass, the many towers atop, and the spread of its wings, has really a very singular and striking appearance, like nothing I saw.[3]

By the time Thomas Pennant and Francis Grose visited the castle, the first when it was suffering the effects of the 9th Earl's improvements, the second of his bankruptcy, it called for little in way of remark save that Grose started, or repeated, the tradition that Inigo Jones had some hand in its design. This story must have come about from the need to account for the magnificence of the building by attributing it to an eminent architect. Since there was no architect more eminent than Jones, whose dates fitted so conveniently with those on the Great Tower, the story was established. That there was not a shred of evidence to support this view, and it would have been beyond belief for the great classicist to have designed in the baronial manner was of no consequence. Sir Walter Scott was quite clear: 'this most splendid mansion (the most modern part of which was the work of Inigo Jones)'; and Billings, quoting Scott, repeats this, though with the *caveat* that there is no evidence to support this claim.[4] The statement 'It is not known whether the final design was that of Inigo Jones or not' appeared as recently as 1985 in the *Inventory of Gardens and Designed Landscapes in Scotland*.[5] It is particularly difficult to explain Scott's statement, since at the time of his visit in 1793 the 'most modern part' of the castle was still being built. But then he could seldom resist believing what he wished to be, rather than that which was.

It was when he was staying with Patrick Murray of Simprin, at Meigle, that Scott first visited Glamis – 'by far the noblest specimen of the real feudal castle, entire and perfect, that had as yet come under his inspection', as Lockhart puts it.[6] The effect it had on him was enormous: he was entertained by Peter Proctor, and seems to have spent the night in the chamber beneath the chapel:

I must own that when I heard door after door shut, after my conductor had retired, I began to consider myself as too far from the living, and somewhat too near the dead. We had passed through what is called the *Kings Chamber*, a vaulted apartment, garnished with stags' antlers and other trophies of the chase, and said by tradition to be the spot of Malcolm's murder, and I had an idea of the vicinity of the chapel. In spite of the truth of history, the whole night scene in Macbeth's Castle rushed in upon me, and struck me more forcibly than even when I have seen its terrors represented by John Kemble and his inimitable sister.

Writing in later years, he tells the story of the secret chamber, the entrance to which can only be known to three people, the Earl of Strathmore, his heir-apparent and any third person they may choose. His writings on Glamis – *Essay on Landscape Gardening* (1829) and *Letters on Demonology and Witchcraft* (1830) – were not written until more than thirty years after his visit, and facts may have become blurred, even if sensations had not, but he speaks only of the secret chamber, and not of the monster. Margaret Mackay of the School of Scottish Studies, University of Edinburgh, agrees that this particular legend 'is of pretty recent origin'.[7]

Far more important is the use that Scott made of the castle and of the circumstances of the family in two of his novels, *Waverley* (1814) and *The Antiquary* (1816). In *Waverley* the silver bear of Tully-veolan, the *poculum potatorium* of the Baron Bradwardine, is taken directly from the great silver and double gilt beaker in the form of a lion, which is one of the treasures of Glamis. Of this Scott wrote: 'The author ought perhaps to be ashamed of recording that he had the honour of swallowing the contents of *the lion*, and the recollection of the feat suggested the story of the Baron of Bradwardine'. The vessel contains upwards of an English pint.

More subtle is the way in which he weaves the strands of family history – and of very recent family history at that – into the fabric of *The Antiquary*, where the Earl of Strathmore becomes the Earl of Glenallan, and Glamis becomes Glenallan House. The Earl of Glenallan's mother, countess in her own right, had married a man of large fortune from the north of England who had predeceased her, and the earl was dependent upon his mother for his fortune. This closely parallels the case of the 10th Earl and his parents. Both earls were at variance with their younger brothers – the heirs apparent – and the plot of the novel turns on a mystery of birth. Lord Glenallan's son is supposed – mistakenly – to be the issue of an incestuous union. The son of Lord Strathmore, although acknowledged by his father, was illegitimate. Scott, with his lawyer's eye, may have foreseen the 'Glamis Cause' that was to resolve the disputed succession when he writes of the likelihood of the 'Great Glenallan Cause'. Although set in the 1790s, *The Antiquary* was published in 1816, five years after the birth of John Bowes; society – polite society, that is – was smaller in those days, and Scott would certainly have been aware of such an event. He could not have been aware of its eventual outcome, but he may have thought, as did others, that the birth was the result of a regular marriage.

It was not only the family that figured in the novel. Glenallan House was 'an ancient building of great extent, the most modern part of which had been designed by the celebrated Inigo Jones', words which Scott used of Glamis, and his description of the furnishings of both houses – gloomy, massive and antique – are interchangeable. At Glenallan 'The most magnificent part of the decoration was a valuable collection of pictures by the best masters, whose massive frames were somewhat tarnished by time'. At Glamis in the 1840s, although Billings notes that they had recently been restored 'in contrast to the grim antiquity of the surrounding objects',[8] there seems to have been little in the great hall other than the pictures – not perhaps by the 'best masters'. And when Billings speaks of 'Some specimens of old armour – chiefly Oriental, and not of much interest or value – are shown to visitors',[9] his comments chime with Scott's description of 'pieces of chivalric armour hanging on the walls' and with his reference at the end of *The Antiquary* to Jonathan Oldbuck's frequent visits to Glenallan to complete his essay on the mailshirt of the great earl.

Augustus Hare, a minor writer with a family connection – he was the great-great-grandson of Lady Anne Simpson, daughter of the 8th Earl – and a frequent visitor to Streatlam and Gibside in the days of John Bowes, has a story in *The Years with Mother*, of which Scott may have been aware:

My grandmother's first cousin, John, Earl of Strathmore, was a very agreeable and popular man, but by no means a moral character. Living near his castle of Streatlam was a beautiful girl named Mary Milner, daughter of a market-gardener of Staindrop. With this girl he went through a false ceremony of marriage, after which, in all innocence, she lived with him as his wife. Their only son, John Bowes, was sent to Eton as Lord Glamis. On his death bed Lord Strathmore confessed to her that their marriage was false, and that she was not really his wife. She said 'I understand that you mean to marry me now, but that will not do; there must be no more secret marriages!', and ill as he was, she had every one within reach summoned to attend the ceremony, and she had him carried to church, and was married to him before the world.[10]

Apart from one mistake – John Bowes was entered at Eton as 'John Strathmore Bowes', and not as 'Lord Glamis' – this story could well be true. Hare knew both John Bowes and his mother, and it would explain the respect in which Mary Millner was always held in a generally censorious world. Hare also tells the story of the secret chamber with its strange history known only to three persons to the intense fury of every succeeding Lady Strathmore, each of whom was to spend her time taking up floorboards and tapping on walls, but without success.

The most famous of the legends, that of the Monster of Glamis, seems to be entirely nineteenth century. It may have its genesis in the birth of their first child to Lord and Lady Glamis in October 1821, a birth recorded in both Douglas's *Scots Peerage* and Cockayne's *Complete Peerage*. The infant did not survive long enough to be baptized, a not unusual occurrence at the time. From this arose the story that a grotesquely deformed creature was kept alive, hidden in the castle until some time between 1865 and 1876. It is worth remembering that Lord and Lady Glamis did not live at the castle, which was abandoned by the family – not from choice, but because of the terms of the 10th Earl's settlements – from 1820 until 1850. Those who cling to belief in this appalling story are best answered with the words Jane Austen puts into the mouth of Henry Tilney in *Northanger Abbey*, when he finds Catherine Morland harbouring similar thoughts about the fate of his mother:

What have you been judging from? Remember the country and the age in which we live. Remember that we are English and that we are Christians. Consult your own understanding, your sense of the improbable, your own observation of what is passing around you. Does our education prepare us for such atrocities? Could they be perpetrated in a country like this, where social and literary intercourse is on such a footing, where everyman is surrounded by a neighbourhood of voluntary spies, and where roads and newspapers lay everything open? Dearest Miss Morland what ideas have you been admitting?[11]

Another story that emerged some time in the nineteenth century, and one which is still assiduously repeated, is that of the destruction of the west wing by fire. That there never was such a fire is confirmed in all the documentary and graphic evidence available, yet the story persists. There is nothing on which to hang this tale, nothing that can be twisted into the least suspicion of foundations for it. It is a story that can be found at other houses, and always where there has been a spectacular destruction. It is as if folk memory is unwilling to accept the destruction of great buildings by human agency – unless it be by Oliver Cromwell – but must involve the power of the elements.

The nineteenth century was a great age for ghosts, and at Glamis they proliferated amazingly and were seen by the most respectable people in the oddest places – those parts of the castle not built until long after the death of the ghostly visitor. It is difficult to impeach the evidence of the Dean of Brechin, baronets, Lord Halifax – an amateur of ghosts – the son of a Speaker of the House of Commons, the Provost of Perth, 'ladies very well known in London society' or Augustus Hare, but some difficulties must be overcome.

From 1865 the castle was full of visitors, and few visitors came away without seeing a ghost: it was as if every guest were a member of the Psychical Research Society on a productivity drive. Both the 13th and the 14th Earls had large and lively families, and for the first time in a hundred years the castle was full of young people. They may have disturbed the ghosts as the Canterville Ghost was disturbed,[12] and with similar results, or the young people may have been tempted by the gullibility of the guests, deciding that if it were ghosts they wanted, then ghosts they should have. In the end Glamis is Gothic, not Gothick, and its history is quite startling enough plain without making it fancy.

APPENDIX A
HERALDIC PANELS ON THE FAÇADE OF GLAMIS CASTLE

Charles John Burnett, Ross Herald

See Figure 6.1 (page 43)

Numbers in brackets refer to the Stenhouse Report[1]

1 [10] Lyon impaling Ogilvie for Patrick, lst Lord Glamis, and Isabel Ogilvy

2 [11] Lyon impaling Crichton for Alexander, 2nd Lord Glamis, and Agnes Crichton

3 [5] Lyon impaling Scrymgeour for John, 3rd Lord Glamis, and Elizabeth Scrymgeour

4 [6] Lyon impaling Gray for John, 4th Lord Glamis, and Elizabeth Gray

5 [7] Lyon, for George, 5th Lord Glamis, unmarried

6 [8] Lyon impaling Douglas for John, 6th Lord Glamis, and Janet Douglas

7 [13] Lyon impaling Keith for John, 7th Lord Glamis, and Jean Keith

8 [16] Lyon impaling Abernethy for John, 8th Lord Glamis, and Elizabeth Abernethy

9 [4] Lyon impaling Murray for Patrick, lst Earl of Kinghorne, and Anne Murray

10 [14] Lyon impaling Erskine for John, 2nd Earl, and Margaret Erskine, first wife

11 [3] Lyon impaling Maule for John, 2nd Earl, and Elizabeth Maule, second wife

12 [1] Lyon impaling Middleton for Patrick, 3rd Earl, and Helen Middleton

13 [9] Lyon impaling Stanhope for John, 4th Earl, and Elizabeth Stanhope

14 [12] Lyon for John, 5th Earl of Kinghorne, unmarried

15 [2] Royal Arms of the United Kingdom [Stewart version] as used in Scotland

16 [19] Arms of Lyon

17 [21] Lion of Lyon

18 [20] Arms of Murray?

19 [23] Arms of Lyon P E K: Patrick Earl Kinghorne

20 [22] Arms of Murray D A M: Dame Anne Murray

21 [17] Monogram PEKDAM: Patrick Earl Kinghorne, Dame Anne Murray

22 [15] Initials: PEK and DAM

23 [18] Date: 1606

Blazons of the Glamis Castle panels

1 [10] Argent a lion rampant Azure, armed and langued Gules within a double tressure flory-counterflory of the Second for Lyon, impaling Argent, a lion passant guardant Gules, armed and langued Azure, crowned with an imperial crown Proper, for Ogilvy.
Supporters, dexter a unicorn Argent, sinister a bull Argent.
PLLG.IOLG: Patrick Lyon Lord Glamis, Isabel Ogilvy Lady Glamis

2 [11] Lyon, as given, impaling:
Argent a lion rampant Azure, armed and langued Gules, for Crichton.
Supporters, dexter a unicorn Argent, sinister a lion Argent.
ALLG.ACLG: Alexander Lyon Lord Glamis, Agnes Crichton Lady Glamis

3 [5] Lyon, as given, impaling:
Gules a lion rampant Or, holding a scimitar Proper, for Scrymgeour.
Supporters, dexter a unicorn Argent, sinister a Lion Or?

JLLG.ESLG: John Lyon Lord Glamis, Elizabeth Scrymgeour Lady Glamis

4 [6] Lyon, as given, impaling:

Gules a lion rampant Argent, armed and langued Or, within a bordure engrailed of the Second, for Gray.

Supporters, dexter a unicorn Argent, sinister a lion Argent.

JLLG.EGLG: John Lyon Lord Glamis, Elizabeth Gray Lady Glamis

5 [7] Lyon, as given, with the usual Lyon supporters, dexter a unicorn Argent, sinister a lion rampant Gules.

GEORGE LYON LORD GLAMIS?

6 [8] Lyon, as given, impaling:

Quarterly lst, Gules a lion rampant Argent, 2nd, Argent a heart Gules on a chief Azure, three mullets of the First, 3rd, Or a lion rampant Gules debruised of a riband Sable, 4th, Argent five piles in point Vert, in base chequy Azure and Argent.

Supporters, dexter a unicorn Argent, sinister a stag Proper

JL8LG.IOLG John Lyon 8th Lord Glamis, Janet Douglas Lady Glamis

[The above blazon is suggested as a result of the original unusual marshalling employed by the sculptor. John Lyon was the 6th, not the 8th Lord Glamis.]

7 [13] Lyon, as given, impaling:

Argent, on a chief Gules three pales Or, for Keith.

Supporters, dexter a unicorn Argent, sinister a stag Proper.

JLLG.IKLG: John Lyon Lord Glamis, Jean Keith Lady Glamis

8 [16] Lyon, as given, impaling:

Quarterly lst and 4th, Or a lion rampant Gules, armed and langued Azure debruised of a riband Sable, 2nd and 3rd, Argent three piles Gules, for Abernethy.

Supporters, dexter a unicorn Argent, sinister a falcon Proper?

JLLG.EALG: John Lyon Lord Glamis, Elizabeth Abernethy Lady Glamis

9 [4] Lyon, as given, impaling:

Quarterly lst and 4th, Or, two chevrons Gules, 2nd and 3rd, Azure three mullets within a double tressure florycounterflory Or, for Murray.

Supporters, dexter a unicorn Argent, sinister a lion rampant

PLEK.AMCK: Patrick Lyon Earl Kinghorne, Anne Murray Countess Kinghorne

10 [14] Lyon, as given, impaling:

Quarterly lst and 4th, Azure a bend between six cross crosslets fitchy Or, 2nd and 3rd, Argent a pale Sable, for Erskine.

Supporters, dexter a unicorn Argent, sinister a griffin Argent.

JLEK.MECK: John Lyon Earl Kinghorne, Margaret Erskine Countess Kinghorne

11 [3] Lyon, as given, impaling:

Per pale Argent and Gules, a bordure charged with eight escallops all counterchanged, for Maule.

Supporters, dexter a unicorn Argent, sinister a greyhound gorged with a collar Gules, charged Argent.

JLEK.EMCK: John Lyon Earl Kinghorne, Elizabeth Maule Countess Kinghorne

12 [1] Lyon, as given, impaling:

Per fess Or and Gules a lion rampant within a double tressure florycounterflory, all counterchanged, for Middleton.

Supporter, dexter a unicorn Argent, sinister an eagle with coronet

PLEK.HMCK: Patrick Lyon Earl Kinghorne, Helen Middleton Countess Kinghorne

13 [9] Lyon, as given, impaling:

Quarterly Ermine and Gules, for Stanhope.

Supporters, dexter a unicorn Argent, sinister a talbot hound ermine.

JLEK.ESCK: John Lyon Earl Kinghorne, Elizabeth Stanhope Countess Kinghorne

14 [12] Lyon as given in 5 but with Earl's coronet over Arms.

No initial panel

15 Royal Arms, lst and 4th Or, a lion rampant Gules, armed and langued Azure within a double tressure florycounterflory of the Second, for Scotland, 2nd, grand quarter lst and 4th, Azure three fleurs-de-lis Or, for France, 2nd and 3rd, Gules three leopards Or for England, 3rd Azure a harp Or, stringed Argent, for Ireland.

16, 17, 18, 19 and 20 repeat the tinctures already given for Lyon, the Murray Arms consist only of: Azure three mullets within a double tressure florycounterflory Or.

Appendix B
Notes on a Copper-plate Engraving of Glamis Castle

John G Dunbar

It seems likely that the engraved copper-plate view of Glamis Castle (*see* Figure 5.3), discovered there in 1974, was prepared in or shortly before 1696 for a proposed second edition of John Slezer's *Theatrum Scotiae*.

Slezer was a Dutch surveyor and engineer who first visited Scotland during the course of a foreign tour made in 1669. He succeeded in gaining the favour of influential members of the nobility, including the Earls of Argyll and Kincardine and the Duke of Lauderdale, and in 1671 was invited to return to take up a commissioned post as an engineer in the Artillery.

Although he retained his military post until well into the reign of Queen Anne, a good deal of Slezer's time and energy was devoted to the publication of a book of engraved 'prospects' of Scottish towns and buildings entitled *Theatrum Scotiae*. Slezer seems to have embarked upon this project chiefly as a financial speculation, although he afterwards claimed to have received the personal encouragement of Charles II himself as well as the support of many of the Scottish nobility. The scheme proved far more costly than anticipated, however, and when Slezer, having expended (so he claimed) 'upwards of one thousand pounds sterling, to almost the exhausting of my small estate and fortune', finally published a collection of fifty-seven prospects in 1693 the book found little sale. Slezer attributed its lack of success partly to the opposition of London booksellers and partly to the fact that the work was incomplete 'which every one delays to buy until it be further perfected'. He therefore proposed to publish an enlarged second edition of the work entitled *The Ancient and Present State of Scotland*, or *Scotia Illustrata*. This was to comprise two volumes, the first containing an historical and descriptive account of Scotland, illustrated by engravings of royal castles, principal towns, universities, etc, and the second containing engraved views and plans of the principal houses of the nobility and gentry, with a description of each place and the proprietor's coat of arms.

Not surprisingly, this project proved over-ambitious and soon failed, despite parliamentary support, and no further edition was published during the author's lifetime. Slezer's financial difficulties became increasingly acute and although he made various attempts to extricate himself, he was finally obliged to seek refuge from his creditors within the sanctuary of Holyroodhouse, where he spent his latter years, dying in November 1717.

No view of Glamis Castle appears in the *Theatrum Scotiae* of 1693. In a statement prepared by Slezer in 1696, however, when he was seeking government support for the proposed second edition, he included a list of various subjects that had already been drawn and engraved in preparation for this work. Among these was 'Glams, with the ground stories', which had cost him £14. This indicates that plans of the castle had been prepared, as well as a view, but in a second and contemporary 'Index of Houses which are already ingraven' no mention is made of the plans. From a similar source it appears that the fifty-seven plates of the 1693 edition had been prepared by the London engraver Robert White, at a cost of £4 10s each, while in 1698 Slezer, alluding to the proposed second edition, complained that 'my work is like to be ruined by my Ingraver, who is fallen very sick at London, and who not only detains all my copper plates, but threatens to sell them if he be not speedily payed'. It thus appears that the plates for this edition, too, were engraved in London, presumably by White. Slezer also mentions the fact, however, that in 1691 '12 plates of prospects' had been spoiled at sea on the way from Holland, which suggests that some engraving, at least, was done there.

In the year following Slezer's death two further editions of *Theatrum Scotiae* were published by a consortium of London booksellers led by D Browne. These included the fifty-seven plates of the original edition together with three additional ones, two of which can be identified with subjects included in Slezer's list of 1696. In 1719 a fourth edition of the *Theatrum* was published by the London bookseller Joseph Smith (who was also a participator in the publication of Colin Campbell's *Vitruvius Britannicus*). Smith's edition omits thirty-five plates of the 1693 edition, but includes nine hitherto unpublished ones, all of which can be identified with subjects in Slezer's list of 1696. It seems clear, therefore, that Slezer's plates had by this time passed from Robert White into the possession of London booksellers, but at some stage in this process confusion arose as to the identification of the various subjects, some of which are incorrectly titled in the published work.

Among the plates incorrectly captioned in the edition of 1719 is a view of Dalkeith Castle, Midlothian, entitled 'Glamms House' (*see* Figure 5.4). MacGibbon and Ross argued that this view 'may be either a copy of an older drawing or else an attempt to represent what existed before the time of Patrick, ninth Lord Glamis',[1] but the survival of the original, correctly captioned, drawing at Dalkeith puts the matter beyond doubt.

Slezer's authentic view of Glamis is, almost certainly, the one engraved on the copper plate by Robert White. This does not appear in any edition of the *Theatrum* and appears never to have been published. The circumstances under which it came to be preserved are not known, but it seems likely that, disappointed with the non-appearance of the second edition of the *Theatrum*, the 4th Earl of Strathmore purchased the plate either from Slezer himself or from the engraver, so that he could have a few copies printed for his private use. Several of these copies remain in the possession of the Strathmore family. So far as can be established, this is the only one of Slezer's original copper plates to survive, the remainder having been lost or destroyed following the publication of the edition of 1818.

The engraving bears the date 1686, but since it was not included in the edition of 1693 it is possible that the plate itself was not engraved until after this date; there is little doubt, however, that it was in existence by 1696. The original drawing, which apparently does not survive, was probably by Slezer himself, the figures and other embellishments being added by the Dutch artist Jan Wyck the younger, whom Slezer is known to have employed for this purpose.

As well as drawing the perspective view (and missing ground-plans) of the castle, Slezer seems to have given architectural advice to the 3rd Earl of Strathmore in connection with the improvements that he was then carrying out. Writing of these in his diary, and apparently referring to the late 1670s, Lord Strathmore says:

> I have indeed been att the charge to imploy on who is to make a book of the figure of the draughts and frontispiece in Talyduce [tailledouce] of all the Kings Castles, Pallaces, towns, and other notable places in the Kingdome belonging to privat subjects who's desyre it was att first to me, and who himselfe passing by deemed this place worthie of the taking notice of. And to this man (Mr Sletcher by name) I gave liberall mony because I was loath that he should do it att his own charge and that I knew the cuts and ingraving would stand him mony.

Slezer is known to have acted as building overseer to the Duke of Lauderdale at Thirlestane Castle, Berwickshire, and at Lethington, East Lothian, *c* 1677–9 and may have been employed for a time in a similar capacity by Lord Strathmore at Glamis.

Appendix C
Archibald Fowler's Report on the Glamis Gardens, 19 January 1866

Report relative to Kitchen, Fruit and Forcing Garden Proposed to be made at Glamis Castle, the property of the Right Honble the Earl of Strathmore, accompanied by two Plans made in January 1866
By Archibald Fowler

THE PLAN

I Ground Plan shewing the position of the Garden and necessary adjuncts.
II Elevations of proposed Fruit and Plant Houses, Pits, etc.

SITE FOR GARDENS

The first and perhaps most important consideration to be kept prominently in view in selecting a site for a kitchen, fruit, and forcing Garden, in an old and extensive place such as Glamis Castle, is to look out for, and try to discover one, where the Garden will fit into the surrounding landscape, without injuring its amenity; but on the contrary be made to add to the dignity and importance of the whole place.

The site chosen possesses these requisites in a high degree, neither occupying too prominent, nor too secluded a position in the Park, being at a convenient distance from the Castle, and not in view from the principal rooms. In other respects the site is equally favourable, being sheltered from the cold cutting north and east winds, but existing plantations. The plantations will answer for a frame work and give support on two sides. Additional plantations will be required to shelter from the west. If all the plantations were done, in some such way as is indicated in Plan No. I, in a few years the effect would be very pleasing as seen from many points in the Park.

This is the only really good site I have been able to discover, sufficiently near the Castle, and taking it altogether by far the best in the Park. Other arguments in its favour will be noticed under different heads in the proper places.

The south wall from some points might appear rather glaring, and will require to be partially draped, this might be done with a few tall growing Cupressuses [*sic*], or other plants of similar habit; supported with small groups of evergreen shrubs, which would break the mass of the wall, and when covered with fruit trees, would remove any objectionable appearance it might otherwise present. The shrubs should be planted in the flower garden and form a part of the decorations, supposing the piece of unoccupied ground betwixt the garden and the Dean River be used for that purpose.

ALTITUDE OF GARDEN

The position is good in so far as it stands a little above the general level, which is a matter of much importance, in saving fruit blossom and early vegetables from late spring and early summer frosts, which are always very destructive in low lying situations. On the other hand it is not so high, as to be exposed to, and suffer from cold winds, being as previously observed, thoroughly sheltered from the north, and east, by plantations which might advantageously be drawn nearer the Garden, and thus fill in the space betwixt the plantations and the garden, and greatly improve the present outlines.

PRESENT LEVELS

The levels on the whole are good, the north and south walls can easily be made level lengthways, there being only about 2 ft of fall to the west on the north wall. The south wall having somewhat less, the levels on this wall being irregular.

There is a fall of about 1 in 40 to the south. This is most important, not only on account of exposure, but also to secure thorough drainage.

SOIL AND SUBSOIL

The soil is in general a good strong loam, on a fine yellow clay sub-soil. Towards the north side of the garden, the soil becomes lighter, where the subsoil changes to sand. The soil averages from two to three feet in depth, and is of a quality very suitable for the growth of most kinds of fruit and vegetables.

SIZE OF GARDEN

As shewn on the Plan No. I the Garden contains 4 acres or nearly so. This at first sight may appear large, but not too large for supplying what may be required in an establishment such as Glamis Castle implies. It must be remembered that a very considerable portion of this space will be occupied with glass structures, walks and flower borders. Rows of dwarf trained fruit trees, will be planted, so as to divide the breaks, and also to support the flower borders on each side of [the] centre and cross walks. When all this is deducted, the space for cultivating vegetables, will be found to be greatly reduced, so much so, that it will be necessary to have additional ground outside, surrounding the garden on the east, south and north, to grow fruit trees, gooseberry bushes, rasps, Asparagus, Rhubarb and other vegetables. As shown on Plan No. I all to be enclosed with a holly or other suitable hedge, and made rabbit and hare proof, with wire netting.

GARDEN WALLS

The Garden walls should be founded on rubble work at least 3 ft below the surface, or till a good foundation is found, and 2 ft in thickness; the brickwork to commence 6 in. below the finished surface. The walls should be built with 9-inch bricks, 18 in. in thickness.

The east and west walls to be 12 ft 4 in. in height, the north wall to vary with the height of the Hot houses, as shown on Plan No. I. The south wall to be 10 ft 4 in. in height, all to be finished with a good freestone coping.

THE GLASS STRUCTURES

A liberal supply of forced fruits and flowers for a large establishment necessitates all the Glass structures I have shown on Plan No. II. The probability is that more will ultimately be required, if so, it will be easy to lengthen the back ranges to any necessary extent. I have studied to keep the forcing houses as much as possible together, so to have them wide enough to prevent their shading each other. This is also desirable both for convenience in working, and economy heating.

They should all be heated from one boiler behind the plant stove. In case of this boiler at any time going wrong, I would advise two boilers being put in at first, and placed near each other and connected, so that either one, or both of them could be used. For instance, in ordinary weather one only would be required, in severe weather particularly when much forcing was going on, they could both be drawn upon, to insure an abundant supply of heat and if at any time one should break down, the other could always be depended upon to work the whole, thus allowing time for repairing or replacing the other. Trusting exclusively to one boiler is false economy although it is frequently done.

The forcing house should all be formed of the best material and workmanship, made plain, substantial and useful, thoroughly adapted to their respective uses. All to be ventilated with machinery on the most approved plans.

The Vine, Peach and Fig house borders should be aerated as at Castle Kennedy, and thus gain during the growing season from 6° to 10° of root temperature, the great advantage of which can best be seen in the quantity and quality of the fruit produced.

GARDEN SHEDS

There is no item in the modern garden, where the first expense is more grudged than garden sheds, and yet, it is impossible to work a large garden economically, and satisfactorily without them, and to secure comfortable accommodation for the young gardeners, and other necessary houses; in short 'to have a place for everything and everything in its place'. I do not therefore see that less shed accommodation, than I have shewn on Plan No. I for a Garden such as is required at Glamis Castle.

ENCLOSURE FOR GARDEN REFUSE, MANURE, SOILS ETC.

An enclosure for Garden refuse, manure, soils etc. is placed at the north east corner, so as to be near the potting shed, Stable etc., and as much out of the way as possible, surrounded with a hedge to keep its contents out of view. The portion where the different kinds of soils are to be kept should be surrounded and divided with low walls as shewn of Plan No. I.

WATER SUPPLY

It will be very desirable to have water laid on to the garden, if it can conveniently be done, if not a supply can be had from the Dean River, by a fixed pump. Provision might also be made to save the rain water which falls upon all the roofs about the garden.

GARDENERS HOUSE

This should be placed somewhere near the glass structure, the exact position for which can best be decided on the spot.

CLIMATE

The climate for garden purposes being superior on the east to the west coast of Scotland, arising from the lesser amount of rainfall, and consequently the greater amount of sunshine, at Glamis accompanied with a good soil, would justify the planting of many of the finer sorts of fruits, which when done might reasonably be expected to come to great perfection in a garden so favourably situated in most respects as the one proposed at Glamis Castle.

To supply first class vegetable an abundant supply of water must be at command, and should be had at different points in the Garden.

APPROACH TO GARDEN

The approach to the Garden from the Castle should enter through an archway in the centre of the south wall, so as to command the best view of the Garden and principal range of glass structures.

The entrance should be made large enough to admit a pony phaeton, or carriage if desirable, a drive could thus pass through the Garden, and betwixt the ranges of forcing houses, pits etc., and connected with the Warren Road as shewn on Plan No. I.

In this way easy access could at all times be had to the Garden, fruit and Plant houses, either walking or driving.

The Garden sheds should be neatly and substantially finished, the open space in front and around the back ranges of forcing houses should be gravelled, and at all times neatly kept and bounded with shrubbery and trees as shown on Plan No. I, so that the most fastidious eye could find nothing to offend at any time.

The entrance to the Garden might also be made at the centre of the west wall, the drive passing at a moderate distance from the Garden, this would admit of building the bridge where previously proposed, and continuing the road in process of formation. The former would make the most imposing and artistic entrance, and on that account I would strongly recommend it.

PROBABLE EXPENSE

Not being in possession of all the necessary data to make an exact calculation, I have sufficient to enable me to make an approximation thereto, which will I believe if the Garden is made be near the real cost.

Groundwork	£600
Garden Walls	£1200
Glass Structures	£3500
Garden Sheds	£1500
Gardeners house	£600
Fruit trees, Pines Plants etc.	£400
	£7800

ANNUAL EXPENDITURE

The Garden will cost from 7 to £800 per annum, less or more as it may be well or ill kept, and would require eight men and occassionally [sic] some boys to work it. A man and horse would also be nearly constantly employed.

GENERAL REMARKS

Should it be decided to go on with the Garden this season, an intelligent, active and experienced gardener, should be at once appointed to superintend the whole of the operations connected with the formation of the garden.

A piece of ground should be enclosed and protected from hares and rabbits, and the necessary quantity of hardy fruit trees procured, and planted in the said enclosure. The standards to be pruned and planted the same as if placed in their permanent positions. The dwarf and standard trained wall trees should be trained to stakes, and pruned and spread out the same as against the walls, and would be ready next winter or spring to place out in their permanent positions, without suffering any perceptible injury, but on the contrary would be benefited by being transplanted. The Garden would thus be brought into a fruit bearing state, one year earlier than if the trees were not provided till the Garden was ready to receive them.

A list of really good and hardy varieties of free bearing sorts, such as would be suitable for the locality and requirements of the place, I would supply, as very much depends on a proper selection being made for satisfactory results.

Preparations for building the walls should be made without unnecessary delay, so as to be ready to commence early in summer, and have them finished before winter.

The Hot houses, Garden sheds etc. should also be proceeded with as soon as possible in part or in whole, as might be deemed advisable.

The foundations of walls and of hot houses etc. could be taken out immediately, the levelling and trenching of the ground in and around the garden proceeded with, as also draining and formation of walks etc.

If operations are vigorously gone into, a first class Garden may be completed within a year, but if the early part of the summer is lost before commencing, the works can neither be so cheaply, so quickly, nor so satisfactorily be carried out.

In this report I have only generally suggested what should be done, the details are left for further consideration.

Castle Kennedy
Stranraer
19th. January 1866

APPENDIX D
ANENT THE GLASS HOUSES OF GLAMIS

(extract from *Gardening World*, 25 September 1897)

Mr. T. Wilson, a young man full of enterprise and a great enthusiast, is the present gardener.

The fruit houses, a fine range, contain fine crops of Peaches, Nectarines, and Grapes, which are everything that one can desire. It is really astonishing what fine Grapes the old vines produce. Mr. Wilson is judiciously replanting, some grand young Vines being on the way.

The plant houses, of which there are many, contain numerous novelties worthy of note. Stove and Greenhouse plants are well represented. I was particularly struck with a grand batch of lovely *Gymnogramme schizophylla*, over 2ft. through, a grand plant for baskets or elevated positions when well done. Standing at intervals between these and some well-grown *Maidenhair Ferns*, what struck me as a beautiful plant for decorative work are many dozens of the scarlet *Clerodendron fallax* plants clothed with foliage to the pots, about 2ft. high, with grand branching spikes of their rich scarlet flowers. They are used here extensively for indoor decorations, and stand well, so I was informed.

Other houses are gay, one with a grand batch of tuberous *Begonias*, many other 2ft. through, as much in height, and superb varieties. These are quite a grand feature. Another house is full of well-grown and profusely-flowered plants of the best zonal, double, and single *Pelargoniums* making a dashing display. *Lilium auratum* and its varieties, *L. lancifolium*, *L. Harrisii*, and *Tuberoses* are grown well, and swell and varied display. Noticeable were some fine *Hydrangea paniculata grandiflora* with enormous heads; the old favourite of mine, *Cassia corymbosa*, with its bright golden flowers; and the grand old *Vallota purpurea*, which is flowering profusely.

Marguerite Carnations, as well as others, are specially well done. A house of these in 48-size pots sown in January is grand. The strain is 'Sutton & Sons'. For variety of colours, flowers of fine form and substance, and most beautifully fringed, they are truly magnificent. As these are just in perfection, they will continue to flower for months to come. The plants are very free, producing enormous quantities of flowers. The *Tree Carnations* and the *Souvenir de la Malmaison* types are likewise well done.

The stove houses contain grand collections of young plants suitable for decorative purposes; and a house of splendidly-grown *Calanthes* of various sorts calls for special comment. They are grown principally in 32-size pots. Many of the pseudo bulbs are fully a foot, and others 15 in. long, and stout in proportion; and judging from their vigorous appearance they will give a good account of themselves later on. A large batch of all the best *Bouvardias* attracts one's attention, flowering profusely.

Tomatoes, Melons, Figs, Cucumbers, etc., are fruiting well and giving every satisfaction. The frames are full of seedling *Begonias, Pelargoniums, Carnations*, and other useful plants. A grand batch of *Chrysanthemums* will soon have to be housed, which will give a good supply of cut flowers, and make a fine display through the winter months. These combined with the scarlet *Salvias* make a good show.

Bedding is well done. The display in front of the large range I shall not forget. Every good annual, combined with all useful bedding plants, is there in full glory, not formally arranged, but broken up, which to me is more interesting. Every kind or style of bedding is well represented. Carpet bedding receives its due attention. Unfortunately the severe frost of a few days ago spoiled the effect of the flower garden on the terrace, the *Begonias, Tropaeolums, Heliotropiums,* etc., being completely cut up and black. The walls in various parts of the grounds are well planted with climbers, *Clematis, Roses,* etc., still making a good display. The pleasure grounds, which are well planted, contain many grand specimens of hardy trees and shrubs, *Coniferae* etc. Every season some new addition to these is being made. The demand for cut flowers, fruit, vegetables, and plants for decorative work is great, but Mr. Wilson is equal to the demand, and I congratulate him upon his success in all-round gardening, which is fully appreciated by his noble employer.

Appendix E
The Cellars, 1895–1970

Although the first mention of a cellar at Glamis is in 1765, when the 'bounkearts', or brick bins, were built in the cellar of the Great Tower, there are a number of references to wine and to wine-related matters among the Glamis papers, quite apart from those in the cellar books themselves. Not usually sources of historical or architectural information, one, at least, of the Glamis books is an exception; that of 1765 tells of the presence at the castle of Mr Bell 'Architect' and Mr Carr.

One of the earliest references, among some miscellaneous accounts of 1695, is not directly to wine: corks were being obtained from Henry Crawford in Dundee, and the purchase of corks in larger quantities – usually by the gross – was to remain a regular feature of cellar expenditure.

The two next oldest papers date from the time of the 4th Earl. The first, of 1701, lists:

1 hogshead Rhoody's Clarett
1 hogshead Vin grave white
1 doz. hogshead Vin grave red
12 bottles sack

The traditional Scots taste for the wines of the Bordeaux region was well developed in Earl John – very well developed if he ordered a dozen hogsheads. The following year there was an order for '1 small casque of Clarett drawn off into ten dozen of ffrench bottles of different sizes' and '1 hogshead of Clarett'. Small wonder that at Glamis corks were ordered by the gross!

Still loyal to France, the 8th Earl was having claret sent to Glamis, though he seems to have been less than clear in his directions, for on 6 August 1743, Archibald Stewart wrote: 'In obedience to your Lordship's orders I have sent you by the bearer Eleven doz. Clarett at 25s. per Doz. Seals Black Wax the impression of a Crown and Grape. I sent you wine at this price being the Price your last was at, and your letter mentioned no particular quality'.

His son, the 9th Earl, had a more catholic taste, as a list of 1765 shows, a list probably prepared as a guide for filling the new numbered 'bounkearts'. It gives no indication of quantities, but shows a far wider range of wines: 'White wine of Lisbon, Port of Lisbon, Port, Old Hock, Mountain, Cape Wine, Muscadine, Madiera, Florence Clarett, London Port, Newcastle Port, Scotch Clarett'. The ports of Lisbon, London and Newcastle are presumably so called after their ports of shipping; Florence Clarett is probably 'clairette', a light Italian red, almost certainly a Chianti. Mountain, a wine now coming back into fashion, is the rich dessert wine from the hills behind Malaga, and Cape from the vineyards of the Cape of Good Hope, South Africa. This was probably the legendary Constantia, which, apart from its more obvious qualities, has the distinction of being the only wine mentioned by name by Jane Austen – in *Sense and Sensibility*, where it is recommended as a cure for the 'colicy gout'. The Muscadine is likely to be the Muscat of modern wine lists. Old Hock, as distinct from Hock, figures frequently in Scottish cellar lists, and is sometimes described as Old Brown Hock. According to Mr Michael Broadbent of Christie's, Old Hock was a tremendously fashionable wine, and frequently figured in their catalogues, adding that he has tasted the 1772, which is rather like a sherry. In the cellars of the Stadthaus of Bremen there are still a number of casks of this wine.

In 1766 the port content of the cellar was increased by the purchase of pipes, on which duty of £84 8s 2d was paid. Depending on whether the pipes were of modern or medieval size, this would have been the equivalent of 3,818 or 3,480 bottles. A further pipe was bought in 1772 at a cost of £31. The same account shows the purchase of five gross of long corks for 12s 6d, and a payment of another 12s 6d to the cooper for drawing and corking the wine, 'Whereof Mr. Menzies got one third and Mr. Gammach another and as they did not choose the whole between them the remaining third was put in the cellar'. Two hogsheads of claret were brought from Leith in the same year, and in 1774 a further two hogsheads were bought for £72. In 1775 a pipe of 'Teneriffe' – the wine of the Canaries – was purchased, together with five hampers of Seltzer Waters.

Following the death of the 9th Earl in 1776, the contents of the cellars, like so much else at the castle, had to be sold (Figure A). Many of the wines were only listed as 'No. 1', 'No. 2', etc, indicating from which bin they came, and these seem generally to have been ports or clarets. One is specifically designated 'Major Balfour's Claret' – the earl having on occasion bought wine from, or in conjunction with, friends. As might have been expected Champagne, Old Hock, Cape, Mountain, Sherry and Madeira were all listed, but there were some new names as well: Muscade Red and White, Côte Rôtie, Syracuse, Frontignac and Calcavello. Both Côte Rôtie and Frontignac (now spelt Frontignan), the rich Muscat from the area south west of Montpellier, have remained popular. The red and white Muscade – perhaps the Muscadine of ten years earlier – could have been from Portugal, Spain or southern France, and Syracuse is another sweet wine, probably a Moscato di Siracusa. Calcavello is more of a problem, but given the general character of so many of the wines in the cellar, it is likely to have been another sweet wine, the amber-coloured Carcavelos from west of Lisbon. In addition there were rum, brandy, liqueurs and Arak.

The presence of so many types of what today would be called 'pudding wines' shows how greatly tastes have changed in the last two hundred years. Today, the preference is for dry wines, and usually the drier the better. This was already evidenced in the 1870s when my grandfather remarked on the contempt shown in some of the Champagne houses for those wines marked 'pour

Angleterre', which were regarded as being of an unpalatable dryness.

The list of wines in the cellar recorded in the inventory taken on the death of the 10th Earl in 1820 was not adduced in evidence in the Strathmore Peerage case in the following years, but it might well have been. On 25 September there were in the castle '25 Doz. Port, 9⅓ Doz. Claret, 2½ Doz. Sherry, 6½ Doz. Madeira AND 10½ Doz. empty bottles'. Valued at £190 8s 4d, this represented a higher value than the contents of any single room in the castle, and 20 per cent of the value of the whole, hardly

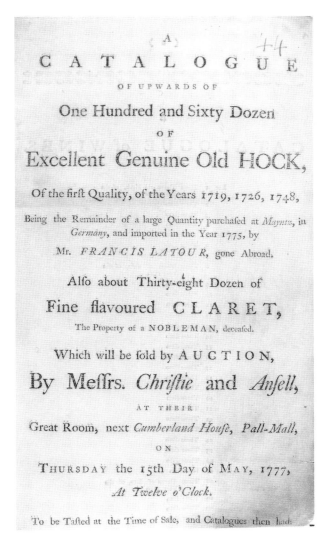

A   Advertisement for the sale of old hock and claret by Christie and Ansell in 1777. The claret may have come from Lord Strathmore's villa (reproduced by permission of Christie's)

enough to suggest that Glamis was the permanent, or even principal, home of Lord Strathmore.

His great-nephew, Thomas, 12th Earl, set out to remedy this oversight, and after his accession in 1846 bought wisely and well. He died in 1865, an embarrassed man, and much of his cellar, amounting to some 4,000 bottles, had to be sold. Of these bottles, 110 dozen were Madeira, Sherry and 1847 Port – considered to be the greatest vintage of the century – and four dozen of Old Hock. Of Champagne (spelt 'Champaign') there were 321 bottles, thirty-six magnums and one double magnum, together with sixteen bottles of Dry Champaign described as 'non-sparkling'. Sweet wines had reduced to twenty-five bottles of Sauternes. The remaining 2,300 bottles were clarets of 1848, 1851 and 1854. Apart from 235 bottles of Tod and James '48 and Tod and Hunter Red Seal '51 – two wine merchants long since vanished – they were all from three châteaux, Margaux, Latour and Lafitte, three of the world's greatest wines. Most of it was in standard bottles, but there was a respectable number of magnums, and six curiosities: six one-gallon Tappit Hen Bottles of Lafitte '48. According to the standard Stirling measure, a Tappit Hen held a Scotch quart, or slightly less than an imperial gallon, and would have been the equivalent of four and a half modern bottles.

To remedy this displenishing, the 13th Earl restocked the cellar with, according to Michael Broadbent, 'the most excellent wines including the very famous 1870 Lafitte, 40 magnums of which we sold ... in December 1970'.[1] *Ichabod*: the glory is departed.[2]

NOTES

Chapter 1 The family and the castle

1 'John, formerly lord of Glamis, sometime son and heir of John, lord of Glamis, is led away on charges of treachery and treason for crimes that he himself committed'.

2 The method adopted for managing elections in the eighteenth century, referring in this case specifically to the Forfar Election of 1770: 'That Lord S. and Mr. L. joyn their interest in the county with Lord P's. to procure his Lordship chose Member for the County while he chuse to represent it. And that Lord Panmure shall joyn his interest in the Boroughs with Lord S. and Mr. L. to procure chose Member for the District, while he chuses to represent it. And that they shall reciprocally engage their Honour to Each other faithfully to perform what is above and to do Every Thing which is in their Power to make sure their respective Elections' – as nice a piece of political stitchery as one could wish to see!

3 See Figure 1.3, in pocket, for the family tree.

Chapter 2 Glamis Castle: the early years, 1379–1480

1 'The king died in the village of Glamis'; Skene 1867, 180.

2 Simpson 1945, 121, where he claims this feature is a mason's hole for the ingress of materials.

3 Cruden 1960, 216.

4 Nisbet 1816, I.305.

5 The theory of fully frontal defence has been obscured by the disrepute – not perhaps entirely fairly – into which the theory of 'bastard feudalism' has fallen.

6 See Figure 2.8, in pocket, for family tree showing the Gray–Lyon connection.

7 Tabraham 1988; Tabraham and Good 1988.

8 Freake *et al*, forthcoming.

9 Gordon Slade 1993.

Chapter 3 The royal occupation, 1537–1542

1 'Three pounds and seventeen pence for the repair of the pile-bridge commonly known as a drawbridge after the other costs had been agreed upon'.

2 'For repairs around Glamis, thought to be around forty-six pounds, nineteen shillings and ten pence more than had been allowed for'.

3 'And the suppliers of pike for the pools around Glamis'.

4 Macivor 1977, 239–62.

5 This suggestion, with its implied use of a ouija board, was made by Professor Charles McKean (pers comm).

Chapter 4 The work of the 1st and 2nd Earls of Kinghorne, 1600–1626

1 Sitwell 1954. This view, which impressed itself deeply on my memory, was contained in an article reviewing Oliver Hill's *Scottish Castles of the 16th and 17th Centuries* (1953, Country Life, London), which appeared in the *Architectural Review*.

2 Similar two-floored rounds existed at Lord Huntly's magnificent house, the Bog o'Gight.

3 Quoted in Stirling 1928, 2, 130.

4 Pitcairn 1830, 168. It is contained in a description of Carrick by Mr William Abercrummie, Episcopal minister at Maybole.

Chapter 5 Earl Patrick and the recasting of Glamis, 1669–1695

1 Apted 1984, 54–61; Apted 1986, 91–115; Apted and Snowden 1981, 232–48.

2 Anderson 1794.

Chapter 7 The chapel, 1679–1891

1 The Revd Dandle French – chaplain to the Earl of Strathmore – has suggested that this picture may be the missing King Charles the Martyr and not a representation of Christ as *Salvator mundi*. He points out that the figure in the painting does not show the nail holes in the hands, as could be expected in a depiction of Christ after the Crucifixion (pers comm).

2 Defoe, III, 166–7.

3 Macky 1723.

Chapter 8 The eighteenth century

1 See Figures 8.11 to 8.13, in pocket, for plans showing the proposed works; the drawings are lodged in the Estates Office at Glamis Castle.

2 Colvin 1995, 409–10.

3 Thurber 1944.

4 National Library of Scotland, MS Acc 4796 FI/48.

Chapter 9 The Interregnum and the dining-room, 1820–1854

1 Recent work at the castle has shown that this inconvenience was of an almost sublime nature. The only access to the embrasures was from the top of an external ladder.

Chapter 10 The 13th Earl, 1865–1904

1 Their account of Glamis is published in MacGibbon and Ross 1887, II, 113–25.

2 Gordon Slade 1977–8, 241.

3 Gilbert, W S, 1885. *The Mikado*, Act II.

4 Austen, J, 1818. *Northanger Abbey*, London.

5 Sir Thomas O'Hagan (1812–85), 1st Baron O'Hagan, twice Lord Chancellor of Ireland, married as his second wife, Alice Towneley.

6 Sir Andrew Fairbairn was MP for the East Division of the West Riding in the Liberal interest.

7 Sir Henry Edwin Chandos Stanhope (1821–87), 9th Earl of Chesterfield, succeeded to the title in 1883, and was not particularly distinguished.

8 Jules Grévy had been elected President in 1879 in succession to Marshall MacMahon. At the end of his first term in 1885 he was re-elected, but resigned because of the involvement of his son-in-law in a financial scandal.

9 At this date, the reigning prince of Monaco was the ageing Charles III. His son, Prince Albert, married, first, Lady Marie Victoria Hamilton, daughter of the Duke of Hamilton, Brandon and Châtelherault, and secondly Alice Haine, Duchesse de Richelieu. There is a flavour of Proust.

10 Charles Crespigny Vivian (1806–86), 2nd Baron Vivian.

11 Edward Augustus Charles Brudenell-Bruce (1811–86), Marquis of Ailesbury (Heneage's spelling is that of the duck), was the father of Lady Ernestine Brudenell-Bruce, who married William Hare, 3rd Earl of Listowel, ie, Mr Heneage's brother's brother-in-law.

12 Richard Bickerton Parnell Lyons (1817–87), 2nd Baron Lyons, Minister in Washington during the American Civil War, and Ambassador in Paris during the equally difficult years of the Franco-Prussian War, the siege and the Commune.

13 The 'consum[m]ate musician' married the Revd Richard Croker, chaplain RN, who retired as chaplain at Gibraltar in 1875 and then served as chaplain at Cadiz, Fray Bentos and Paysandru.

14 This was the earthquake of 25 December 1884, which had caused widespread devastation across Andalucia, with thousands of victims.

15 This is unlikely to have been possible. Bishop John Jackson had died on 6 January, and his successor, Frederick Temple, had not yet been nominated.

16 Possibly one of the Bradshaws of Lifton Park in Devonshire; the dates of Mr Bradshaw of that family (1821–1909) would fit.

17 Prince Xavier Saphieha, a member of a distinguished Polish family.

18 The Medical Directory of 1885 lists no doctor of that name at that address. The most likely candidate is Dr John Batty Tuke of Charlotte Square, Edinburgh, and the Royal Lunatic Asylum, Montrose.

19 Edward Heneage (1840–1922), elder brother of Charles Heneage, inherited the family estate of Hainton on the death of his father in 1864. He married Lady Eleanor Hare, daughter of 2nd Earl of Listowel. He sat as MP for Lincoln and for Grimsby in the Liberal interest, became Chancellor of the Duchy of Lancaster in 1886 and was created Baron Heneage of Hainton in 1896.

Chapter 11 The twentieth century

1 Gordon Slade 1977–8, 241.

Chapter 13 The policies and gardens

1 Higgs 1986, 110.

2 Tait 1980.

3 Pers comm.

4 D/ST.C2/10/1.

5 National Library of Scotland MS, Acc 4796 Fl/48.

Chapter 14 Glamis: literature, legend and letters

1 Defoe, III, 166–7.

2 Gray, 1935 edn.

3 Ibid.

4 Billings 1845–52, IV.

5 Countryside Commission for Scotland 1985.

6 Lockhart 1845, 59.

7 Pers comm.

8 Billings 1845–52, IV.

9 Ibid.

10 Hare 1952, 146.

11 Austen, J, 1818. *Northanger Abbey*, London.

12 See 'The Canterville Ghost' in *The Complete Works of Oscar Wilde* (published by Harper Collins, 1994, Glasgow, 184–204) for the story of how an American family finally laid to rest the 300-year-old ghost of an English ancestral home.

Appendix A Heraldic panels on the façade of Glamis
Castle

1   Historic Scotland letter EWO 04303.051, 7 May 1991.

Appendix B Notes on a copper-plate engraving of
Glamis Castle

1   MacGibbon and Ross 1887, II, 114–15.

Appendix E The cellars, 1895–1970

1   Pers comm.
2   From the Hebrew: see I Samuel 4:21.

Bibliography

Adams, I A, 1979. *Peter May, Land Surveyor 1749–1793*, Scottish History Society, 4th ser, 15, Edinburgh

Anderson, J, 1794. *A General View of the Agriculture of Aberdeen*, Edinburgh

Apted, M R, 1984. 'Arnold Quellin's statues at Glamis Castle', *Antiq J*, 64, 54–61

Apted, M R, 1986. 'The building and other works of Patrick, 1st Earl of Strathmore, 1671–1695', *Antiq J*, 66, 91–115

Apted, M R, and Snowden, R L, 1981. 'The De Wet paintings in the chapel at Glamis Castle', in *Studies in Scottish Antiquity* (ed D J Breeze), 232–48, Edinburgh

Baynes, J, 1970. *The Jacobite Rising of 1715*, London

Beard, G, 1975. *Decorative Plasterwork in Great Britain*, London

Billings, R W, 1845–52. *The Baronial and Ecclesiastical Antiquities of Scotland*, 4 vols, Edinburgh

Burke, J, 1949 edn. *Burke's Genealogical and Heraldic History of the Peerage, Baronetage and Knightage*, London

Burton, J (ed), 1877. *The Register of the Privy Council of Scotland*, Edinburgh

Cavers, K, 1993. *A Vision of Scotland*, Edinburgh

Colvin, H M, 1995. *A Biographical Dictionary of British Architects 1600–1840*, 3rd edn, London

Cornforth, J, 1989. 'Was there a Scottish baroque?', *Country Life*, 15 June, 184–7

Cornforth, J, 1990. 'Ornamentally Scottish', *Country Life*, 9 August, 58–61

Countryside Commission for Scotland, 1985. *Inventory of Gardens and Designed Landscapes in Scotland*

Cruden, S, 1960. *The Scottish Castle*, London

Defoe, D, 1827 edn. *A Tour thro' the Whole Island of Great Britain*, London

Dunbar, J G, 1974. 'Lowlanders in the Highlands: Dutch craftsmen in Restoration Scotland', *Country Life*, 8 August, 372–6

Dundee Courier and Argus, 1866. 'The re-opening of the chapel of Glamis Castle', 1 October

Freake, D, *et al*, forthcoming. *Peel Castle Excavation Report*

Gordon Slade, H, 1966–7. 'Druminnor Castle', *Proc Soc Antiq Scotl*, 99, 148–66

Gordon Slade, H, 1974–5. 'Lickleyhead Castle', *Proc Soc Antiq Scotl*, 106, 161–71

Gordon Slade, H, 1976–7. 'Craigston Castle', *Proc Soc Antiq Scotl*, 108, 262–99

Gordon Slade, H, 1977–8. 'Castle Fraser', *Proc Soc Antiq Scotl*, 109, 233–300

Gordon Slade, H, 1978–80. 'Arbuthnott House', *Proc Soc Antiq Scotl*, 110, 432–74

Gordon Slade, H, 1984. 'Fyvie Castle', *Château Gaillard*, 12, 152–66, Caen

Gordon Slade, H, 1985. 'The Tower and House of Drum', *Proc Soc Antiq Scotl*, 115, 297–356

Gordon Slade, H, 1993. *Old Cromarty Castle*, Cromarty

Gordon Slade, H, 1994. 'Glamis Castle 1372–1626', *Château Gaillard*, 16, 232–9, Caen

Gordon Slade, H, 1995. 'John Elphinstone and the castle of Glamis', in *Scottish Country Houses 1600–1914* (eds I Gow and A Rowan), Edinburgh

Gray, T, 1935 edn. *The Correspondence of Thomas Gray* (ed P Toynbee and L Whibley), 3 vols, Oxford

Guilding, R A, 1986. 'The De Wet apostle paintings in the chapel of Glamis Castle', *Proc Soc Antiq Scotl*, 116, 429–46

Hare, A, 1952. *The Years with Mother*, London

Hay, G, 1984. 'Scottish Renaissance architecture', in *Studies in Scottish Antiquity* (ed D J Breeze), 196–231, Edinburgh

Higgs, S R, 1986. 'The building and other works of Patrick, 1st Earl of Strathmore at Glamis, 1671–1695', *Antiq J*, 66, 110

Hill, O, 1947. 'Glamis Castle', *Country Life*, 9 May, 860–3, and 16 May, 910–13

Livingstone, M (ed), 1908. *Registrum Secreti Sigilli Regum Scotorum*, Edinburgh

Lockhart, J G, 1845. *Life of Sir Walter Scott*, Edinburgh

MacDougall, N, 1982. *James III: a Political Study*, Edinburgh

MacGibbon, D, and Ross, T, 1887–92. *The Castellated and Domestic Architecture of Scotland*, 5 vols, Edinburgh

Macivor, I, 1977. 'Craignethan Castle, Lanarkshire: an experiment in artillery fortification' in *Ancient Monuments and their Interpretation* (eds M R Apted, R Gilyard-Beer and A D Saunders), 239–62

Macky, J, 1723. *A Journey through Scotland. In familiar letters* (1st edn)

Millar, A H (ed), 1890. *The Glamis Book of Record*, Scottish History Society, 1st ser, 9, Edinburgh

New Statistical Account of Scotland, 1845. XI, 337–50, Edinburgh

Nisbet, A, 1816. *A System of Heraldry, Speculative and Practical*, 2 vols, Edinburgh

Paul, Sir J B (ed), 1904–14. *The Scottish Peerage*, Edinburgh

Pitcairn, R, 1830. *Pitcairn's Historical and Genealogical Account of the Principal Families of the Name of Kennedy* (ed W Abercrombie), Edinburgh

Pitcairn, R (ed), 1833. *Criminal Trials in Scotland 1488–1624*, Edinburgh

Pride, G L, 1975. *Glossary of Scottish Building*, Alexandria, Scotland

Robinson, M (ed), 1985. *The Concise Scots Dictionary*, Aberdeen

Scott, Sir Walter, 1814. *Waverley*, Edinburgh

Scott, Sir Walter, 1816. *The Antiquary*, Edinburgh

Scott, Sir Walter, 1829. *Essay on Landscape Gardening*, Edinburgh

Scott, Sir Walter, 1830. *Letters on Witchcraft and Demonology*, Edinburgh

Scott-Moncrieff, D, 1950. 'Glamis Castle', *Country Life*, 27 October, 1408–13

Simpson, W D, 1945. *The Earldom of Mar*, Aberdeen

Sitwell, S, 1954. 'Plastic baronial Scottish castles of the sixteenth and seventeenth centuries', *Architectural Review*, 115, No. 689, May 1954

Skene, J (ed), 1871. *Johannis de Fordoun Chronica Gentis Scotorum*, Edinburgh

Skene, W P (ed), 1867. *Chronicles of the Picts, Chronicles of the Scots*, Edinburgh

Somerville, A R, 1987. 'The ancient sundials of Scotland', *Proc Soc Antiq Scotl*, 117, 233–64

The Statistical Account of Scotland, 1792. III, XIII, 124–9

Stirling, A M W, 1928. *Fyvie Castle*, London

Stirton, J, 1938. *Glamis Castle*, Forfar

Stuart, J (ed), 1878. *The Exchequer Rolls of Scotland*, Edinburgh

Tabraham, C J, 1988. 'The Scottish medieval towerhouse as lordly residence in the light of recent excavation', *Proc Soc Antiq Scotl*, 118, 267–76

Tabraham, C J, and Good, G L, 1981a. 'Excavations at Threave Castle, Galloway', *Medieval Archaeol*, 25, 90–140

Tabraham, C J, and Good, G L, 1981b. 'The artillery fortifications at Threave Castle, Galloway', in *Scottish Weapons and Fortifications 1100–1800* (ed D H Caldwell), 55–72, Edinburgh

Tabraham, C J, and Good, G L, 1988. 'Excavations at Smailholm Tower, Roxburghshire', *Proc Soc Antiq Scotl*, 118, 231–66

Tait, A A, 1980. *The Landscape Garden in Scotland 1735–1835*, Edinburgh

Taylor, A and H, 1936. *1715: The Story of the Rising*, London

Terry, C S, 1922. *The Jacobites and the Union*, Cambridge

Thomson, J M (ed), 1882–1914. *Registrum Magnum Sigilli Regum Scotorum*, Edinburgh

Thurber, J, 1944. 'Men, women and dogs', *The Thurber Carnival*, New York

INDEX